MY MAN

For almost fifty years, my husband, *Michael Pearl*, and I have functioned as one. Our art, writing, ministry, family, and fun have all been done together. This book is no exception. It bears my name as the author, but it is loaded with his wisdom, creative play on words, and divine Biblical knowledge. Two are better than one.

CONTENTS

I am the aged woman found in **Titus 2:3, "...the aged women likewise, that they be...teachers of good things..."**

As you read this book, please allow me to be your mother, your grandmother, your sister, your friend, your counselor, or perhaps your advocate. I want you to flourish, to be healthy, happy, and of a sound mind. I want you to learn, and I want your children to love learning.

I want you to find reward in your role as a wife, mother, and homeschool teacher.

Walk with me just a little while as we delve into the wonderful world of neuroplasticity and discover how this knowledge can help you not just survive, but thrive.

-Debi Pearl

A MANUAL FOR *Mamas*

Create
A BETTER
BRAIN
-through-
NEUROPLASTICITY

DEBI PEARL

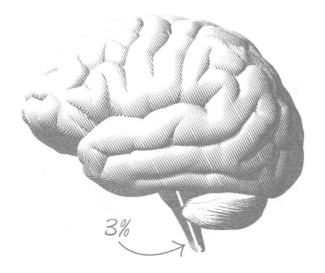

3%

What Is Neuroplasticity?

CHAPTER 1

Neuroplasticity has taught us that the brain can remap itself and, in doing so, can bring healing.

Why should you want to read a book about the strange-sounding, relatively new science called neuroplasticity? How could knowledge of this science help you? More than you could ever believe.

What if I told you that if you changed a few simple habits in your life you could actually increase your IQ or that of your child? Sounds good, doesn't it?

And what if I could show you what you could do to make you and your child naturally happier and more confident, get rid of your brain fog or sluggishness, and be more motivated to get things done? It is not as hard as you may think, in fact, brain scans show us that it is really just a matter of knowing how to direct our actions and thoughts to make it happen.

This book is written to bless you, to show you how to make your and your child's lives better, and to help you be the best you can be.

What do you want for your life?

Today millions of people all over the world are learning about applied neuroplasticity, and it is drastically changing their lives for the better. This book is Neuroplasticity 101.

Get ready to create a better brain.

NEUROPLASTICITY

Where scientists once thought we were the product of our brains, it is now understood that our brains are the product of us. The research that we examine will show how our children are not born with depression, ADHD, optimistic confidence, or any particular mindset; we create it. It is true that we are all born with physical propensities, weaknesses, and strengths. And we all get hit with outside influences; some suffer brain accidents or diseases. What we have learned through neuroplasticity is that we are not at the mercy of our genetics or the mishaps of life. What we do with these propensities, influences, mishaps, and diseases is our choice. You can design or redesign your brain for your own good, and we'll discuss how. This is a book of HOPE—hope because we are not bound by preset intelligence, character or capabilities.

Dr. Norman Doidge, a Canadian-born psychiatrist and best-selling author, said, "Thought changes structure...I saw people rewire their brains with their thoughts, to cure previously incurable obsessions and trauma."[1] Neuroscientists say with certainty that the brain is capable of re-engineering, and we are the engineers. By means of brain scans, scientists can see it happen.

The brain is not limited to changes that make us smarter or more emotionally balanced; it responds to training that helps us recover from all sorts of injury, diseases, and emotional ills. Now that is almost a miracle.

THE MOMENT THAT CHANGED EVERYTHING

Pedro Bach-y-Rita's brain, lying on the autopsy table, provided the evidence that would shatter the 400-year-old "holy grail" of brain science. Professional dogma about the nature of the brain was challenged in 1966 when neuropathologist, Dr. Mary Jane Aguilar, was asked to do the autopsy on Pedro. Both of Pedro's sons were psychiatrists, and they were curious to know the extent of the damage done to their father's brain from the stroke he'd had seven years earlier. Their father's complete recovery had been perplexing, considering how debilitating the stroke had been. On that September day,

1 Doidge, Norman. (2007). *The Brain That Changes Itself.* New York: Viking Books.

Stroke - A sudden disabling attack or loss of consciousness caused by an interruption in the flow of blood to the brain, especially through thrombosis.

Paul, the elder son, stood totally flabbergasted as he stared at his father's brain. No less than 97% of the brain stem had clearly been destroyed by the stroke, leaving only 3% to have served Pedro after the stroke. "It was shocking," Paul said. "My father had recovered so much that we'd figured he didn't have much brain damage."[2] This event was the beginning of neuroplasticity—the science of how the brain is rewired by our thoughts and actions. [3]

In the year 1958, Pedro was a 65-year-old widower and a professor at City College of New York. His beloved Jewish wife, Anne Hyman, the mother of his two sons Paul and George, had died a few years earlier. After she passed, Pedro poured his life into getting his two young sons educated. Now, his oldest son Paul was a psychiatrist working to establish his practice in New York, and his younger son George was in medical school back home in Mexico. As with most strokes, Pedro's came unexpectedly and was profoundly devastating.

The brain stem sits at the top of the spinal column centered at the base of the brain, and carries information between the body and the brain. As well as voluntary movement, the brain stem handles basic functions like breathing, swallowing, heart rate, blood pressure, sleeping, and vomiting.[4] Their once-intelligent, active father was now reduced to less than an infant, being unable to walk, talk, feed himself, or control his bodily functions. They needed to decide how they were going to handle this unfortunate turn of events.

It was decided that older brother Paul would continue his medical practice in New York and provide the needed income for his younger brother George, so he could finish his medical studies while caring for their dad.

2 Abrams, Michael, and Winters, Dan. (2003). "Can You See with Your Tongue?" *Discover Magazine.* Retrieved from: discovermagazine.com/2003/jun/feattongue

3 Doidge, Norman. (2008). "Brain that Changes Itself: into the abyss." *The Telegraph.* Retrieved from: www.telegraph.co.uk/news/health/3355721/Brain-That-Changes-Itself-into-the-abyss.html

4 Caswell, John. (2017). "When Stroke Affects the Brain." *Stroke Connection.* Retrieved from: strokeconnection.strokeassociation.org/Winter-2017/When-Stroke-Affects-the-Brain-Stem

George would take their father back home to Mexico and place him in a nursing facility. After a short time in the facility, due to a lack of results, George decided his father would do better at home. The stroke had left their father in an almost catatonic state. It is rare for victims of completely debilitating strokes to make a full recovery. Considering the severity of Pedro's condition, most people would not have seen the use of trying. But George was curious to see if it could make a difference so he tried anyway.

George bought his father knee pads and heavy gloves, propped him against the outside fence, and using a rope tied around his waist to hold him up, began teaching his father how to crawl. Neighbors who remembered the fine, sophisticated professor, now being treated with such a lack of respect, complained to the authorities.

In keeping with the family tradition, George ignored the ridicule and continued the experimental training sessions. He added to the regimen simple physical tasks such as tossing dice, rolling marbles, and playing cards. With progress, he employed circular movement inside a pan, forcing the inactive arm to respond.

THE MAP MADE THE DIFFERENCE

Since the late 1700s, medical science had been mapping the human brain. The area of the brain that makes the left hand work is laid out just like the hand itself: the thumb is at one end, with the index finger beside it, then the middle and ring finger, and on the end, the pinkie. Doctors can stick a probe into the brain and touch the part that corresponds to the thumb and the thumb jumps. It was thought that if the part of the brain that moves a finger was destroyed, that finger would be forever unresponsive. This science was all but written in stone and no one questioned it until sheer fate (or maybe divine providence) stepped in through Papa Pedro's recovery. With therapy, over the next few months Pedro began to improve. His sons assumed their dad's stroke did not affect a large area of his brain due to his full recovery.

Over the next year, little by little, the paralyzed man made improvements until he was able to conduct his own training sessions. Watching the movements of his mouth in a mirror, he regained his ability to speak. It was grueling labor, but in time, Pedro had his life back.

Imagine having been confined to a body that couldn't move or speak. Or how humiliating it would have been to have your mental faculties and know your son was changing your diaper. This was a magnificent and new opportunity to live again! He returned to teaching young students and loving his sons who had worked so hard for his recovery. He embraced life in finding love again and remarrying!

But no man lives forever and in 1966, at the age of 72, Pedro suffered a fatal heart attack while mountain climbing.

Being a scientist, the older son, Paul, had an autopsy performed on his father. The nature of their father's miraculous recovery still puzzled the two brothers. They wanted to see his brain with their own eyes so they would know what had taken place.

Paul recounted that as he approached the autopsy room, he remembered having a strange tingling at the thought of viewing his father's brain. What would he find? Would he be able to detect any variations in the structure of the brain? Did the stroke leave any trace of damage after his father's apparent healing?

Examining the brain, Paul stood in shocked amazement because 97% of the nerves in the brain stem had died. It was incomprehensible. With so much damage, how had his father regained function—walking, talking, and even teaching again—with only 3% of his brain stem? With what Paul thought he knew about the brain, it didn't make sense. The brain map that doctors had been refining for over 400 years clearly showed the area of the brain that controlled each action of the body. But now Paul could see that the undamaged 3% had learned to take control of all body functions. Amazingly, the brain had remapped itself and found new pathways to function. The concept that the brain can remap itself with training is an amazing idea—and completely unorthodox!

When Paul saw his father's brain, he knew that healing would not be limited to stroke victims. Children who suffered minor brain disorders from such things as falling off monkey bars could utilize this same rerouting technique. Those playing football, soccer, or boxing often suffer some brain impairment. Concussions from car accidents, diseases that affect the brain, or slight damage that causes the eyes to move out of line or the ears to be deaf can be corrected. If Pedro could find total recovery from this extensive brain trauma, then what brain disease, disorder, or damage couldn't be helped with training?

BRAIN ENGINEERING

Within the last few years, thanks to rapid development in the spheres of brain imaging and neuroscience, researchers now say with certainty that the brain is capable of re-engineering, and we are the engineers.

The ramification of Pedro's recovery was far greater than just one man returning from near-brain-death; it opened up the wonder of how we can remap the brain. A brain that can adapt is said to be *plastic*—moldable, not fixed or limited. This is the hope that I want to convey in this book, not just for those suffering from brain injury, but for anyone who wants to utilize this discovery to improve their day-to-day life.

EUREKA

As a scientist and psychiatrist, while Paul Bach-y-Rita stood looking at his father's brain, he knew that he bore the profound burden to make this information known. Paul was faithful to the task. He would spend the rest of his life finding ways to use this information to bring healing to as many as possible. The information garnered from this one autopsy would eventually revolutionize the world of neuroscience. But it would be a hard sell, as is most medical innovation.

A PREPOSTEROUS IDEA

Dr. Paul Bach-y-Rita began to test the hypothesis of the brain's plasticity. He surmised that neurons (brain cells) could adapt to whatever you needed them to do. The trick was to find a way to help facilitate this wonder of creation. Paul was awed like King David who said, **"...for I am fearfully and wonderfully made: marvellous are thy works; and that my soul knoweth right well" (Psalm 139:14).**

The young doctor-turned-researcher decided if part of the "wiring" was destroyed, then he must devise a way to help the brain detour around the blockage. That would be like a house rewiring itself after a circuit was cut. This seemed ludicrous according to the standard thinking of that day, and Paul's research was treated with ridicule. No one would even publish his findings. *Neuroplasticity* was a bad word used by only a few behaviorists, and no serious researcher dared use it to describe the physiology of the brain. But once you see a miracle—as he did with his father—it changes you. Paul persevered, regardless of the mockery he would endure.

THE BLIND SEE

Paul didn't blame the world of science for being skeptical, for they had not seen the autopsy of his father's brain. He decided he would do the unthinkable in providing proof: he would cause a blind man to see. And to remove all doubt, he would choose a subject with no eyes. Paul hoped he would be able to train a different area of the blind man's brain—the area that controlled other senses—to provide the sense of sight. If this worked, it would seal the deal and no one would question his claims. He confidently announced to his colleagues, "We don't see with our eyes; we see with our brains." Sounds pretty far-fetched, doesn't it?

> **FURTHER READING**
>
> The history of neuroplasticity, and the trail-blazing men that helped open up this new frontier, are found in Dr. Norman Doidge's book, *The Brain That Changes Itself*.[1] It is an excellent book on the subject that I recommend, but only for mature readers, as it does cover some sexual topics.
>
> 1 Doidge, Norman. (2007). *The Brain That Changes Itself*. New York: Viking Books.

Paul's team set to work creating electrical devices that would stimulate healthy neurons and "train" them to process sight. After many experiments with various contrived devices constructed from bits and pieces of electronics, Paul and his team finally came up with what they called the "lollypop." It actually looked like the end of a computer cable. With this device placed on the subject's tongue, it could send signals that the brain could recognize as visual sensory information. The resulting vision was a sensation described as "pictures being painted with tiny bubbles." To this day, the device is so effective that a blind man can throw a ball into a can ten feet away, or even know what is written on a small card in front of him. Blind men have been known to climb mountains utilizing this device.[5] This was a feat no one expected, and it gained the attention and respect of his critics. The technique

5 Twilley, Nicola. (2017). "Seeing with Your Tongue." *The New Yorker*. Retrieved from: www.newyorker.com/magazine/2017/05/15/seeing-with-your-tongue

is called sensory substitution, using one sense to take over the task of another. The actual event can be seen on YouTube.

All over the world, scientists were electrified by this miraculous new research. In a few short years, it would open up many new research studies. Paul Bach-y-Rita died at age 72, knowing he had made the amazing science of neuroplasticity a byword. He had helped the lame to walk, the blind to see, and the dumb to speak.

Over the years technology has advanced. With the use of fMRI, SPECT, and other machines, doctors are able to clearly see the damaged areas of the brain and document the "rewiring" that takes place. This has tremendous application to more than just brain damage. This science has been shown to be capable of raising the intelligence of our children, increasing their capacity for learning, and addressing learning disabilities.

THE GIFT OF MANY ROADS

The brain is composed of billions of neurons in a web of pathways like interconnected roads. Thoughts, feelings, and sensory input activate a web of connections formed by past experiences. Every stimulus creates or utilizes a network of these pathways. With the use of an fMRI (a machine used for measuring and mapping brain activity), one can see what resembles major thoroughfares with intersections, main avenues, and small streets that zigzag throughout every area of the brain. We make our own "roads" with our thoughts and actions: what we see, think, feel, and strive to learn. The use of music, art, laughter, exercise, study, etc. is making us who and what we will become. Our default tendency in life is to do the familiar: drive familiar roads, think familiar thoughts, eat familiar foods. All of these repeated actions of familiar things create familiar pathways. The more a pathway is used, the broader it becomes. If there is damage along the route of a familiar pathway, information is blocked. Neuroplasticity has taught us that we can train our brain to use pathways that were previously dedicated to other functions.

In the case of Papa Pedro it meant recovery from brain damage. Most of Pedro's "roads" had been destroyed by the stroke. His brain had to learn how to run all the traffic through only those undamaged pathways.

But the brain's ability to do this is not limited to overcoming brain injuries. For most of us mamas, this science can be applied to child development, homeschooling, correcting bad habits, overcoming addictions, breaking negative attitudes, etc. Harmful emotional behavior grooves roads leading to destructive results the same way any repeated thought or action does. With positive repetition, we can create new roads built by better thoughts and actions, so we no longer have to be stuck in the familiar rut of resentment, anger, bitterness or other undesirable attitudes. The more we utilize these new healthy roads, the larger they will become, and the smaller and weaker the old negative ones will become. What you focus on expands. Truly we are **"...fearfully and wonderfully made..." (Psalm 139:14)**.

Romans 12:2 says, **"...be ye transformed by the renewing of your mind..."**

I CHARGE YOU

Become informed; educate yourself for your family's sake. Start by asking yourself, "What would you want neuroplasticity to do for you and your loved ones?"

Some examples might include: help you recover from brain injury, help you break the bondage of depression, resentment, or fear, raise your IQ. Neuroplasticity has taught us that you are the captain of your ship; it's time to take charge.

"The fear of the Lord is the beginning of wisdom:
a good understanding have all they that do his commandments:
his praise endureth for ever" (Psalm 111:10)

Little Children, Little Children

CHAPTER 2

Neuroplasticity has taught us that the first year of a child's life is critically important to the quality of their intellectual and emotional development. The study of Neuroplasticity can help you know how to help your child develop a better brain.

WONDERFULLY MADE

When the ultrasound technician rushed from the room to call the doctor, Mama and Daddy both knew something was very wrong with their unborn baby. The doctor came into the room and barely spoke as he studied the ultrasound image. The room was charged with tension. One look at the doctor's face made it clear he had news he dreaded sharing. "Your baby is missing her corpus callosum, and it looks as if there is other damage as well."

Mama wasn't a medical professional, so she asked in a stunned, confused voice, "Her WHAT?"

"Part of her brain is not there. The brain is divided into two separate hemispheres. The corpus callosum connects the two sides. Without that part of the brain, the hemispheres can't communicate or share information."

Mama was still in a state of confusion. "What does that mean?"

The poor doctor just wanted to tell them the news and leave, but doctors are often called upon to be more than they wished for. "I have no idea what it might mean or whether your daughter will even survive, but I suspect she will be extremely mentally and physically challenged, and she will have seizures. It might be better for everyone if you considered another option."

Mama's voice cracked as her soul was tearing into pieces. "Option? What 'option' for our precious baby?"

A few months later, baby Janessa was born. Mama wrote this: "Extensive sonogram testing showed major concerns on the development of Janessa's brain. Cysts, stroke (leaving a portion of her brain damaged), and no corpus callosum were the grave diagnoses. We cried, not knowing what the future held. Would she ever walk, talk, or live a normal life? Through it all though, we had peace and an overwhelming love swept over the cords of our hearts that God had placed this precious baby girl in our care for a reason. We have prayed over her every night since she was born, and trusted—trusted a sovereign God. We trusted that HE would give us the strength no matter what."

Let's think back to Pedro Bach-y-Rita's recovery and the brain map. If the map area of the brain that makes the thumb work is destroyed, then how could the thumb ever be functional? Neuroplasticity has taught us that another area of the brain can be trained to do the work of the part destroyed. Remember how Dr. Paul Bach-y-Rita wired the sensory neurons in the brain of the blind man so that he could see? In the same way, Janessa's brain could be trained to use other areas to do the work of the destroyed neurons normally dedicated to that particular function. At around two years of age, Janessa's brain will have more synapses (brain connectors) than she will ever have at any time in her life. Every time her brain is stimulated by feelings, sight, smell, hearing, etc., connections are being made, and learning is taking place. Also, remember just how much Pedro had lost. He only had 3% of his brain stem left, yet he recovered.

Although baby Janessa's doctors cannot see any connection between the hemispheres, it is possible, and maybe even likely, that there are a few neurons making a connection. If this is the case, then they can be strengthened with use. This part of Janessa's brain development is still a mystery, but with neuroplasticity, it is a hopeful mystery.

The truth is Janessa's mama had never heard of the corpus callosum, nor had she ever heard of neuroplasticity. She also didn't have two curious psychiatrists at her beck and call as Papa Pedro did with his sons. What Mama did have was hope, lots of love, and a great desire to do everything she could to make her baby girl feel loved. Mama also had another asset that was even greater than her hope: she had twelve other children ready to spend every minute loving on their baby sister, singing to her, and talking non-stop. That is a lot of positive brain stimulation. And to round off an already great opportunity, little Janessa happened to be born into a family that travels and sings in churches. This means a lot of music being practiced regularly. Every day of baby Janessa's life, usually all day long, there is some sort of music being played or sung. Later you will read how music is being used for all kinds of brain recoveries, as well as developing higher intelligence.

Music opens up both sides of the brain. The key to all learning is utilizing many areas of the brain for each learning experience. For example, if you are teaching a child to memorize a Bible verse, then put it to music and teach them dance steps as they sing the Bible verse. Look into their eyes and smile at them as they sing. Show them the words so they can read them as they sing them. This will open up the part of the brain that is used for reading. Each activity—singing, dancing, feeling appreciated by your smile (happy feelings open up a lot of brain area), reading, and saying the words—all employ a different area of the brain. This forms a multifaceted network, each related to the others. The child is storing a memory of the Bible verse in all those different areas of the brain at one time. When it is time to recall the verses, memories come from several areas of the brain, making recall much easier.

Baby Janessa had twelve helpers giving her first-class "therapy" and opening up several areas of her brain for every session. Her damaged areas would still show up as dark, empty spots on a SPECT scan (3D medical imaging) because they were destroyed before she was born. The missing part of the brain would still be obvious, but the remaining areas of the brain still functioning would be learning to take on new duties and storing information with every experience.

Janessa is now about one year old. Here is an update straight from Mama: "To this day, Janessa has shown NO signs of being behind developmentally. She tries to talk, walk, and is RIGHT on target for her age. The doctors scratch their heads...eager (it seems) to find SOMETHING in which she is lacking, behind, or slow. They find NOTHING.

"What a great God we serve! Now, we understand and appreciate that not all situations have such happy and successful endings. But we are grateful to a God that still works miracles.

"As I snuggle my nose against her soft cheek, a tear runs down my face. I raise my eyes toward Heaven and thank God for this precious little gift from God...our sweet, little Janessa Ruth."

Neuroplasticity = HOPE

YOUR BABY'S BRAIN

The science of neuroplasticity was born out of what was learned from Pedro's brain damage. The door of understanding that was opened has given science a whole world of possibilities. Many new sciences have arisen as more and more research reaches into yet-unknown areas. With this new knowledge, people can learn to excel in every mental endeavor, can learn to overcome emotional and physical trauma, and we can apply this knowledge to train our children to excel like never before. We can use this new science to train our children to be more self-controlled and self-motivated. If a mother will start with her newborn, applying the principles of neuroplasticity, she can impart skills to her child that would not be possible otherwise. Applied neuroplasticity is amazingly simple and very akin to common sense, as you read in Janessa's story.

> **BABY'S BRAIN**
>
> Talking, singing, playing, laughing, cuddling, and reading establish productive links in a baby's brain.

STARTING AT THE BEGINNING

Barring a birth abnormality, we are all born with similar brain structures. Our brains change and adapt according to how we use them. Amazingly, the number of brain cells we are born with is ten times the number of stars in the Milky Way galaxy, or twenty times the number of people on earth. At birth, the human brain is extraordinary, yet it is in an unfinished and undeveloped state. Most of its 100 billion neurons are not yet connected into networks.

Forming and reinforcing these connections are the vital tasks of early brain development. In the first decade of life, a child's brain forms trillions of connections, or synapses. Although the brain continues to change through-out life, these early months and years are the most active because the brain emerges from the womb with every page empty, waiting to be written upon.

Science has proven that your child's emotional strength and mental well-being are not inherited but are a product of what we introduce into their world. Every experience—or lack of experience—is shaping our child's brain and laying the foundation for their future. Every person in their life, every babysitter, every playmate, everything they see, hear, and feel, is con-tributing to their eventual emotional and mental framework.

WOMB BABIES LEARN

Babies are learning and developing in the womb long before birth. Research has demonstrated that when a happy mother reads or sings to her baby after birth, the infant shows obvious recognition of his mother's voice and the songs and stories he has heard.

Newborns soon differentiate between human faces and objects. They pre-fer a smiling, adoring face to anything else. These tiny new people can even discriminate between happy and sad expressions as soon as they are born. How can that be? Neither their IQ nor their emotional disposition is formed.

Babies have little ability to control their movements; they can't see very well and have limited cognitive abilities. Most babies react to their mother's voice and instinctually nurse, but other than their affinity for their mother, it is evident that the baby's brain is a book yet to be written. The newborn emerges into a world of sensory stimulation. He has gone from dark to light, from warmth to changing temperature, from a soft, watery bed to the tex-tures of fabric and mother's skin. Sensory experiences of every kind turn on switches in the brain and begin the process of brain development.

NEURONS, SYNAPSES, AND NEUROTRANSMITTERS

The brain is composed of cells called **neurons**. Extending from each neuron are thousands of tube-like connectors seeking to link up to other neurons. At the end of each tube is a **synapse** that grabs hold of other synapses (like a plug and a socket), creating a connection between those two neurons. At the instant of the synapse connection the brain releases a chemical/hor-mone called a neurotransmitter. "Neuro" means brain and transmitter is something that carries information. In this book you will read a lot about neurotransmitters because they play a critical role in learning, moods, and a host of other brain functions. This is a key list in the book that you may want to reference.

The most common neurotransmitters:

1. *Dopamine* is often called the happy chemical.

2. *Serotonin* makes you feel important.

3. *Cortisol* is known as the stress hormone.

4. *Noradrenalin* is the fight and flight chemical and works with *adrenaline.*

5. *Endorphin* is the love hormone.

6. *Oxytocin* is known as the bonding hormone.

7. *Melatonin* is the hormone that helps you sleep.

Our feelings decide which neurotransmitter will be released. A pleasant feeling will release dopamine. A stressful moment will release cortisol. A baby's brain will release noradrenalin when alarmed. Neurotransmitters intensify the feelings as well as seal the synapse connection.

Moment-by-moment connections:

1. Baby hears Mama's soft, soothing voice. Neurons immediately start the process of making connections in the hearing section of the brain.

2. The room light is turned on, so now neurons connect the sight area of the brain to the hearing.

3. The baby's body senses a different temperature; therefore, both the hearing and the seeing connections are linked to temperature change.

4. The sound of music plays while Daddy's voice sings along in the background. This connects to Mama's voice, light, and temperature.

5. An older child chattering over the music is heard in the distance, which creates an ever-widening net of connections.

6. The overall feeling of comfort is associated with Mama and forms connections with all previously pleasant sensations.

Such a momentary event could create millions of connections to form a web to be accessed and built upon in the future. When any one of these events or sounds occurs again, the established connections will light up together. Brain scans reveal that synapses appear to compete for connections. A small child has many more synapses than will ever be used, but this overabundance guarantees the availability of connections as they are needed.

Things we don't notice, such as white noise in the background, doors slamming, mother suddenly yelling at another child, or shrill sounds coming from digital media, have a significant impact on a baby's brain. This is because children have so many synapses that the brain is electrified by the overpowering input. The brain is overstimulated. Just as pleasant sensations form a web of connections, the unpleasant, startling sensations also form associations. A nervous, agitated baby could be reacting negatively to Mama's voice because the last time he heard Mama's voice, there was a sensation of cold, a sudden jerking movement, hunger, or a loud, startling bang from the TV. Repeats of these negative experiences will create a nervous and discontented child.

THE IMPORTANCE OF TOUCH

Researchers at Baylor College of Medicine (2001 study)[6] have found that small children deprived of touch, play, and interaction with others have brains 20–30% smaller than normal for their age.

Simple touch makes a big difference in your baby's brain growth. This is just one reason why I strongly advocate that Mom and Dad (and siblings) keep their baby skin-to-skin with just the family for the first few days. That means not passing the infant around for others to hold. Those first few days are critical for brain development as bonding occurs and for development of the immune system without introducing any outside disease.

There is a great deal of skin-to-skin research that can easily be found on the internet, but one study really caught my attention: "Effects of father-neonate skin-to-skin contact on attachment."[7] This randomized, controlled trial included 83 first-time fathers, aged 20 years and up, with their newborns. Half of the fathers and their babies experienced sessions that lasted at least 15 minutes in which they held their infants skin-on-skin; the other half did

6 Nash, J. Madeleine. (2001). "Fertile Minds." Time Magazine. Retrieved from: content.time.com/time/magazine/article/0,9171,137214,00.html

7 Chen, Er-Mei, et al. (2017). "Effects of father-neonate skin-to-skin contact on attachment: a randomized trial." Hindawi. Retrieved from: www.hindawi.com/journals/nrp/2017/8612024/

not. Researchers then applied the Father-Child Attachment Scale (FCAS). The measurements were found to be significantly higher in those who held their child skin-on-skin. The experience engendered strong feelings in the father for his newborn, increased the infant's alertness to his environment, provided critical emotional support, and encouraged the father to become actively involved in caring for his infant. The study concluded that touching, massaging, and hugging an infant is a critical bonding experience for both.

BABY BONDING

Physical connection is a critical element in the parent-infant bonding process.

The first skin-to-skin contact the infant experiences sets off a cascade of hormones. Simple touch can lower levels of the stress hormone cortisol in your baby's body, which leads to better sleep patterns in infancy. The bonding hormone oxytocin rises during physical contact and increases the feeling of attachment between you and your new baby. Even his motor skills are improved with each skin-to-skin attachment to Mother or Father. Fathers caring for their newborn also have a hormonal release that creates bonding. This is beautiful in its simplicity.

"Our findings add to our understanding that more exposure to these types of supportive touch can actually impact how the brain processes touch, a sense necessary for learning and social-emotional connections," said lead study author Dr. Nathalie Maitre of Nationwide Children's Hospital in Columbus, Ohio.[8]

KANGAROO CARE

Kangaroo Care (KC) is well known for its advocacy of skin-to-skin contact between a nursing mother and her newborn. It often goes a step further than the intermittent skin-on-skin experience; babies are tied to their mothers' bodies and carried like a kangaroo carries her joey. According to the University of Edinburgh Global Health Society, this natural care is effective in reducing mortality among preterm and low birth weight infants. There is

8 Rapaport, Lisa. (2017). "How Touch Can Shape Babies' Brain Development." *Reuters*. Retrieved from: www.reuters.com/article/us-health-preemies-touch/how-touch-can-shape-babies-brain-development-idUSKBN16O2IH

an abundance of evidence that KC, when compared to conventional neonatal care in resource-limited settings, significantly reduces the risk of mortality in infants.[9] It has also been shown that KC enables the premature infant to achieve a balanced core body temperature more readily than when placed in an incubator.

Another intriguing study, found in AAP News & Journals Gateway, studied 47 healthy mother-infant pairs. Half of the infants received KC beginning 15 minutes after delivery and lasting one hour. The control group babies were taken straight to the nursery as is the standard maternity procedure. The study showed that as soon as four hours postnatally, the KC infants slept longer, were mostly in a quiet sleep state, and exhibited more flexing movements with fewer extensor movements—stiffening of limbs.[10] The conclusion was that KC babies fared much better.

As we stated, skin-to-skin touch is a necessary part of your baby's brain development. Without the cuddling care in their first days babies often do not thrive, and neither do their brains. The Romanian orphanage study is the most infamous of all research done on children. During the 1980s and 90s, in many Romanian orphanages, care-takers of infants were told never to look at, hold, talk to, cuddle, or give any emotional support to the babies. Basically, the children were fed, diapered, kept warm and dry and left lying in their cribs. This experiment was to determine if intentional emotional neglect would cause lasting mental disorder. Since the program was forced to close, many researchers have followed the unfortunate orphans. The follow-up researchers have documented extreme lack of normalcy in the children who were part of that terrible study. Basically, the children's brains simply never developed properly. The Harvard Gazette called the unethical research "Breathtakingly awful."[11]

9 (2019). "Research on Skin-to-Skin Contact." *UNICEF.* Retrieved from: www.unicef.org.uk/baby-friendly/news-and-research/baby-friendly-research/research-supporting-breastfeeding/skin-to-skin-contact/

10 Ferber, Sari Goldstein and Makhoul, Imad R. (2004). "The effect of skin-to-skin contact (kangaroo care) shortly after birth on the neurobehavioral responses of the term newborn: a randomized controlled trial." *Pediatrics.* Retrieved from: pediatrics.aappublications.org/content/113/4/858?sso=1&sso_redirect_count=1&nfstatus=401&nftoken=00000000-0000-0000-0000-000000000000&nfstatusdescription=ERROR%3a+No+local+token

11 (2010). "Breathtakingly Awful" *The Harvard Gazette.* Retrieved from: news.harvard.edu/gazette/story/2010/10/breathtakingly-awful/

WHISKER SENSATION

Animal studies have shown that newborn mice must experience whisker sensation in the first few days of life to enable them to develop normal sensorimotor skills. Cats must be allowed normal visual input during their first three months or their vision will be permanently impaired. Monkeys need consistent social contact during their first six months or they will end up extremely emotionally disturbed. The same critical periods appear to hold for human development (zerotothree.org).

The brain grows in direct response to any and all stimuli. For a newborn, skin-to-skin is an essential part of successful brain development. A baby's mental and emotional intelligence will be higher when he spends time in skin-to-skin contact with Mama, Daddy, and in some cases, siblings.

BE CAREFUL LITTLE EYES WHAT YOU SEE

"Window of opportunity" is a term used in research to describe sensitive periods in the lives of children when specific types of learning are optimal. At birth, the eyes are fully developed, but the area of the brain that controls sight has not grown or developed to the point of processing all of the visual information. The first two years are the "window of opportunity" for the brain to develop its potential to process what the eyes see.[12]

For the first few months, an infant's sight is pretty fuzzy. The BabyCenter Editorial Team says, "By the end of the first month, a baby can make eye contact and focus on objects about 12 inches away. By the time a baby is three to four months old, he can distinguish between colors and focus on smaller objects."[13]

Scientists know that the neurons for vision begin sending messages back and forth at great speed around two to four months of age and then peak

12 Graham, Judith. (2011). "Children and Brain Development: What We Know About How Children Learn." *The University of Maine Bulletin* #4356. Retrieved from: extension.umaine.edu/publications/4356e

13 "When will my baby see clearly?" *BabyCenter*. Retrieved from: www.babycenter.com/404_when-will-my-baby-see-clearly_1368493.bc

at eight months. As your baby's eye/brain functions are developing, he will need a variety of natural sights in addition to lights, darkness, shadows, and sunlight to develop the brain to its full potential.

The cerebellum is that part of the brain at the back of the skull which triples in size during the first year. The cerebellum is an important structure within a widely distributed neural network that coordinates and controls movements, including those of the eyes.[14] As the visual areas of the cortex grow, the infant's initially dim and limited sight develops into full binocular vision. He can now see fairly clear at one year old, but his vision won't be fully developed until he is a few years older.

From the day your child is born, his eyes will aid in his physical, mental, and emotional development by allowing him to take in visual information. This information will create new synapse connections that will grow his brain. Eyes are indeed a wondrous gift from God that aid in brain development. William Shakespeare is credited as saying, "The eyes are the window to your soul." Jesus Christ said it better: **"The light of the body is the eye: if therefore thine eye be single** [single focus]**, thy whole body shall be full of light" (Matthew 6:22).**

A baby's brain does not interpret the flashing screens of digital media. A baby placed in front of a TV as a way of distraction will focus on the screen, but this has been shown to be damaging to the development of the eyes and brain. He needs to be in a real environment where he is provoked to utilize his peripheral vision and experience depth of field. Digital viewing promotes tunnel vision. The connecting neurons that cause the little eyes to properly function must be provoked by variations in focus and visual stimuli. The screen holds the attention but leaves the brain undeveloped. When multiple senses—sight, smell, touch, hearing—are stimulated together, the brain forms multiple connections, enhancing the functionality of each sense.

Researchers from Proceedings of the National Academy of Sciences have found that when babies reach two to four months and are able to look into the eyes of adults, their brain waves sync with the adults'. This creates what researchers call a "joint-networked state."[15] It has been found that babies

14 Pouget, P. (2015). "The cortex is in overall control of 'voluntary' eye movement." *Eye*. Retrieved from: www.ncbi.nlm.nih.gov/pmc/articles/PMC4330293

15 (2017). "Speaker gaze increases information coupling between infant and adult brains" *PNAS*. Retrieved from: www.pnas.org/content/114/50/13290

vocalize, or try to communicate more, when this network state is active. It appears that the baby's synapse connections are kicked up a notch by an adult's gaze. This starts a new area of development in regard to socialization and will result in what is commonly called one's EQ, or emotional quotient. This quality has been proven a surer indicator of later success and happiness than IQ.

Surely, if a child could speak his need, he would say, **"Keep me as the apple of the eye, hide me under the shadow of thy wings" (Psalm 17:8).**

The Bible speaks of infants and small children who have died and gone to heaven. In keeping with the laws of childhood development, it says, **"Take heed that ye despise not one of these little ones; for I say unto you, That in heaven their angels do always behold the face of my Father which is in heaven" (Matthew 18:10).** If you have a child who died, or even one who died in the womb, be assured, they are getting the necessary socialization and development children need as they constantly look into the face of the Lord Jesus Christ. That is much better nurturing than any of us could provide.

HEARING

It is like poetry to see expectant mothers gently caress their baby bump and speak loving words to their womb baby. It is instinctive to know that as you do these things, he loves your voice and gentle touch. Are our instincts correct? Does your baby hear your voice while still in the womb?

> **MASSAGE THERAPY**
>
> Every malady responds to massage in a positive way according to Touch Research Institute in Miami, Florida.

By the time your tummy has barely begun to stress the zipper of your pants, your baby is hearing your voice. Healthline.com states that at 18 weeks, your little one is just five inches long and weighs about seven ounces, but he hears you sing to him.[16] The hearing ability rapidly develops at this point so that sensitivity to sound becomes apparent. Hearing your heart beating, he become accustomed to your particular rhythm. He hears the sound of air moving in and out of your lungs, and know when your stomach growls with hunger. He can even hear the blood moving through the umbilical cord. Noises from the outside are muted by half because there is no open air in the uterus to convey sound.

16 McDermott, Annette. (2017). "18 Weeks Pregnant: Symptoms, Tips, and More." *Healthline.* Retrieved from: www.healthline.com/health/pregnancy/18-weeks-pregnant#your-baby

SYNAPSES

At birth, the number of synapses per neuron is 2,500, but by age two or three, it's about 15,000 per neuron. The neural network expands exponentially. If the synapses are not used repeatedly or often enough, they are eliminated. In this way, experience plays a crucial role in "wiring" a young child's brain.[1]

1 (Shonkoff, J.P., and Phillips, D.A. (Eds). (2000). *From Neurons to Neighborhoods: The Science of Early Childhood Development.* Washington, DC: National Academies Press.)

By the beginning of the third trimester, your baby will respond to your voice, distinguishing it from others. He will respond to your increased heart rate and will be more alert when you are speaking. You are already building their brain by means of various sounds and vibrations. Connections are being formed with every stimulus. Your peace, laughter, and serenity are felt and heard by your womb baby. Hearing is his primary learning tool at this stage. But the wrong kind of sound or too much volume during these delicate months can be detrimental.

THE USE OF ULTRASOUNDS

Research suggests that noise exposure may be linked to fetal hearing loss. Ultrasounds (high-frequency sound wave imaging) allow us a peek into the mother's womb. Most expectant mothers want to have one or more while pregnant, if only to learn the gender of their baby. Ultrasound waves reach a high frequency of about 20 megahertz, or 20 million cycles per second, greater than the upper limit of human hearing. These **waves are strong enough to penetrate the flesh and bounce back for measurement.** According to the Canadian Medical Association Journal, research suggests that ultrasounds are a likely factor in higher incidences of poor speech development.[17]

According to the American College of Radiology, physicians should be prudent about the use of ultrasound, using it only when medically necessary or when benefits outweigh the clear risks. This advice comes from a

17 Campbell, J.D., et al. (1993). "Case-control study of prenatal ultrasonography exposure in children with delayed speech." *Canadian Medical Association Journal.* Retrieved from: www.ncbi.nlm.nih.gov/pmc/articles/PMC1485930

study by Yale researchers that link animal prenatal ultrasound exposure to brain damage.

During fetal development, neurons of the brain migrate to their correct positions. In a study of 335 mice, the researchers found that exposing pregnant mice to ultrasound waves could interfere with this normal migration in their fetuses. This interference could potentially result in brain abnormalities such as mental retardation and seizures. Results were published in the Proceedings of the National Academy of Sciences. Further research is needed to determine whether the results would apply equally to humans.

The study has unveiled a risk not previously known, according to Dr. Carol Rumack, head of the American College of Radiology Ultrasound Commission. It provides further proof that ultrasound keepsake videos should not be performed and that ultrasound equipment should be used only by qualified individuals. [18]

Ultrasounds are fun because we all love to see our tiny baby wrapped safely in our womb, but unless they are necessary to sustain life, they should be avoided. Doctors have been alerted to explain this to their patients, but the caution has yet to fully catch on.

USING A DOPPLER ULTRASOUND

The National Center for Biotechnology Information says concerning Doppler ultrasounds: "It is a form of energy and, as such, may have **effects** on tissues it traverses."[19]

The FDA suggests that you avoid using home Dopplers. Although they are generally safe, using them too much—and without medical supervision—could pose risks to your baby.[20]

Although there has been no study in the U.S. to duplicate it, a German study strongly warns against the use of Dopplers, stating that the ultrasound could be detrimental to the womb baby's hearing; and heating of embryonic

18 (2006). "Yale study links prenatal ultrasound to brain damage." *The Natural Child Project*. Retrieved from: www.naturalchild.org/articles/research/yale_ultrasound.html

19 Abramowicz, J.S., et al. (2012). "Obstetrical ultrasound: can the fetus hear the wave and feel the heat?" (translated). *Ultraschall in der Medizin*. Retrieved from: www.ncbi.nlm.nih.gov/pubmed/22700164

20 (2018). "Avoid Fetal 'Keepsake' Images, Heartbeat Monitors." *US FDA*. Retrieved from: www.fda.gov/ForConsumers/ConsumerUpdates/ucm095508.htm

fluid could be detrimental to the baby itself.[21]

Hearing is extremely important for language learning. It is also vital for the brain's continued development. As a grandmother and a person with lifelong partial hearing impairment, I would suggest that if either an ultrasound or Doppler is necessary for you or your baby's health, then do it; otherwise, better safe than sorry.

LANGUAGE LEARNING

According to TheConversation.com, "Babies begin to learn language sounds before they're even born. In the womb, a mother's voice is one of the most prominent sounds an unborn baby hears. By the time they're born, newborns can not only tell the difference between their mother's language and another language, but also show the ability to distinguish between languages."[22]

Language "circuits" in the frontal and temporal lobes become consolidated in the first year of a child's life. The child's brain is challenged by every word it hears, and as it processes the sound, it makes millions of new connections every day. Though the brain is developing the fundamental patterning necessary for future excellence, there will be little obvious manifestation of the change taking place in the brain. The six-month-old child cannot yet speak, but the foundation for all future speech is being laid.

God did an amazing thing in the brain of the womb baby that extends for just a few months after birth. He made the early brain to have an extra-sensitive ability to process sounds.

At birth, the baby's brain has an unusual opportunity: it can differentiate between all of the 800 sounds that comprise the world's languages. During the first year, infants can learn any language to which they are exposed. We can actually see in scans that during the first few months of a child's life, he can distinguish between the sounds of a foreign language and the language of those whom he loves. The child is not saying these sounds nor interpreting them, but he is able to easily differentiate the sounds. Memory neurons

21 Helmy, Samir, et al. (2015). "Measurement of thermal effects of Doppler ultrasound: an in vitro study." *Public Library of Science*. Retrieved from: www.ncbi.nlm.nih.gov/pmc/articles/PMC4547707

22 Ramirez, Naja F. (2016). "Why the Baby Brain Can Learn Two Languages at the Same Time." *The Conversation*. Retrieved from: theconversation.com/why-the-baby-brain-can-learn-two-languages-at-the-same-time-57470

are developed in the child's brain in relation to these sounds, which will make it much easier for him to learn languages. A baby loses this ability to differentiate between the 800 sounds by the end of his first year. Though he is yet unable to speak, the language he hears spoken by the person he wants to understand has been imprinted on their brain.

TheConversation.com says, "In fact, early childhood is the best possible time to learn a second language. Children who experience two languages from birth typically become native speakers of both, while adults often struggle with second language learning and rarely attain native-like fluency."[23]

The process of learning two or more languages increases the number of connections, and bilingual children have been shown to be more creative and better at processing complex problems.

TALKING *WITH* OUR CHILDREN

Research shows that you can increase the IQ of children by simply having a two-way conversation with them. Their mental and emotional strength increases in direct proportion to adult conversation, and it is not predicated by the educational level of the parents. Average parents can produce bright kids by simply talking with them. It is not the quality of information exchanged that increases the IQ; it is the mechanics of a two-way conversation that stimulates the formation of new neural connections.

The *Journal of Psychological Science* published an article discussing a study called, "Beyond the 30-million-word Gap: Children's conversational exposure is associated with language-related brain function."[24] Rachel Romeo and her colleagues began their study with 36 Boston-area children, ages four to six. Their end goal was to determine if back-and-forth conversations

> ### LANGUAGE
> Long before your child can speak or even understand words, it is important to be talking to him because this establishes foundations for learning language.

23 Ramirez, Naja F. (2016). "Why the Baby Brain Can Learn Two Languages at the Same Time." *The Conversation.* Retrieved from: theconversation.com/why-the-baby-brain-can-learn-two-languages-at-the-same-time-57470

24 Romeo, R.R., et al. (2018). "Beyond the 30-million-word gap: children's conversational exposure is associated with language-related brain function." *Psychological Science.* Retrieved from: www.ncbi.nlm.nih.gov/pubmed/29442613

with parents made a difference in a child's brain activation (learning power).

They tested the verbal and reasoning skills of each child, and then placed them in an MRI brain scanner. While the children relaxed in the machines, they listened to an audio story. Researchers were able to view the brain in real time and document its response to the audio recording. The children were then sent home with a digital voice recorder in their pocket. Parents were told to turn it on during the child's waking hours for the entire weekend. Algorithms analyzed the recordings, counted the number of words spoken by adults, and noted conversational turns. The algorithms were able to discern real, live human voices and discard words that the child heard from the television or other devices. If the recorder picked up a caretaker talking on a cell phone, it would be categorized as adult speech and the words counted.

Finally, the researchers compared the children's test scores and brain images in the laboratory with the audio patterns at home. They found for every 11 back-and-forth conversations with a parent, a child's verbal test score increased by one point. And they saw that the part of the brain involved in processing language lit up more for children who had experienced more conversation at home. This was a remarkable find. Simply talking with your child will increase his ability to learn.

"What we found is that the sheer amount of language, the number of adult words, was not related to brain activation or verbal skills," said Rachel Romeo. "But what was related, strongly related, was the amount of back-and-forth conversation between children and adults. We think this research finding suggests, instead of talking at or to your child, you really need to talk with your child to have meaningful brain development and language development."

This type of interaction should start early in a baby's life and continue throughout his formative years. Your child will hunger for your interaction because it will stir his imagination and creativity. This is meaningful bonding.

As parents, we do talk to our children, or maybe at our children, but we often fail to have regular, meaningful, and interesting conversations WITH them. God knew the importance of parent-child conversation long before medical science, for in **Deuteronomy 11:19** we read, **"And ye shall teach them your children, speaking of them when thou sittest in thine house, and when thou walkest by the way, when thou liest down, and when thou risest up."**

Child development cannot be done only in a classroom; it is an ongoing family lifestyle.

WORDS OF WISDOM
By Shoshanna, my youngest child

Talk. People often talk around their babies but don't actually talk to them. Your baby is learning rapidly and needs to know he is being spoken to. I talked to my baby every single day, all day long. He heard me while he was in my womb, and he heard me continue when he was born. Every day he hears me say, "I love you baby, I love you, I do, I do." I know people will think I am crazy, and I am sure it was just an echo from him, but when he was eight days old he said, "I love you, I do." My husband and I were sitting on the bed and we heard him echo that, and we thought, "Whaaaaaat?" We stared at each other like, "DID YOU HEAR THAT?" We were totally shocked. I know that babies are absorbing everything. I know that my baby's brain is making language connections that he will soon be able to use, but when he spoke, I was beyond surprised. I'm sure you are wondering if he kept saying it after that. No, but he echoed basic sounds of words from the very beginning.

When we are talking to our little ones, our language, our body language, and our tone are all important. We need to engage our children. When I was growing up, I saw a lot of parents who communicated well with everyone else, but I never saw them really talking to their children. You may have noticed kids who don't quite make eye contact. It's because they are not accustomed to having adults look them in the eye unless it is to fuss at them. Not my children. They are the most important people in my life, and I let them know it by how I talk with them. I start the day by saying, "Hey kiddo, how are you doing? Oh, it's so good to see you this morning! I'm so glad you're up with the sunshine! Your face is like sunshine itself! Gimme a big ol' hug. I need some sugar from you!" I make sure the words, as well as the sunshiny tone, are clearly there. It's going to start their day off with such positive, happy thoughts.

My baby knows he is an important part of the party and an integral piece of the project. He wants to be in the center of everything. For example, I'm cooking and he's (at nine months) on my countertop. I hand him a big spoon and show him how to hold it and say, "Hold this." I wait, and then say, "Now give me the spoon so I can stir, but now hold this other spoon." After one or two times, he will stare at me with great concentration, knowing he is part of what's going on and that what he is doing is important. Of course, he isn't actually helping, but he's part of the current activity; he's included

> **BABY TALK**
>
> During the first few weeks of life, a babbling baby utters almost every sound of every known language. Later, the ability to make some sounds vanishes, which is the result of pruning.

in the project. He feels valued and needed. When he is helping, I have a conversation with him, and when someone takes note of him helping, we speak of him being a good helper. By the time he is two, he will be actually serving people. He will be useful in this world and in our home. I have raised my other two children this way and they both love serving others. My parents raised my siblings and me to serve others; it was one of the most important aspects of our youth, and I am thankful. There is nothing nastier than a lazy girl, unless it is a lazy boy who avoids work and thinks it is funny to skip out. Give your children a purpose by allowing them to be an active part of everything you do.

Children like sameness—same cup, same seat, same blanket, same bed, etc. But in life, everything isn't always the same. When we are going to go somewhere, do something, meet new people, or see new sights, we can make these experiences something of wonder or dread depending on how we introduce them to our children. I have heard parents say, "Ooooh, what are we going to do? Don't be scared!" This is the wrong approach. You build confidence in your child by your tone, words, and body language. If your child is going to be sliding down a big slide, say, "Pfff, you've got this! No big deal!" You may be freaking out on the inside, but to your child, you must show confidence. Watching my nine-month-old learning to walk has me on pins and needles, but I remember I am training him to have confidence. Generally, but not always, daddies can be rougher than mamas. I can be cringing inside, but I don't show my panic on the outside. I just say, "Wooo! Good job, kiddo!"

We all have moments of hurt, panic, or confusion; we want our children to be able to handle them as a matter of course because they were trained from the beginning. *-Shoshanna*

SLEEP SAFELY AND WAKE SOFTLY

One of the most common concerns of parents is the inconsistent sleep patterns of their young children. It is also one of the most common behavioral issues brought to the attention of pediatricians, occurring in approximately

20–30% of infants and toddlers. Most pediatricians recommend instituting and maintaining a bedtime routine. Research shows that daily routines lead to less stressful environments for young children and are related to parenting competence, improved daytime behavior, and lower maternal mental distress.[25]

It is not only the bedtime routine that is important; it is the bonding that occurs as you impart the feeling that you and your husband are watching over them. Children need a sweet, secure close to their day. It gives them assurance to hear their parents pray for their safety and for a good night's sleep. They need to spend a little time recounting what they did that day and what they think is going to happen tomorrow. A short Bible story or family story is great at this time, but if you don't have time for a story, then be sure you have time for a two-minute connection and a little kiss goodnight. The time spent is like the sun going down. It says the day has ended and the time of sweet sleep begins. It quiets their souls and kicks in the melatonin—the sleep hormone.

Wake-up time is an important time for the child as well. Small children need to sleep as much as their bodies dictate, and they need to wake softly. Every child needs the first few minutes after waking to be spent with a parent. It reinstates them into the family fellowship and recognizes them to be a vital part of the order of things. If your child wakes up crying, you are likely doing something wrong. The mood may last all day. Without this bonding time, you will have cranky kids because they will feel emotionally detached.

Children are happiest when they wake and know they are welcome to run and hop in bed with Mama and Daddy. Each family is different. Some children just need a warm cuddle and a back scratch, while others will want a boisterous tussle filled with giggles. The release of oxytocin (the bonding neurotransmitter in the brain) is crucial for the child.

I know that Daddy is usually off to work before little ones wake, but Mama can always crawl back into bed when the kids get up, allowing them that special time with her. This is the easiest technique to institute, yet the best child-training tip you will ever receive.

HUMOR OR STRESS

Laughter is good for the brain. A study published in the journal *Cognition*

25 Mindell, Jodi A., et al. (2009). "A nightly bedtime routine: impact on sleep in young children and maternal mood." *Sleep*. Retrieved from: www.ncbi.nlm.nih.gov/pmc/articles/PMC2675894

> ### CUDDLE CHEMICAL
>
> Oxytocin is known as the cuddle chemical. It is the bonding chemical that is released when we interact with our loved ones. A German study published in 2014 stated that singing together nearly doubled the level of oxytocin in comparison to just interacting with friends. This and many other studies have proven music has a powerful effect on family and social bonding.

and Emotion suggests that laughter helps children learn new tasks.[26] The act of laughter, or simply enjoying humor, increases the release of endorphins and dopamine which aid the learning process. These hormones are active in the brain, providing a sense of pleasure and reward. When you connect any learning with the release of these "feel good" neurotransmitters, it substantially increases learning. Humor is great at reducing stress hormone levels. Conversely, the hormone cortisol, which is brought on by stress, decreases memory neurons. This means if you really need to learn or remember something, it is best not to be stressed.

Your child's brain needs a low-stress, joyful environment if he is going to learn effectively. Every parent, regardless of their own stress, needs to learn to laugh and laugh often.

ROUGH AND TUMBLE

As we discussed in the skin-to-skin section, researchers at Baylor College of Medicine have found that small children deprived of touch, play, and interaction with others have brains 20–30% smaller than is normal for their age. [27]

In the animal world, the young have rough-and-tumble play. In the humans world, daddies (and occasionally mamas) share the same instinct with their toddlers. Why is this a universal activity of nature, and what is missing

26 Ceschi, Grazia & Scherer, Klaus. (2003). Children's ability to control the facial expression of laughter and smiling: Knowledge and behaviour. Cognition and Emotion. 17. 385-411. 10.1080/02699930143000725.

27 Frost, Joe L. (1998). "Neuroscience, Play, and Child Development." Paper presented at IPA/USA Triennial National Conference, Longmont, Colorado. Retrieved from: https://files.eric.ed.gov/fulltext/ED427845.pdf

in the human family when this tendency is suppressed?

Dr. Anthony T. DeBenedet, a practicing physician and behavioral-science enthusiast, teaches in his books *The Art of Roughhousing* and *Playful Intelligence* that roughhousing is key to a child's mental and emotional development. Here's how it works: "When your child starts roughhousing, the brain recognizes this as a small stressor. As heart rate increases, the brain thinks he is fighting or fleeing some bad person. To protect his brain from stress, brain-derived neurotrophic factor (BDNF) is released. BDNF is nature's medicine for healthy brain growth and development. It protects and improves memory by stimulating neuron growth in many areas. This is why children love roughhousing and feel more connected after a good struggle."[28]

Even as adults, men bond with each other through roughhousing. Just observe a group of "buddies" hanging out. Likewise, dads have an instinct to tussle with their sons and even their daughters. Kids often will initiate a confrontation, striking the first blow and then running with a delighted squeal, expecting pursuit and retaliation. Many mothers stop dads from roughhousing for fear it will end in the little one crying. And it may. But Mother is not serving her child well; without this rough play, the child's confidence can be stunted.

Rough-and-tumble play provokes a touch of fear and anxiety in the child, which is exciting and healthy, while remaining in a circle of security and trust. Small pains may be remembered, but more so the grand excitement. The child wildly attacks Dad again for another tumble. It is a major bonding with the male figure. Mama nurtures, soothes, feeds, and tenderly embraces. Dad thrills, taking children to the edge of their emotional endurance, imparting confidence and toughness. It is nature. And it is wholesome, as brain scans prove.

A word of caution: The Bible does warn, **"...fathers, provoke not your children to wrath..." (Ephesians 6:4).** God knew that dads can get worked up, having too much fun at the expense of the little one and thus become bullies. There are limits; exercise them. Grow the brain, not the pain. Let the child's emotional state be your guide. It is going too far when the child flees in fear or pain. In our house, we had a motto that was oft repeated: "If it is not fun for all, it is not fun at all." Bullies make new bullies or broken boys; sparring partners make bosom buddies.

28 DeBenedet, Anthony T. (2011). *The Art of Roughhousing.* Philadelphia: Quirk Books.

ADULT SENSITIVITY

Roughhousing not only helps your child have confidence in childhood, it translates into adult confidence and self-assurance. But not all mamas were blessed by being toughened up as children. As adults, you may be emotionally weak, sensitive, and get your feelings hurt. It is perpetuating weakness to justify your hurt feelings and expect people to accommodate your emotional sensitivity.

To remain overly sensitive is a selfish choice, one that perpetuates your inadequate childhood. It is certainly easier to build confidence as a toddler with roughhousing, but as an adult, you will need to take responsibility for your own emotional toughening. This issue is vital for yourself and your child. Continue reading for ideas on how to take on this responsibility.

I CHARGE YOU

Start new habits that will increase your child's mental, emotional, and spiritual growth. When it's time to put him to bed at night, retell the day's events, have a short Bible story or connection time, pray with him, allow him to sleep as much as his body dictates, and upon waking, let him have several happy minutes with you to help re-center him. This is the easiest to accomplish, yet best child training tip you will ever hear me give.

SPECT SCAN

SPECT stands for single-photon emission computerized tomography. This type of imaging provides a non-invasive way for doctors to evaluate certain parts of your body. SPECT scans are different from other types of scans in that they can reveal irregular blood flow.[1] The Bible says **"For the life of the flesh is in the blood..." (Leviticus 17:11)**. Where there is not proper blood flow, permanent damage to that organ can occur. Hence, the importance of using SPECT scans in order to locate these areas. They can help to find the location of seizures in epilepsy patients as well as to gather information about changes in the brain due to such diseases as: Alzheimer's, Parkinson's, and Lyme disease.

1 www.verywellhealth.com/spect-scan-uses-side-effects-procedure-results-4173223

"Whom shall he teach knowledge? and whom shall he make to understand doctrine? them that are weaned from the milk, and drawn from the breasts" (Isaiah 28:9)

The Gift of Music

CHAPTER 3

Neuroplasticity has taught us that music is among the strongest neural-connecting activities and can aid in boosting IQ, memory retention, recovery from brain maladies, and improve learning in math, science and other subjects.

When viewed through an fMRI scanner, tasks such as reading or math light up particular areas of the brain relevant to that task alone. But when people are intently listening to quality music, multiple areas of the brain light up at once, areas not even directly related to music. Millions of connections are formed as the brain processes music.

Playing a musical instrument engages practically every area of the brain simultaneously, especially the visual, auditory, and motor cortices. It increases the volume and activity in the brain's corpus callosum, which is the mass of nerve fibers that connects the left and right hemispheres. Consequently, the brains of musicians adapt to the challenges involved in learning and playing an instrument by creating a larger corpus callosum. It is like building brain muscles through music exercise! This allows messages to get across the brain faster and through more varied routes.

Learning to play an instrument has been shown to raise the brain's cognitive skills. It can even increase IQ by seven points in both children and adults. Every time musicians pick up their instruments, thousands of connections are firing all over their brains. Music becomes the gateway to increased brain power for all areas of learning, including math, science, and memory.

THE GIFT OF GENERATIONAL MUSICIANS

I have a friend who sings publicly with his very young daughters. This past Sunday, the baby, about nine months old, was loudly humming on tune long after the congregation finished the song. How can a baby that can't talk stay on key? Her sisters, too young to go to school, can sing harmony. How did that happen? It is commonly thought that it is just in their genes—you are born with it or you are not. Now we know better. It was brain grooving/ synapse connections that made it happen. The little singers' daddy was raised in a home where all his siblings played instruments and sang, but neither Mom nor Dad have any musical ability. This unmusical mom decided that her children would be musicians. So she opened the door to the field of music by providing teachers and instruments, organizing demanding practice, and encouraging them to play and sing together. That is how a generationally musical family started. Supermom didn't know it, but she was also raising her family's IQs for generations to come (more on that later).

If there was a surefire way to improve your child's brain and emotional stability, would you do it?

THE GIFT OF PERFECT PITCH

The "gift" of perfect pitch is imparted before most parents think it is possible. Perfect pitch is the ability to recognize the pitch of a note or to produce any given note at will. It is estimated that from one to five people per 10,000 have a sense of absolute pitch. Through the study of neuroplasticity, researchers have discovered that a baby's brain is more malleable to the perception of pitch than at any other stage in life. It is in those first two years that children exposed to quality music develop perfect pitch. You will remember that up until about one year of age, an infant can distinguish between all 800 sounds that are made by all the languages on earth. That ability diminishes thereafter.[29]

"Whom shall he teach knowledge? ...them that are weaned from the milk, and drawn from the breasts" (Isaiah 28:9).

The lack of musical ability doesn't seem like such a loss until you read the academic scores and statistics of countries and individuals that have developed musically. Now we know it is worth a little effort to introduce your baby—even your womb baby—to quality music.

THE GIFT OF INTELLIGENCE THROUGH MUSIC

The academic scores of children increase significantly when music is part of the curriculum, as is evidenced in several nationwide experiments.

In a study of 17 countries examining the academic scores of 14-year-old science students, it was found that the top three countries—Hungary, the Netherlands, and Japan—all included music in their curriculum from kindergarten through high school. In the 1960s, Hungary noted the higher academic achievement of students enrolled in their "singing school", and sensibly responded by providing the Kodály method of music education for all their students. This method uses a child-developmental approach that introduces skills according to the capabilities of the child. Today, there are no third graders who cannot sing on pitch and sing beautifully. In addition, the academic achievement of Hungarian students—especially in math and science—continues to be outstanding. The Netherlands began their music program in 1968 and Japan followed suit, having observed the success of these two countries.[30]

It has been disclosed that almost all the foremost technical designers and engineers in Silicon Valley are practicing musicians. Wow! That says a lot!

The famous Donald Hebb, one of the earliest pioneers of neuroplasticity and neuropsychology, coined the phrase "Neurons that fire together wire together." Music fires basically every area of the brain, and in its wake,

29 Dingfelder, Sadie F. (2005). "Pitch perfect." *Monitor on Psychology. Retrieved from: www.apa.org/monitor/feb05/pitch.aspx*

30 Dickinson, Dee. (1993). "Music and the Mind." *New Horizons' On the Beam. Retrieved from: http://archive.education.jhu.edu/PD/newhorizons/strategies/topics/Arts%20in%20Education/dickinson_music.htm*

millions of new connections are formed. Every one of those connections increases brain power by making more sections of the brain available to process more information.

Listening to music requires no effort, but becoming a musician requires diligence, self-discipline, and perseverance. Are you or your child up for the task? As the research has shown, it is well worth the effort.

THE MECHANICS OF MUSIC UPON THE BRAIN

When we perform various motor skills—walking, typing, etc.—we utilize limited parts of the brain. But, as stated earlier, when we perform or listen to quality music, we are using many different parts of the brain in both hemispheres. Music has the power to change how we think, feel, and perform. It even has the power to heal.

Music stimulates many different areas of the brain all at once:
- Auditory cortex (volume, melody, speed, frequencies in song)
- Cerebrum (recalling the lyrics and sounds, using memory)
- Cerebellum (coordinating body movements and muscles)
- Limbic system (emotions in lyrics or melodies)

According to Piano Central Studios, "The corpus callosum is the part of our brains that connects the right hemisphere to the left. It allows both sides to communicate with each other, and is responsible for eye movement and helping us maintain our balance."

They continue by saying, "...the corpus callosum is the communicator for the brain. Current research from Anita Collins suggests that when our students play their instruments, they are working on their fine motor skills. *Both* parts of our brain are responsible for these fine motor skills. Additionally, as the right side of the brain is responsible for the creative process, while the left side is responsible for our linguistic prowess, musicians use both of these hemispheres simultaneously when they create. Consequently, musicians adapt to these challenges by creating a larger corpus callosum, much the way an athlete would grow his or her muscles."[31]

31 (2015). "Your Brain on Music: The Corpus Callosum." *Piano Central Studios. Retrieved from: www. pianocentralstudios.com/your-brain-on-music-the-corpus-callosum/*

THE GIFT OF MUSIC FOR WOMB BABIES

As previously stated, at 18 weeks gestation, a baby in the womb is able to hear external sounds. It has been observed that after birth, the baby responds differently to music that was played when he was still in the womb. This implies that he was experiencing the music and developing neural connections relating to music even before birth. In the first years of life, this child will be well equipped to learn music. Pity the infant exposed to rap and most pop music.

Dr. Kathleen M. Holland agrees, "Human responsiveness to music begins in the womb. Babies are brought into the world with the ability to detect beat."[32]

Introducing your sweet womb baby and newborn to quality music is one of the easiest and smartest things you can do for your child's developing brain. When he is in the crawling stage, buy a simple instrument and encourage your child to play. Lastly, find a way for him to take lessons. This will enable a fuller development of his potential.

THE GIFT OF MUSIC BRINGS PEACE

Schools around the world are now using music to set a mood and inspire children to participate in cleanup or fun activities. Teachers know from experience that singing cute, short songs like "Itsy-Bitsy Spider" to children provoke them to immediately focus their attention. Only speaking to the children would arouse a limited part of the brain, whereas music stimulates a web of responses from many places in the brain. The more connections made, the more learning there will be, and the greater the cooperation in doing routine chores. Have you ever noticed that military troops sing cadence as they march and drill? The practical results were appreciated long before anyone knew anything about the brain.

Dopamine levels in the brain rise when *pleasurable* music is playing. Dopamine is a neurotransmitter released when a person experiences pleasure. It helps regulate attention, working memory, and motivation. Dopamine is found to be low in ADHD brains. Obviously, if we can increase dopamine in a child, we can improve mood, focus, and participation. "Music

32 Howland, Kathleen M. (2015). "How Music Can Heal Our Brain and Heart." TEDx Talks. Retrieved from: https://www.youtube.com/watch?v=NlY4yCsGKXU

shares neural networks with other cognitive processes," says Patti Catalano, a neurologic music therapist at Music Works Northwest. "Through brain imaging, we can see how music lights up the left and right lobes. The goal of music therapy is to build up those activated brain muscles over time to help overall function."[33]

As your child sits on the floor playing, you can greatly enhance his brain by quietly playing quality music in the background. Any positive stimulus, especially involving multiple senses, causes the brain to respond by building new connections, and new connections mean a bigger brain. Bigger is better.

POWER OF TWO

Humans have more brain cells at the age of two than at any other time of their lives.

PNAS (Proceedings of the National Academy of Sciences) did a study that enlisted 39 infants (nine months old) in social play, some with waltz-type music and some without. After twelve sessions, the infants' temporal information processing was assessed in speech as well as music using magnetoencephalography. The brains of the babies who were exposed to music exhibited enhanced neural responses in the area of music and speech—the auditory and prefrontal cortices. This showed that the music had been instrumental in awakening in the brain those patterns that are utilized in speech and music.[34]

In summary, this means that exposing your newborns and young children to softly playing, quality music will improve their speech as well as their musical ability. Exposure to good music will expand your child's brain to be able to accommodate new areas of information. Music is a healthy stimulant for many areas of knowledge.

THE CURSE OF NOISE

There are many expressions of music, but if it does not include pattern and structure, the brain registers it as random noise, not music. On brain scans,

33 Rodgers, Anni Layne. (2012). "Music Therapy: Sound Medicine for ADHD." *ADDitude Magazine.* *Retrieved from: www.additudemag.com/music-therapy-for-adhd-how-rhythm-builds-focus/*

34 Zhao, T. Christina, and Kuhl, Patricia K. (2016). "Musical intervention enhances infants' neural processing of temporal structure in music and speech." *Proceedings of the National Academy of Sciences. Retrieved from: www.pnas.org/content/113/19/5212*

MOZART

Listening to Mozart has a long-term effect in helping children with ADD gain focus and mood control, and improve social skills.[1]

1 Amen, Daniel G. (n.d.). "Music and the Brain." *Didpuzzle. homestead.com.* Retrieved from: didpuzzle.homestead.com/music-and-the-brain.html

it is easy to discern music from noise because the brain doesn't know what to do with noise. It must be patterned and have consistent structure to be interpreted as music. The brain finds music easy to encode. Music makes us smarter as seen by researchers at the University of California Frances H. Rauscher, PhD, and her colleagues. They conducted a study with 36 undergraduates from the department of psychology who scored eight to nine points higher on a spatial IQ test after listening to ten minutes of Mozart. One of the researchers, Gordon Shaw, said, "We suspect that complex music facilitates certain complex neuronal patterns involved in high brain activities like math and chess."[35]

Music is influential from a very early age—even womb babies respond to Mozart. Thomas Verny, in his book *The Secret Life of the Unborn Child*, cites scientific experiments showing that fetuses preferred Mozart and Vivaldi, even in the earliest stages of pregnancy. He reported that fetal heart rates steadied and kicking decreased, while other music, especially rock, "drove most fetuses to distraction."[36]

Some "music" is noise. Noise does not help in the release of soothing neurotransmitters like dopamine. Research in animal models has shown that exposure to noise can induce stress and impair both cognition and memory by suppressing long-term potentiation in the hippocampus.[37] There are forms of sound that have been referred to as music, but instead of releasing happy neurotransmitters, they actually stimulate the release of chemicals that are detrimental to the brain. Noise is bad, but *loud* noise is

35 Amen, Daniel G. (n.d.). "Music and the Brain" *Didpuzzle.homestead.com. Retrieved from: didpuzzle. homestead.com/music-and-the-brain.html*

36 Verny, Thomas. (1982). *The Secret Life of the Unborn Child.* New York: Dell Publishing.

37 Barzegar, Marzieh, et al. (2014). "Prenatal exposure to noise stress: anxiety, impaired spatial memory, and deteriorated hippocampal plasticity in postnatal life." *Hippocampus. Retrieved from: www.researchgate.net/publication/265605350_Prenatal_Exposure_to_Noise_Stress_Anxiety_Impaired_Spatial_Memory_and_Deteriorated_Hippocampal_Plasticity_in_Postnatal_Life*

worse. It is extremely debilitating to the brain as well as the ear.

"Prolonged exposure to loud noise [or even white noise from things like fans and motors] alters how the brain processes speech, potentially increasing the difficulty in distinguishing speech sounds, according to neuroscientists. Exposure to intensely loud sounds leads to permanent damage of the hair cells that act as sound receivers in the ear. Once damaged, the hair cells do not grow back, leading to noise-induced hearing loss."[38]

According to Parenting and Child Health, "Because of their thinner skulls, babies and young children are at greater risk from loud sounds than are adults. If at all possible, avoid exposing young children to loud noises, such as car racing events or loud music, as the damage could last all of their life." Even noise from power tools, fans, kitchen appliances, electronic entertainment, and general racket are all detrimental to the brain.[39]

Sound travels in waves that keep moving. When a person is in a closed-in

NOISE POLLUTION

The World Health Organization reports that 40% of Europe's population is exposed to noise levels in excess of 55dB at night[1] (50dB is a quiet office and 60dB is a normal conversation): a level that disturbs sleep, concentration, and productivity, raises blood pressure, and increases incidences of heart disease. How about your home...do you sleep in peace?

Sound waves arrive at the brain in the form of electrical signals via the ear, which in turn causes the body to react. In particular, the amygdala (emotion) is activated, which leads to the release of the stress hormone cortisol.

1 WHO. (n.d.). "Noise: Data and Statistics." *World Health Organization, Europe.* Retrieved from: www.euro.who.int/en/health-topics/environment-and-health/noise/data-and-statistics

38 (2014). "Study: Noise-Induced Hearing Loss Alters Brain Responses to Speech." *UTD News Center. Retrieved from: www.utdallas.edu/news/2014/7/31-31061_Study-Noise-Induced-Hearing-Loss-Alters-Brain-Resp_story-wide.html*

39 Parenting and Child Health. (2017). "Children with Hearing Loss: Hearing Impairment." *Women's and Children's Health Network. Retrieved from: www.cyh.com/HealthTopics/HealthTopicDetails.aspx-?p=114&np=304&id=1584*

QUALITY

It takes something of substance to create good brain cells.

area where the sound waves are trapped, there is a greater possibility of damage. Putting anything in your ear (earbuds) or over your ear (headphones) for listening purposes can be detrimental to your hearing. This is because sound waves become trapped in the ear canal and, as stated earlier, can damage the delicate auditory hair cells in the cochlea. This is one critical reason why there is an increase in the number of people becoming hearing impaired.

Otherwise-educated couples drop their babies and young children off at childcare centers where there is constant racket of screaming babies, TV blaring, loud noise/music playing, and toddlers shoving things across the floor, adding screeching sounds to the bedlam. The children are exposed to this emotionally exhausting trauma ALL DAY LONG. In their most delicate stage of brain development, children are handicapped by extreme and negative environmental forces. Research has proven this to be damaging to the brain and the emotional well-being of small children. Some children do survive that environment to become normal, healthy adults, but what of the many who do not? And what might the child have become if he had been in a brain-healthy environment his entire youth?

THE GIFT OF HEALING

In the world of music therapy, the word *miracle* is spoken daily. Music therapists are using music to bring healing to children with autism, ADHD, and Tourette syndrome, as well as mental and mood disorders. It is employed to help overcome stuttering, open up reading to non-readers, and even reverse hearing and sight disorders that originate in the brain. Those trained in the field of music therapy are being introduced to a world of possibilities never before imagined.

A person's brain can be damaged in many ways. An infant can be born with brain damage or suffer damage at birth. It could occur as a result of an accident, medication, a high fever, oxygen deprivation, or various diseases. Often, it is an unknown element that brings on ADHD or other similar brain disorders. When the idea of neuroplasticity first emerged, researchers used animals to demonstrate its healing power, but the focus quickly shifted to older adults with debilitating brain maladies. Researchers reasoned that if an OLD brain could recover, then the sky would be the limit where young brains are concerned. Remember, young brains are even more plastic—able to change more quickly.

Several years ago, well-known Congresswoman Gabby Giffords was speaking to a crowd when an assailant shot her in the head, damaging her left hemisphere. She survived the horrific, brain-shattering blow, but was left with many disabilities, including the inability to speak. Until the application of neuroplasticity, recovery would have been a hit-or-miss experiment, possibly with little result. Her family chose to turn to a little-known treatment—music therapy. She learned to sing words before she could speak them. True to its promise, it did indeed rewire her brain. It was not a miracle, but it felt like one to all who knew her. Multiply this by the thousands and you will appreciate why I said at the beginning that neuroplasticity is so close to a miracle that it should be spelled H-O-P-E.

BYPASS

It has been shown that humor and music both bypass higher reasoning.

THE GIFT TO THE OLD FOLKS

It is common for elderly people to have brain damage. With reports of amazing success, music therapists quickly began their own research. Could new pathways be generated in old brains through the use of music? Could even severely diseased brains respond favorably to music therapy? The answer, they discovered, is a resounding YES.

PARKINSON'S DISEASE

A friend was explaining to me why she couldn't be part of an upcoming event: her husband had recently developed Parkinson's disease. "At this point," she said, "he is not even able to lift his feet to walk to the bathroom. It is like his feet are glued to the floor."

I was shocked at the seemingly helpless situation and asked, "Why don't you just sing to him?"

"Sing?" she blurted out incredulously, as if I had suddenly developed a bad case of Alzheimer's. "What does that have to do with anything?"

"You know, sing. Music activates both sides of the brain, so when a person with Parkinson's disease gets locked up, the problem is in the brain, not in the feet. When you sing and activate large areas of the brain, the Parkinson's brain is able to shift commands to the other side of the brain, which then allows the neural signals to reach the feet. Amazingly, they can now walk, talk, or feed themselves. Surely, the VA hospital taught you all this stuff! Your daughters are nurses—ask them!"

She just stared at me as if I were telling her a really bad joke. "No, I don't know, and no, the VA didn't tell me to sing to Tom. And no, my daughters didn't tell me; so are you sure you know what you are talking about? I never heard such a crazy thing in my life."

THE GIFT OF MUSIC THERAPISTS

In a TED talk, music therapist Dr. Kathleen M. Holland said, "Music is being used to help with the mobility of people with Parkinson's disease, a long, chronic disease process. What we are looking at here are brain-based treatments for brain-based disorders. We're not looking at the paralyzed leg; we're not looking at the symptom. Our goal is to address the cause changing the underlying neural mechanisms—the place in the brain that Parkinson's has destroyed, thus can no longer communicate to the body. Music is being used by music therapists with great success across a variety of brain disorders."[40]

"Parkinson's disease is a degenerative, progressive disease that affects nerve cells deep in the parts of the brain called the basal ganglia and the substantia nigra."[41] When symptoms first appear, through music therapy, the patient can reroute neural signals to parts of the brain not yet affected. There is wonderful hope for these patients to regain many functions. Parkinson's patients struggle with feeling as though their feet are glued to the floor, but when they even think about music, they are able to walk within seconds. People who have lost their ability to walk, talk, pick up a cup, and many other motor skills, can often function normally while music is playing or when

40 Howland, Kathleen M. (2015). "How Music Can Heal Our Brain and Heart." *TEDx Talks. Retrieved from: www.youtube.com/watch?v=NIY4yCsGKXU*

41 Mandybur, George, MD, and Gartner, Maureen, RN, (reviewers). (2018). "Parkinson's Disease." *Mayfield Brain & Spine. Retrieved from: www.mayfieldclinic.com/PE-PD.htm*

they hum, or even think of humming a song. Music is powerful. There are host of YouTube videos where you can actually see these results.

I love what Elizabeth Stegemoller, PhD said in her TED talk: "But perhaps the most powerful component of music therapy is the social benefit derived from making music together, which can help patients combat depression. When patients with Parkinson's engage in music therapy, often one of the first behaviors to emerge is smiling. The flat effect and masked face, characteristic of the disease, fade away."[42]

MUSIC IDEAS TO GET YOU STARTED

Lullabies/Quieter Songs (good for bedtimes/quiet times)

Sleep Sound in Jesus by Michael Card

Bless My Little Girl/Bless My Little Boy by Kelly Willard

Baby's First Hymns: An Instrumental Lullaby Collection by Dream Baby

Classical Music

Beethoven's Wig: Sing-Along Symphonies (3 different albums)

Essential Mozart: 32 of His Greatest Masterpieces

Maestro Classics (12 CD Collection)

Handel's Water Music

Peter and the Wolf, Op. 767 by Sergei Prokofiev (The Philadelphia Orchestra/David Bowie narration is an excellent album)

Meet the Great Composers Book/CD sets

Classical Music Albums from Composers such as: Johannes Brahms, Franz Liszt, Peter Tchaikovsky, Frederic Chopin, Antonin Dvorak, Sergei Rachmaninoff, Johann Strauss, Felix Mendelssohn, Antonio Vivaldi, Franz Schubert (Opal Wheeler children's biographies are great children's books for bedtime reading.)

Hymns

Hymnworks by Lynda McKechnie (2 volumes)

42 Stegemoller, Elizabeth, MD. (2017). "Music Therapy and Its Impact on the Brain." *TEDx Talk. Retrieved from: https://community.sfn.org/t/tedx-music-therapy-and-its-impact-on-the-brain/7069*

I CHARGE YOU

Download quality music and play it softly in the background while your children are at play. If you have toddlers, buy a few toy instruments that they can play with. Make it a habit to sit your little ones in your lap and sing along with good music. Check into music lessons for you and your children. Learn to be particular in your choice of music as it is either doing something positive or negative to your brain as well as your child's. Now is the time for some serious evaluation and purging. You only have one brain. Love it and treat it well.

"O sing unto the Lord a new song: sing unto the Lord, all the earth. Sing unto the Lord, bless his name; shew forth his salvation from day to day. Declare his glory among the heathen, his wonders among all people" (Psalm 96:1-3).

Many Roads

CHAPTER 4

Neuroplasticity has taught us that learning is accelerated
when we are using several areas of our brain at once.
The more areas used, the greater the recall.

THE GIFT OF MANY ROADS

The brain is like a spider's web, composed of billions of neurons in a web of interconnected pathways. A thought, idea, word, color, or smell activates a system of connections formed by past experiences. Every stimulus creates or utilizes a network of roads. As we have discussed, music creates many more pathways than any other activity. Through fMRI, one can see major thoroughfares with multiple intersections, main avenues, and small streets that zigzag throughout every area of the brain.

It reminds me of the Google navigational road map on my phone. When I see a red line alerting me that the interstate has come to a standstill ahead, I could stop and wait for possibly hours. Instead, I look for alternate routes. It might be a longer route with slower traffic and more red lights, but at least the traffic is moving and the detour will eventually get me to my destination.

Many diseases or brain traumas impair the existing connections and can cause major "interstate" blockage. A stroke or other debilitating condition is like a bridge being out—nothing is moving down the old, familiar road. A part of the brain that controls an arm or leg or one of the senses is not able to communicate with that member of the body. Traffic stops. These damaged areas of the brain are clearly seen on scans as black spots—black because there is no electrical activity or blood flow crossing the darkened void.

Previously, doctors knew that the darkened area of the brain was dead, thus an irreversible tragedy. Believing the brain to be an organ fixed in its attributes and knowing there was no way to repair the old pathway, they had to accept the inevitable. But then came the understanding of neuroplasticity. The brain is a changing, adapting, moldable wonder. With skillful therapy that is still being developed, the brain can find a detour that will bring signals to the desired location. In time, it can be enlarged into a major interstate, carrying brain traffic just as efficiently as before.

If music has been a part of your life, especially if you play an instrument, then your brain already has so many alternate byways in place that it can more easily find a workaround to complete the circuit. For non-musical people, it might take more effort and time to form new pathways around the damaged part of the brain. But, just as with Parkinson's patients, music helps make it happen even if you can't sing on key.

I am 68 years old and have been hearing impaired since I was born. But yesterday, I learned how to play the old song "Victory in Jesus" on the piano. I practiced it over and over to groove it deeply into my brain. Then I took a 15-minute break and came back to practice again. Today, my brain is more connected. I know this because scans have proven music is that powerful. What I have learned as I have researched and written this book will provoke me to continue learning music even though it means stumbling around on the piano like a six-year-old. I know it could yet make the difference in my life! Michael Merzenich, PhD, now recognized as perhaps the world's most renowned neuroscientist in the field of neuroplasticity, says, "It is never too late to rewire the brain."

ENJOY

One of my favorite YouTube lecturers is Dr. Deforia Lane, PhD. Watch her lecture called Music Is Beautiful. You will enjoy learning from her gifts.

An old brain is in the winter of life—basically in a state of decay—yet music therapists are seeing some recovery in almost every area of brain damage and even in brain diseases. The young brain is in the spring of life—new, just beginning to fire, wire, and create pathways. If your baby has any sort of brain issue, regardless of where in the body or mind the damage might manifest itself, know that there is hope through music and therapy. Study what is happening in the world of neuroscience, find a good music therapist to help your child, and don't stop until you know you have done all there is to do.

MY PERSONAL EXPERIENCE

I was not aware of neuroplasticity when I was young and raising my family. But I was always searching for a better way to train my children. This is my story.

I have potty-trained our babies beginning on their first day by simply making a noise every time I felt wet heat in their diapers. Those two things happening simultaneously, over and over, created an association that triggered their bladders to release when they heard the noise. It was a brain link or connection that was being formed, but at the time, I had no idea this was how the brain functioned. Now my grandchildren are being trained. By the time they walk, they take themselves to the potty. Amazing, right?

Babies quickly learn to be comforted by their mama's style of handling them. Some time ago during a church meeting, I was babysitting a newborn, but I could not comfort the screaming child. I rocked, sang, and cuddled the baby, but she continued to cry. Someone went into the meeting to get the mother, thinking the child must be hungry. As soon as the mother saw her baby being held and gently rocked, she just laughed and said, "Give her to me." The mother began this hard rocking motion along with a high-pitched hum. The baby immediately stopped crying and began contentedly sucking her thumb. The newborn's brain had been grooved to a different kind of security. The mother handed the baby back to me and I mimicked the mother's style, which resulted in a happy little girl. If a tiny baby can find quiet comfort in that rough and bouncy treatment over my gentle grandma style, then grooving is important to comfort.

The first few years of a child's life are an opportunity to be grooving them into confidence, thankfulness, joyfulness, self-discipline, and an eagerness to learn. In these early years, your child is in a heightened state of learning;

it is the time when neural links are most easily and quickly formed. His physical, mental, and emotional states are forming strong neural pathways. Today through the use of fMRI scanners, we are learning exactly what actions, moods, and sounds create positive, lasting grooves on the brain and what things we have been doing to train our children that are really just a waste of time.

When my first child was born, I had just finished reading a book about introducing your infant to good music. The book showed how children are not born with a gift for music; rather, their early exposure to music grooves the brain to love music and develop musical abilities. For the first three months of my baby's life, I had music softly playing most of the time. Later, I read how reading poetry to your toddlers would imprint the concept of rhyme into their brains. Millions of brain connections were being made that would be building blocks for music and poetry for all of her life. I really wanted to give my child all that I could, so I was faithful in these exercises. Of course, my gratification was delayed because it was YEARS before I realized how successful my endeavors were. But it REALLY worked.

I was reading another baby book when my next child was born. It showed how you could use dots to teach math concepts to infants. I faithfully made large cards with big dots on them. Several times a day, I would hold up that day's card of dots and say to my two-year-old, "This is eight dots. Eight." And my toddler would excitedly yell out, "Eight dots!" He never actually counted the dots. I reviewed often, going back to one dot, and when I reviewed, I intentionally hesitated before I called out the number so my baby boy would call it out before I could. The book warned me not to challenge him by asking, "How many dots?" I finished with 35 dots arranged randomly on a card. He knew them all. But to me, if there were more than 15 dots, it was just a guessing game. I couldn't identify the number but he could. Amazing! That boy grew up to be a master at math—not reading, not music, but really good at math.

Now when my third child came around, I was reading, *How to Teach Your Baby to Read* by Glenn and Janet Doman. He had flash cards of words. Not easy words, but words with lots of letters. I taped words to everything in the house, identifying the objects. The fact is, I read too much and I love experimenting. I have a habit of getting excited and wanting to try everything I read. You would have to meet Nathan (the third child) to believe what I am telling you. He is a master with words; he LOVES words. Ask anyone who knows him and they will tell you he has a rich vocabulary, far beyond any-one they know. I never actually taught him how to read. When he was just a small child, people would ask him, "Who taught you that?" and he would always answer, "Nobody did. I just always knew." Since the brain connec-tions were made when he was just a few months old, he did "just always know." He only did a few school lessons with workbooks (at the most ten pages) in his whole life. Yet he can discuss most any subject with any edu-cator, lawyer, or scientist and maintain parity; in most cases, he is capable of explaining it better. He does have major holes in his education: his hand-writing is terrible and he can't spell. But because he loves words, he loves reading, so he's been able to learn a good deal about almost every subject. I grooved his brain deeply with the love of words.

When my fourth child was born, I recorded myself reading books so she could listen and "read" along with the tape any time she wanted. She loved playing the tapes and liked showing her friends. I was sure this was a great way to homeschool because she could listen over and over. Repetition was considered to be the mother of all education, but surprisingly, she had the hardest time learning to read. I now **know** through my study of neuroplas-ticity that nothing takes the place of a real person sitting and reading along with a little one. The brain reacts differently when you sit next to your child as you teach her how to read. Her neurons are firing in areas of companion-ship, love, safety, and reading, creating a much wider net of connections. The child is learning, not just because she likes to sit by someone, but be-cause more of her brain is being activated; the bigger the net, the greater the number of connections; and the more connections, the more memories are being established. The neurons for fellowship are more extensive, so when you combine learning with love and safety, you are greatly multiplying the child's learning ability.

Remember the example I gave in baby Janessa's story? It's a good exam-ple, so here it is again. "If you are teaching a child to memorize a Bible verse, put it to music and teach them dance steps as they sing the Bible verse. Look into their eyes and smile at them as they sing. Show them the words so they can read them as they sing them. This will open up the part of the brain that is used for reading. Each activity—singing, dancing, feeling appreciated by your smile (happy feelings open up a lot of brain area), reading, and saying the words—all employ a different area of the brain. This forms a multifacet-ed network, each related to the others. The child is storing a memory of the

Bible verse in all those different areas of the brain at one time. When it is time to recall the verses, memories come from several areas of the brain, making recall much easier.

On a side note and jumping ahead to the adult section of the book: If you listen to the audio of this book as you read it, your brain will store the information in several different areas of the brain simply because you are using different parts of the brain. Your recall will be greater due to the multiple areas that are tapped. This will greatly aid your study.

HIGHER IQ

Your baby's IQ is not fixed. You, as his mama, have the power to increase his intelligence with just a few, simple things added to his life.

Sadly, I didn't understand the power of neuroplasticity: touching, feeling, smelling, laughing, and singing as you learn. I thought the repetition of a recording would be better than Mama doing it only once or twice a day. Thankfully, my daughter developed strong, confident leadership skills from caring for her little sister and playing house, which helped make up for my lack.

The fifth child caught me in the middle of studying herbs. Like every research topic I get into, I was passionate about herbs. I checked out and studied every herb book in every library in Memphis, Tennessee. My kids—from my ten-year-old down to the newborn—studied with me. We scrutinized pictures of herbs and then went into the wild to find them. We bought herb seeds to grow and then harvested and dried the plants. We cooked with herbs, healed with herbs, and puked together when I misused them. My oldest child learned a lot about herbs, as did the other children, but it was the baby I carried on my hip (Shoshanna) who became a renowned herbalist. Did you know brain links are also made by sniffing? That young brain was creating synapse connections by the millions as she was smelling, touching, tasting, and understanding herbs. Her network of learning was happening all over her brain, and the amazing thing is, those connections are still there!

By the time my baby was nine years old, she was bringing in a good amount of money selling her plants. When she was thirteen, she took over a tiny herb business that we had established a few years earlier for our children as a way to allow them to make a little money and develop business skills. Within three years, she had a huge, thriving business, and people from all over the world would write, asking her questions about herbs, to which she knew the answers.

When I was studying herbs, I got my children involved because it allowed me to follow my own interest. I had no idea that by sharing ideas, concepts, and basic knowledge, we were sharing neural activations. Also, it was grooving their brains much more deeply and in a more lasting way, than if I had been teaching them school as usual. Research has proven that shared experiences and feelings cause neurons in each person's brain to activate together, so shared learning is much more productive than learning alone.

There is one thing I did as a mother that was just perfect: I gave my children my presence. I didn't have a cell phone to pull my attention from them, and I didn't wear earphones to listen to music. I was present. They never had to yell out, "Hey, Mom, watch me," when they were doing some silly, childhood show-off thing. I was always watching! I am sure my lack of hearing had a lot to do with my constant eye contact and intense interest in their lives, and for this, I count my hearing loss a glorious gift. I am most thankful. Nothing you can do in life will take the place of your undivided presence in their lives. Sharing life with your children is more important than your friends or your business, even if you go completely broke. When your mind, heart, and soul are attentive to what they are doing, you are sharing brain neuron activations with them. God says, **"Train up a child in the way he should go: and when he is old, he will not depart from it"** (Proverbs 22:6).

Brain scans, such as fMRI, clearly demonstrate a much more extensive learning experience when learning occurs in a group. If the group is comprised of family, the learning is even greater. If the experience is shared, such as with the study of music, singing, math, science, and any other discipline, it is greatly enhanced. This should change your methods of schooling. Reading to all your children at the same time should become a habit. Learn science together as a fun project. Don't waste your time sticking to old methods established in 1837 by Horace Mann. Neuroplasticity has shown us the old ways of public schooling are not the best.

HINDSIGHT

What have I learned from my experiences and what would I do differently now that I know about neuroplasticity and can see the results in my children? Well, of course, ALL my children would have the opportunity to hear classical music as newborns; in fact, even as womb babies they would have been quite familiar with Mozart and Vivaldi. I would also provide many types of musical instruments for my little children to play as they grew up. I would even provide some instruments for them to play as small children— not electronic, except for a keyboard. As stated earlier, music makes connections all over the brain, and the more connections, the smarter they will be. Every one of my children would have had dots on cards and words on furniture. All would have had their senses stirred by herbs. But you only get one shot at being a mom, and I have had mine. You now have the science of neuroplasticity to steer you on the path that I accidentally stumbled across here and there. I write this to you so that by reading this one book, you can learn what took me a lifetime to discover.

What has impressed me more than words on a wall, dots on a paper, or growing herbs is the fact that my babies' brains were being grooved with my moods, my actions toward others, my attitude toward their daddy, and all the things that made up my days. I was molding their brains to become weak or strong, pitiful or resourceful, needy or thankful, overbearing or longsuffering. I am my children's mother. Their bodies were formed in my womb; their souls were shaped in my care. I have learned that everything I did shaped their brains. I am thankful we did not have electronics to put into their hands. They always had something more brain-building and important to do. I am profoundly thankful my children spent their days playing in the dirt, swimming in the creek, inventing rocket ships, and making spear-fishing guns. These childhood things turned out to be critically important in brain development. No one had a clue these things were important for mental and emotional intelligence. We just did them because they were fun and there was nothing else to do.

PERIPHERAL VISION

Peripheral vision is what is seen on both sides when looking straight ahead. Cell phone use or excess viewing of small screens can disrupt the development of peripheral vision. The lack of normal peripheral vision is a handicap that can often be avoided.

You, young mamas, can do the same. You can proactively help your children create quality brain connections that will aid them all their lives. We don't need to shrug our shoulders and use our own lack of high intelligence or creativity as an excuse. Our intelligence and gifts are what we make them.

THE CURSE OF WASTED TIME

The study of neuroplasticity conforms to the ancient wisdom of King Solomon, who said **"...but a child left to himself bringeth his mother to shame"** **(Proverbs 29:15b)**.

When children are allowed to disengage from society and spend hours focused on a digital screen, their brains are being left idle. The offensive noises and psychedelic, flashing colors that emit from the screen are unhealthy. God created the brain to operate at its optimum, in the simple, physical, and social environment of a multi-stimulus society of fellowship and communion. Brain cells cannot be produced in brainless entertainment. The narrow focus of the two-dimensional screen will not allow eyesight to develop correctly. Children's brains will not be challenged to adjust to depth of field and to a wide panorama of sights that call for the development of peripheral vision. The brain/hearing relationship will not be challenged in a two-dimensional, sound-modulated environment. Because of this, children's intellects will be limited. Their social bonding will be nil, and they will grow up to live in an artificial world of limited possibilities, predetermined by the masterminds of mindless entertainment. As the body is what you feed it, so much more is the brain.

"The light of the body is the eye: therefore when thine eye is single, thy whole body also is full of light; but when thine eye is evil, thy body also is full of darkness" (Luke 11:34).

Researchers Kayla Bois and Brad Bushman of Michigan University summed up the cartoon consumption in the average child's schedule as follows:

- 2- to 5-year-old children watch cartoons 32 hours per week.
- 6- to 11-year-old children watch cartoons 28 hours per week.
- In 51% of homes, the TV is switched on most of the time.

Researcher Sharmin at BRAC University concluded:

- Most parents prefer to leave their children in front of the TV in order to finish their work or to have a rest.

- Putting a child in front of the TV is the best way for a parent to make their child eat their food, which could, in part, explain the trend toward obesity.[43]

Cartoons are often violent and have characters that act silly. They don't express normal childhood behavior and, as a rule, train children to reflect such undesirable behavior.

"While children are watching cartoons, there is a learning process going on. Whatever children learn while watching cartoons, they tend to act out, thereby influencing their mode of socializing with other children and with the world in general."[44]

On September 12, 2011, the respected medical journal *Pediatrics* published a fascinating study called, "The Effects of Fast-Paced Cartoons." In the study, researchers divided sixty 4-year-olds into three groups. Each group was put into a room and directed to do one of the following activities: draw with crayons, watch a PBS show called *Caillou*, or watch a fast-paced cartoon show called *SpongeBob*. After nine minutes, the children took a battery of tests that required focus, concentration, patience, working memory, and manipulation. Researchers wanted to observe the "executive function" of children's brains.

It came as no surprise that the children who watched the fast-paced cartoon performed significantly **worse** on attention and memory testing than the children in the other two groups. What the researchers concluded was that the *unnatural pace* of the cartoon sequences was overstimulating and stressful to the children's brains.

In an editorial in *Pediatrics*, Dr. Dimitri Christakis of Seattle Children's Hospital said: "Connecting fast-paced television viewing to deficits in executive function, regardless of whether they are transient, has profound implications for children's cognitive and social development that need to be considered and reacted to."[45]

Many children spend hours watching cartoons or engaging in some

43 Habib, Khaled, and Solimon, Tarek. (2015). "Cartoons' Effect in Changing Children's Mental Response and Behavior." *Open Journal of Social Sciences.* Retrieved from: file.scirp.org/Html/17-1760575_59815.htm

44 Baran, Stanley J., and Davis, Dennis K. (2009). *Mass Communication Theory: Foundations, Ferment, and Future,* 6th Ed. Boston: Wadsworth, Cengage Learning.

45 Christakis, Dimitri A. (2011). "The Effects of Fast-Paced Cartoons." *Pediatrics.* Retrieved from: pediatrics.aappublications.org/content/128/4/772

other equally useless yet noisy pursuit. The unnaturally rapid stimulation of odd sounds and imagery taxes the child's brain and is not conducive to good development. It is crucial to understand that a child's intellect, as well as his soul, will not develop into anything more than what is poured into him. Nothing comes out of nothing, and nothing ever will.

Dr. Christakis is right; we need to react to this issue by giving our children better options for occupying their attention. Fast-paced cartoons are the white bread, candy bar, and Cheetos of mental food. They're nutritionally empty, and a diet full of them will result in poor development.

"I will walk within my house with a perfect heart. I will set no wicked thing before mine eyes: I hate the work of them that turn aside; it shall not cleave to me" (Psalm 101:2–3). Read all of Psalm 101. My husband calls it the digital media psalm.

SAND PILE SCHOOLING BY DEBI

When our first child was born over 45 years ago, dyslexia was an issue little known to the public. However, universities were highly interested in how to detect it and how to fix it. Some young students had already come up with a few interesting and effective ideas, although they had no idea why they worked so well. I was totally unaware of any of this.

The public library was my source for all things intriguing, and I was always looking for something new to try. When I was carrying our first child, as I mentioned, I had read that keeping classical music softly playing in the background while pregnant and during the first year would provoke the child to become musical. As the book suggested, I started the music playing before my first child was born. No one knew why music worked, but, like most all young mamas, I wanted more for my child than I had available for myself. Since I was born with an extreme hearing impairment, any background noise, including music, is a problem for me because it creates just enough sound to drown out voices. But for my baby, no sacrifice was too great, so soft music played all day every day. I felt gratified that I was giving my baby a real head start in life.

One day, as she sat in her highchair eating, I noticed she reached out her hand for an object on her tray, but she reached for it on the opposite side of where it was located. I started watching her, testing her, and I grew concerned. It appeared to me that her lovely, pale blue eyes were not working correctly. The library resources offered no information, but the young librarian gave me the phone number of a research department at Memphis State University. Through these students, a whole new world of learning opened up to me and my little girl.

According to one website's definition, Dyslexia is neurobiological in origin. The defect is intrinsic to the individual and occurs at the level of neuronal activity.[46] This means her problem was not in her eyes, but her brain.

Apparently, my child's neurons were not connecting correctly. Every child seems to have a slightly different brain response, but my little Beka seemed to see life as if she were looking into a mirror. The MSU students helped me come up with a plan that might help her, especially since I had caught the malady so early in Beka's life. Following instructions, I put a shallow box in front of her containing an inch of sand spread evenly across the bottom for her to play in. It was grand play that kept her occupied while I cooked dinner. According to the researchers, her fingers would fix her brain. They didn't know why, since neuroplasticity was not part of medical science at that time, but through experimentation, they knew it worked. It was new enough research that the students called me regularly to see how she was responding to the sand/finger project.

My baby girl started just playing in the sand but soon recognized I had a plan for her in how she used it. I added food coloring, divided the areas into sections, and she started creating art. The researchers admonished me to always make it a happy occasion that she would anticipate with pleasure because they had noted that **the child's pleasure was integral to the effectiveness of the conditioning**. Now, after studying neuroplasticity, I know that the joy we shared together released dopamine, a neurotransmitter that greatly enhances learning. I began to hold her tiny finger as we drew letters in the sand and I softly made the sound of the letter in her ear. I laid a bright red, plastic letter A in the sand so she could see it as we drew with her finger. She loved the mama time and her sand box. Learning became the highlight of our days.

The research students continued to call me with other suggestions, and they followed up to document their effectiveness. I think we were their project. I used clay, mud, and flour-and-water mixtures to make balls to count, and we made letters out of M&M candies. Finally, I began to make peanut

46 (2002). "Definition of Dyslexia." *International Dyslexia Association.* Retrieved from: dyslexiaida. org/definition-of-dyslexia/

butter play dough for her to mold shapes. I added food dye to make it more interesting and to teach her colors at the same time. Her fingers touching the different textures and her joy in doing something fun with Mama released happy neurotransmitter chemicals, causing her synapses to connect new neurons to work their magic.

Forty-something years ago, I had no idea about neurons or synapses, though I often wondered how the fingers could retrain the brain. Researchers had discovered the effectiveness of the techniques and there were various theories about how and why they worked, but today, thanks to the availability of brain scans, it is an absolute science.

It worked! We play-doughed and finger-painted our way out of dyslexia. She could read well by the age of four, although when she was tired or sick, her dyslexia would reappear, but only slightly. I didn't consider at the time that this was homeschooling, since there were no books, schedules, or tests involved.

This personal, hands-on schooling took little of my time, but it kept my daughter (and later my sons and then two more daughters) busy for many happy hours. The cost was minimal, yet the rewards were great. It did require a vacuum cleaner!

My husband and I realized that we as parents could provide a better education for our children than was possible in any government classroom, so that was the year we started talking about educating our children at home. The term "homeschooling" was unknown to us or anyone we knew. It was a radical concept at the time. That year, my husband and I became movers and shakers in Memphis, Tennessee in what was to become known as the homeschooling movement.

SUGGESTIONS

- *Animal care* – Let them play with, exercise, feed, and train animals.

- *Discovering how things work* – Give them non-functional devices and machines to take apart and put back together. This is a great way to help them understand how things work, and as they get older, they may be able to start fixing the items. I know a two-year-old who has been at this type of play for months.

- *Art* – Give them a subject to draw or a book/video lesson to follow. Have them start field sketchbooks in which they draw items they find in nature (in the yard) such as leaves, trees, feathers, and flowers. Turn on some background music and let them color with markers. There are "grown-up" coloring books full of beautiful designs that are enjoyable for teens and adults.

- *Board games* – Quality games promote critical thinking, socializing, math skills, managing resources, learning to deal with victory and defeat, and more. Some suggestions to get you started: Scrabble, UpWords, Settlers of Catan, Ticket to Ride, Qwirkle, Scotland Yard, Blokus, and Chess.

- *Puzzles* – These are great for little ones developing spatial reasoning and eye-hand coordination. An intricate puzzle can take many hours to put together but also be easily put away when not in use.

I CHARGE YOU

Sit down and write five new projects you want to do with your children. They can be simple. Make word cards to put up in several places around the house. Let them do sand box writing once a week or every time it rains. Think of something that you can research with your children, such as herbs or cooking. Involve all the children in cleaning out the kitchen drawers and pantry shelves, and then assign each child an area to keep clean.

"And let the beauty of the Lord our God be upon us: and establish thou the work of our hands upon us; yea, the work of our hands establish thou it" (Psalm 90:17)

Bring Back PLAY

CHAPTER 5

*Neuroplasticity has taught us that using our
bodies is critical for brain development.*

BRING BACK PLAY
by Dr. Ellen Easley, PT, DPT (Doctor of Physical Therapy)

Early environments dictate early circuitry—brain grooving! The first few years of life are when the brain is most malleable with the highest potential for neural plasticity. So malleable, in fact, that a baby who suffers a stroke that wipes out an entire hemisphere (one side) of the brain can still mature into a highly functional adult. The brain retains its ability to mold like hot plastic until the day we die; however, most of this grooving occurs in the "little" years.

As a physical therapist, I am fascinated by how a moving body grooves and literally grows the brain larger. Physical therapists who work in pediatrics are focused on getting their little patients to meet physical developmental milestones to ensure the brain and body grow properly. Our culture vigorously pushes academic milestones and educational success, while physical development suffers. We do this despite research proving that developing a strong body through play actually makes a child smarter.[47] Free, unstructured play will ensure these physical milestones are met.[48] As fine and gross motor skills progressively develop, they secure the foundation for a healthy adult body alongside a well-grooved brain.

If you grew up in a public or private school system, you likely have fond memories of recess. It was the part of the day when you were finally free to run off pent-up energy through freeze tag, swing upside down by your knees, play hopscotch, and soak up sunshine. With the notion that this playtime could be better spent on academics, an alarming number of U.S. schools now offer no recess;[49] and yes, that includes kindergarten programs. With schools' hands tied between state academic requirements and shortages of playground staff, recess time continues to be reduced and even deleted. When out of school, the rest of the modern child's day and weekend is typically rigid and over-scheduled. Between after-school programs, sports, and music practice, parents shuffle their kids from one structured activity to the next. While incorporating some of these rich experiences is wonderful, setting aside time for free play and exercise to develop the body and, subsequently, the mind should be top priority. Physical activity increases cognitive function and literally grows new brain cells.[50] And don't think this only applies to those three feet tall and under; the advantages are also seen in adults. Getting sweaty makes you smarter too.

When modern children do have free time, they tend to "play" using technology. The upcoming chapter by Dr. Dawson, DC, shows how digital media overuse is evidence enough of its danger. Sedentary bodies bombarded with chaotic sensory stimulation from video games and the TV have resulted in delays in attaining developmental milestones. Not enough proof? Think on

47 Basch, C. E. (2011). "Healthier students are better learners: high-quality, strategically planned, and effectively coordinated school health programs must be a fundamental mission of schools to help close the achievement gap." *Journal of School Health*, 81(10): 650-662.

48 Dewar, G. (2014). "The cognitive benefits of play: Effects on the learning brain." Retrieved from: www.parentingscience.com/benefits-of-play.html

49 Pappas, S. (2011, August 14). "As Schools Cut Recess, Kids' Learning Will Suffer, Experts Say." Retrieved from: www.livescience.com/15555-schools-cut-recess-learning-suffers.html

50 Maheedhar Kodali, T. M. (2016). "Voluntary Running Exercise-Mediated Enhanced Neurogenesis Does Not Obliterate Retrograde Spatial Memory." *Journal of Neuroscience*, 36 (31) 8112-8122.

this: one in six American children has a diagnosed developmental disability[51] and one in three is overweight or obese.[52] It is alarming how many teenagers I have treated for neck pain and headaches due to poor posture. These young people have symptoms and stiffness worse than my elderly patients simply from looking down at their phones all day. Technology is a damaging substitute for play. Limiting screen time and providing exciting physical activities will maximize quality brain grooving.

PLAY MAKES ANIMALS SMARTER

Kittens wrestle, puppies nip, and birds peck and chase each other. Wolves, dolphins, chimps, and even octopuses play. But are animals doing this to simply develop their hunting and fighting skills so as to be able to survive in the wild? Research says no. If an adult cat is deprived of play as a kitten, for example, it has no trouble killing a mouse.[53] Play must have other, less obvious benefits. A study done by neuroscientists examined the brains of two groups of rats. One group was raised in boring, solitary confinement, while the other in an exciting, toy-filled colony. The "play group" was found to have thicker cerebral cortices than their deprived peers; playing literally grew their brains bigger. Subsequent studies confirmed these results and proved that the play groups were, in fact, smarter and able to find their way through mazes more quickly.[54]

Other research done by the famous psychologist Harry Harlow entitled "Monkeys without Play" showed that when deprived of play while young, juvenile monkeys show highly aggressive and bizarre behavior.[55] They appear to completely lose touch with social norms and accepted behavioral

51 Diament, M. (2011, May 23). "CDC: 1 In 6 Kids Have A Developmental Disability." Retrieved from: www.disabilityscoop.com/2011/05/23/cdc-1-in-6/13146/

52 American Heart Association . (2018, May 15). "Overweight in Children." Retrieved from: www.heart.org/HEARTORG/HealthyLiving/HealthyKids/ChildhoodObesity/Overweight-in-Children_UCM_304054_Article.jsp

53 Pellis, S. M. (2005). The Development of Social Engagement: Neurobiological Perspectives. New York: Oxford University Press.

54 Dewar, G. (2014). "The cognitive benefits of play: Effects on the learning brain." Retrieved from: www.parentingscience.com/benefits-of-play.html

55 Harlow, H. F. (1958). "The Nature of Love". Classics in the History of Psychology. Retrieved from: psychclassics.yorku.ca/Harlow/love.htm

protocols of their species. That outcome sounds eerily similar when compared to the socially awkward, angry, and even violent teenagers modern society seems to be producing.

PLAY BUILDS BIG BRAINS

While ethical considerations obviously prevent experimenting like this with children, there are retrospective studies that show human brains respond to play and exploration in similar ways. As Debi mentioned previously, the researchers began studying children in Romanian orphanages after the brutal and repressive government was overthrown in 1989. The orphans grew up in play-deprived, overcrowded, and harsh conditions. Researchers have closely tracked the progress, or lack of it, in these children. MRI studies show that the fully developed brains of those children, who are now adults, are significantly smaller in comparison to orphans in the same geographical area who were randomly assigned to foster care.[56] The brain is dependent on experience to develop and grow normally. Normal childhood free play is a crucial experience that needs to happen. When key experiences like regular play do not happen, circuits either fail to develop or develop atypically. Rich experiences really do develop rich brains.

LOOSE PARTS

I was served grass "french fries" last night. I paid my jolly, two-year-old waitress a handful of leaves for my delicious snack. Open-ended play materials such as these are what 1970s architect Simon Nicholson called "loose parts."[57] This refers to parts of our environment that empower creativity. Loose parts are items like colorful paper, fabric, cups, and leftover Costco boxes. These are things with no designated role or purpose; they can be adapted to anything the child imagines. A child must then flex his brain's imagination neural circuitry, a wiring process that eventually forms adult creativity and problem solving skills.

A trip to the Wal-Mart toy aisle reveals playthings that are the opposite

56 Windsor, Jennifer, L. E. (2007). "Language Acquisition With Limited Input: Romanian Institution and Foster Care." *Journal of Speech, Language, and Hearing Research*, Vol. 50, 1365-1381.

57 Nicholson, S. (1971). "How not to cheat children; the theory of loose parts." *Landscape Architecture*, 62(1), 30-34.

AS THE BODY DEMANDS, THE BRAIN EXPANDS

Body movement is also an essential part of the brain plasticity. The fine-motor movements of the body are all controlled by the brain. Think of it this way: when a person has a stroke and suddenly can't move their arm or leg, or even talk, is it their body that is damaged or is it their brain? The brain, of course. Then, if the brain is rewired, bodily functions are restored. The body continues to function because the brain learns to support it again. The ability to stand on your head is a brain function. The ability to play ball is a brain function.

The soul finds expression through the brain with all its neurons, electrical exchanges, hormones, and wiring. The brain finds expression through the body, with its ability to gather sensory information from the environment and relate it back to the brain. There is an integral, two-way, back-and-forth link between the body and the brain. Each is dependent upon the other, and each grows or diminishes with feedback from the other. *-Debi*

of loose parts. Toys that flood the market are "role-specific;" they don't generally stimulate curiosity and innovation. A Superman action figure, a flashy battery-operated egg that hatches, or a plastic barn with animals—items such as these do not offer much variability. That being said, we have several of these types of toys in our home. Everyone does, and that's okay—they're fun! In an interesting research study, a large group of toddlers were each given either four or sixteen of these commercial toys to play with for a set amount of time. It was found that the children with fewer toys were far more creative, thinking up additional uses for each toy, and had twice as long an attention span.[58] Having fewer toys, it turns out, results in healthier play and, ultimately, deeper cognitive development. The secret is having a limited quantity of commercial toys and an abundance of loose parts. Most of our toys are packed away and I rotate a small number regularly. Being reunited with a previously cherished toy seems to bring our toddlers even more delight than getting a brand new one.

58 Dauch, Carly, M. I. (2018). "The influence of the number of toys in the environment on toddlers' play." *Infant Behavior and Development*, vol. 50, 78-87.

PINECONES, MUD, STICKS, AND STONES

While commercial toys do offer great excitement, loose parts are superior in stimulating quality brain architecture. The best loose parts are found in nature. Take a stick from the yard, for example. It could be used as a golf club, light saber, magic wand, or balance beam. Rocks can be used as currency, served as cookies, or stacked to make a tower. Enjoying nature's supply of playthings has many benefits, as seen in Debi's treatment of Beka's dyslexia. When little Beka's fingers were learning through the sand, mud, and clay, it rewired and remapped parts of her brain that a standard pen and paper could not.

Playing in the natural elements is also good for a child's health. Outdoor play has been shown to expose the body to *Mycobacterium vaccae*,[59] a friendly soil bacterium that stimulates the immune system. This healthy immunity boost has been found to cause the brain to release serotonin, the endorphin used to regulate mood. A lack of serotonin in the brain has been linked to depression. So playing in the dirt not only enhances a child's immunity, it grooves the "happy" neural connections in the brain.

BDNF...WHAT?

Yesterday with the baby on my hip, I walked our kids to a waterfall about head height. My head is six foot, two inches high, so it is fairly tall. The waterfall comes from our drinking spring. After he played in the small pool, I encouraged our three-year-old to climb up the side of the waterfall. I showed him how to pull up on sturdy tree roots and place his feet on little limestone shelves. He was nervous at first but took on the challenge and made it to the top with a huge grin. This little aerobic, challenging activity actually made him smarter. Being active in the outdoors like this is the best way to stimulate production of brain-derived neurotrophic factor (BDNF).[60] This is the "fertilizer" for your mind; it builds and maintains brain circuitry. It causes the brain to grow new cells and connections and keeps existing cells functioning at the optimal level. It specifically builds the hippocampus, a part of the brain associated with higher cognitive functions such as memory.

59 University of Bristol. (2007, April 10). "Getting Dirty May Lift Your Mood." Retrieved from: www.sciencedaily.com/releases/2007/04/070402102001.htm

60 Liou, S. (2010, June 26). "Brain-derived neurotrophic factor (BDNF)." Retrieved from: web.stanford.edu/group/hopes/cgi-bin/hopes_test/brain-derived-neurotrophic-factor-bdnf/#can-exercising-promote-bdnf-production

BDNF generates with activities that involve aerobic exercise, especially if a little risk is involved. Activities like rock climbing, trail running, hunting, team sports, and even roughhousing will increase its levels. The benefits are not only for children; adults can increase their levels also by getting more active. Low levels of BDNF in adults have been associated with depression, anxiety, poor memory, and brain degeneration diseases. How exhilarating it is to know there is a way to combat conditions that eat away at the brain such as Alzheimer's, Parkinson's disease, and dementia. The more BDNF in the brain, the better, so get moving!

BUCKET BABIES

Did you know that movement and "play" are also important for a newborn? The best position for a tiny baby to develop his brain and body is on his tummy. In 1992, the phrase "back to sleep" was coined to help parents remember to place their baby on his back while sleeping. This practice reduced the occurrence of sudden infant death syndrome (SIDS); however, it also led to parents generally avoiding infant tummy time. Time on the tummy while awake is the best position to encourage a baby to "play." In this posture, the baby can build early back, neck, and shoulder strength as well as coordination. In opposition to this, baby registries are filled with "buckets" that keep baby face-up. Baby is moved from the baby swing to the car seat, to the bouncer, the stroller, and then the rocker. When baby gets a couple months older, a Bumbo Floor Seat®, ExerSaucer®, and door jumper are added into the container shuffle. These devices can be a lifesaver when Mom needs a shower; they do keep baby happy and quiet for long periods of time. I'll be the first to admit that we all need some help and convenience from time to time, but it is important to limit time in these containers. Overuse can lead to what physical therapists refer to as "bucket babies." These are babies with developmental delays who are failing to form those important strength and body awareness brain grooves because they are always positioned on their back or in a confined, fully supportive commercial device.

Tummy time should start from day one on a firm surface while baby is awake. In this position, the baby is free to flex, extend, and move in diagonal patterns, forming the coordination brain circuitry for rolling, crawling, sitting, and walking. The pressure through their hands helps to strengthen and define the arch of the hand, which is needed for being able to hold a pencil later on. The tummy is the optimal position for play.

BAREFOOT BRAINS

Our preschoolers were born on a Hawaiian island, and our newest two babies were born here in the Tennessee countryside. In both of these cultures, youngsters go barefoot everywhere, and oftentimes, the adults do too. In fact, we keep our kids' shoes in the car because they're only worn on the occasional drive to town. A study found that the physical movement of and the sensory stimulation through a baby's bare foot is a factor in accelerating proprioceptive (or body-awareness) and intellectual development of the child.[61] Sense of touch is dampened and messages to the brain are diminished when wearing shoes. A bare foot strengthens the balance neural connections of the brain. Close your eyes and stand on one foot. Can you feel your foot and ankle make small automatic movements to keep you from falling? You just exercised this foot-to-brain connection.

The sole of the foot is one of the most sensory-rich parts of the body, having as many proprioceptors (or nerve endings) as the entire spinal column.[62] The brain needs this many connections with our ticklish feet to make us safer and better able to adapt to the ground beneath us. Going barefoot also strengthens the feet and lower legs, making the body more agile and less prone to injury. Wearing shoes as soon as the child starts walking creates tender feet with soft, thin skin. Lack of calluses, however, is not the only reason walking barefoot is painful for these shoe-wearing children. It is also due to a chronic lack of sensory stimulation from the ground. So on the rare occasion when the child or adult does go barefoot, this strange sensory overload is perceived by the brain as being painful.

While shoes are more of a social convention than a biomechanical necessity, there is, of course, a time and place for them. So what type of footwear would be best for an early walker? A stiff bootie or "cute" high-top sneaker is a common yet poor choice. These shoes limit the ankle and foot's ability to strengthen the balance system, as well as hinder optimal foot arch development. When purchasing shoes for a child, turn the shoe upside down and bend the sole; I like to try to smash it into a ball in my hand. If you can't, the shoe is too stiff. On a side note, there are rare exceptions for

61 (2017). "Barefoot Babies: Happier and Smarter?" *You Are Mom*. Retrieved from: youaremom.com/babies/barefoot-babies-happier-and-smarter/

62 Flegal, Kacie. (n.d.). "Barefoot Babies." *Natural Child Magazine*. Retrieved from www.natural-childmagazine.com/1210/barefoot-babies.htm

80/20

The Pareto Principle teaches that the first 20% of a person's life has a disproportionally large impact on the outcome of the remaining 80%. The same is true when an arrow is drawn in a bow, where a small adjustment in the angle will make a disproportionally large difference in where that arrow will go. **"Train up a child in the way he should go: and when he is old, he will not depart from it" (Proverbs 22:6).** Even if the first 20% of your life didn't set a good trajectory, "it is never too late to rewire the brain," according to Michael Merzenich, PhD. The worst thing you can do at this point is do nothing.

certain children who need more support. If you are concerned about your child's foot position or the way he walks, consult with your physical therapist or pediatrician. Adults also need to talk to a physical therapist or podiatrist if they are considering a less supportive shoe, as this can cause injury to a foot that is not conditioned for such footwear.

CONCLUSION

The brain is moldable like hot plastic until the day we die, hence the term, "neural plasticity." Based on the experiences it has, it bends and builds connections. It is the most pliable to new grooves in the first few years of life; however, the potential remains until the day we die. Albert Einstein, the greatest scientific mind of the twentieth century, once said, "Nothing happens until something moves." Movement of the body is absolutely required to create quality brain circuitry. Babies', children's, and adults' brains alike all benefit from physical movement, especially when it is done in the outdoors. Perhaps ADD (attention deficit disorder) should be renamed NDD (nature deficit disorder). Let's change the meaning of "social media" back to GO PLAY OUTSIDE.

-Dr. Ellen

NEUROSCIENCE OF EXERCISE

How exercise affects the brain is a real issue that neuroplasticity researchers from all over the world are chasing with all their might, indicating they believe it is a critical issue that must be addressed.

The US National Library of Medicine and National Institutes of Health says in an October 13, 2016, article titled "Neuroscience of Exercise: Neuroplasticity and Its Behavioral Consequences": "The human brain adapts to changing demands by altering its functional and structural properties (neuroplasticity) which results in learning and acquiring skills. Convergent evidence from both human and animal studies suggests that enhanced physical exercise facilitates neuroplasticity of certain brain structures and, as a result, cognitive functions as well as affective and behavioral responses. This special issue is being proposed at a very challenging time. There is evidence linking increased physical exercise with an enhancement of neurogenesis, synaptogenesis, angiogenesis, and the release of neurotrophins as well as neuroendocrinological changes, which are associated with benefits in cognitive and affective as well as behavioral functioning (such as fine motor functioning)."

I CHARGE YOU

Get a box for each of your younger children and allow them to gather things to add to their box that will be a part of their play. Decorating the box can be fun. Start them off by gathering three things such as: a few interesting rocks, sticks, or leaves—whatever interests them. Add to their box: tape, string, markers, and other items that encourage creativity.

Also, when the weather is nice, set up an area in the yard where the children can create a mud town. Allow them to use water to make mud roads and sticks for houses. A little of this type play, and you will be raising future engineers.

"And the streets of the city shall be full of boys and girls playing in the streets thereof" (Zechariah 8:5).

The Young Child's Brain

CHAPTER 6

Neuroplasticity has taught us that we can literally damage or retard our children's brain structure or we can enhance it by what we allow or disallow in their lives.

My friend has a three-year-old son named Roger. When you speak to him, he shifts his eyes away and stays as still as a statue until you stop focusing on him. He withdraws from people socially with the exception of several small children with whom he is familiar. What is wrong with Roger? I am sure we have all known small children like this. Did you ever wonder what is going on in the brain of a child who is so unnerved by your focus that he avoids your gaze? Other children—normal children—desire to look into your eyes so they can read your feelings: "Does she like me?" "Is she a nice lady?"

FACTOID EXPLAINED

Neurons are brain cells, and each neuron has thousands of long, arm-like extensions with connectors at the end called synapses. Neurons communicate with other neurons by means of these synapses. Every connection expands the brain's overall ability.

When I think of how neurons function, it reminds me of telephone lines. Neurons are little social cells that love to "talk" on the phone and share what they know with other neurons; and as the brain's version of a telephone landline, the synapses connect two neurons that want to talk to each other. The synapses love ringing up neighboring neurons and making new connections every chance they get! It is good that God created neurons to be so interested in linking up because every connection makes us more capable humans. When new information comes down the phone line, synapses try to connect neurons that may know something about that subject.

For instance, let's say you are trying to learn a new word that has a strange sound. **You hear the word**. Many synapses in the area of the brain that deals with sound will begin swinging over, trying to connect to other neurons that have to do with sound. Usually, it takes a great deal of effort for synapses to make lasting connections.

The word still eludes you. You need to make a little extra effort. So **you see the word and say it.** Your hearing, seeing, and speaking neurons are now all involved in the learning process, which means additional areas of the brain have now been activated, resulting in a widening of the network. In saying the word, many synapses in the speech area of the brain swing toward each other in an effort to link up, but just a few thousand latch on—not enough to make a lasting memory in all areas of the brain. These synapses need help. So God made the brain to have neurotransmitters. The word is self-explanatory: *neuro*=brain and *transmitter* describes their function. These chemicals (some of which also function as hormones) make connections more likely and lasting. I think of neurotransmitters as glue that makes the connectors sticky. With multiple senses now engaged (hearing, seeing, and speaking), neurotransmitters are released to pour over the synapses, causing them to stick together and form connections. Next, you take pencil in hand and write the new word as you speak it, spelling each letter in your mind as you go.

Some minds do best with pictures, especially people who are artistic and expressive. If you could bring your attention to an object and draw a picture, it will use different areas of the brain which will make learning more complete. Pictures in the mind have an amazing ability to stick with us. As I write this, I recall reading a book about 45 years ago about increasing your memory capacity. Although I can't remember the author or title, I do remember the capitals of most states in this country because the author created pictures in my mind to help me remember those details. For instance, for the state of Pennsylvania, he said to think of a man holding a pencil in his hand, who's getting a haircut, while eating a burger. The pencil is to remind me of "PENNSYL" from Pennsylvania. His hair is "HARR" and the burger is "BURG", both from Harrisburg. Now everyone who has read this will be able to remember that the capital of Pennsylvania is Harrisburg. Let's hope they don't change the capital city! Now without any effort your brain has created a word picture pulled from this story. A very effective means of recall is pictures being tied to a word or phrase you are trying to memorize. Many areas of the brain have been stimulated, and synapses everywhere have made connections corresponding with the areas of the brain for each learned skill—hand movement, sound, sight, and word picture.

The sounds you learned from this one word have made connections that will make learning additional words easier because a network of sound is now established. You own the word. You own the sound, the shape of the letters, and much more. If this were a foreign language, you would have learned the sounds of many words just by learning this one word. This is because sounds are connected to like sounds. Without effort, the word will readily come to mind when needed. You are connected.

Your neurons have thousands of synapses swinging around, ready to make connections in response to your feelings and thoughts. It all happens at the speed of thought. The more synapse connections in the brain, the greater your knowledge, abilities, and gifts.

But what does this have to do with little Roger who cannot look into your eyes? Everything. But before we diagnose the source of Roger's reluctance to socially engage, we need to lay further foundation.

> **DOUBLE SPEED**
>
> A three-year-old's brain is twice as active as an adult's in creating links and those links will be building blocks that last a lifetime.

MANY SYNAPSES

A newborn baby has 2,500 synapses per neuron. But when he is two or three years old, he will have 15,000 synapses for each neuron, more than at any other time in his life. Thanks to this high number, he is learning at incredible speeds, so it is the most important period of brain development. During this accelerated time of learning, every child NEEDS to have as many opportunities to experience a great variety of physical and mental stimuli as possible. All the things we discussed in the first chapter about the unique ability of babies to learn several languages before age two now make sense. It is understandable why a toddler can develop perfect pitch, but the ability is lost by the time he is five. Once you understand how the neurons are connected, you can see that as more areas of the brain are stimulated in any learning experience, brain function increases.

Adults are sometimes perturbed by children constantly moving, fidgeting, and manipulating objects or their bodies. But the child needs movement in order to develop coordination between body and brain. He needs many challenges like music, art, digging in the dirt, climbing, and swinging on ropes to build neural connections. All physical movements are establishing brain connections that will enable balance, depth perception, distinguishing sounds, analyzing concepts, expressing feelings, etc. Though it will be years before the child expresses competence in these areas, the neural groundwork is being laid that will later boost his development. That is why it is so critical that a child's time is not wasted on digital entertainment. Brain scans reveal that the young brain cannot compute cartoons and digital trifles that are not based in reality.

BABY SUE'S SYNAPSES

Baby Sue is in church with her mother, her head turning this way and that, taking in all the people and sights. She senses the peace and joy of Mom and all present. The music, laughter, and joyous words combined with security and good feelings are creating many positive synapse connections. Her learning is peaking, and her parents don't have a clue how important this time is to her future. Thankfully, they are just doing what comes naturally for them as loving parents.

Later, Baby Sue lies on her mother's lap nursing while her mother softly hums a song. The warm milk and the sucking sensation, the pleasure of tenderness and security, as well as the sound and feel of her mother's breathing and beating heart, when combined with the music create a much wider net of connections. As stated earlier, music is unique in its ability to open up additional areas of the brain. Learning connections happen best when a person is at peace.

Another time, Baby Sue is sitting on Daddy's lap in church as he sings and taps his foot. Now fresh, new synapses are connecting with the same network formerly associated with Mom. The infant is also developing an awareness that this place means sitting quietly for a while. She is learning self-restraint in the context of pure pleasure. Self-restraint becomes a pleasure rather than a pain to be protested. The whole church experience creates memories of goodness. Over the years, parents have asked us how they can train their small children to sit quietly in church. Now you know. This entire, delightful neural network creates a strong association between deep pleasure derived from multiple senses and music—even with a particular song that is sung or a tune that is hummed.

In the child's brain, music becomes more than lyrics and rhythm; it is pleasure, peace, and all things good and wholesome. There is a reason born of instinct that mothers have traditionally sung lullabies to their infants. Unknown to these parents, they are imparting not only a love of music, but actually the "gift" of music—to be realized later.

SIDE NOTE ON CHILD TRAINING

When my husband and I began teaching and writing on child training, we knew nothing of the neural network. But from experience, we did know children, and we appreciated their need for constant, physical movement. We always encouraged parents to provide crayons, paper, play dough, or soft toys (no clanging or banging sounds) to fiddle with during the church services or any time they would be subject to boredom and possible complaint. It is a win-win concept. When they color or manipulate an object, they are opening up additional areas of the brain that provide association with the things they are hearing at the moment. The thoughts combined with the coloring find a wider area of lodging. In the future when the child colors a picture, the areas of the brain that house Bible teaching will also light up. By your example, you are also training your children to be respectful of other people. Therefore, if your church is not accustomed to the presence of children, plan on joyfully sitting in the back. If your child is not yet trained to sit quietly in church, then set up training sessions at home rather than disrupt the harmony of the moment. When Jesus was speaking to large crowds, the disciples considered the children to be disruptive and sought to usher them away. Jesus responded by saying, **"...Suffer little children to come unto me,** and forbid them not: for of such is the kingdom of God" (Luke 18:16). In heaven, Jesus keeps all the little children very close to him (Matthew 18:10).

In former days, I remember that many of the ladies brought their knitting to church. The preacher knew they were listening much better than the hypnotized people staring at him as he spoke. It is a law of nature practiced by young and old long before we understood the science of it.

LET A LITTLE CHILD LEAD YOU

A couple years ago, we received a letter from a middle-aged preacher who was part of our Bible studies when he was a child. His disturbed parents never came to the meetings, but dropped Bez and his siblings off as a way to obtain free babysitting. Our very young Bible student was a genuine pest. Bez loved coming because there were always snacks and other children with whom he could be annoying or wrestle. This all happened while the adults were engaged in Bible study. His yells, laughter, and crying, young voice can be clearly heard in our cataloged recordings. His grandchildren will doubtless laugh with delight when they listen to Bez's yell while they enjoy Pastor Pearl's recorded teachings from the book of Romans.

Bez is now the pastor of a church, and I am sure he has his own share of "drop-off kids" at Bible studies. I smile at this, knowing he is getting his just recompense. In his letter, he reminisced of his upbringing. His take was intriguing. He reminded us of all those many Bible studies he came to as a very young child, right up through his late teens. He wrote to Mike saying, "I was recalling those Bible studies and the people who came, and I thought of something interesting. You taught so faithfully over the years, but who among the students is carrying the torch? Who is preaching and teaching the Word? Those that were adults then are still coming to meetings and listening, but those of us who were children, crawling at your feet and interrupting the meetings, are the ones that are now busy in the ministry. Our little minds were drinking in the Word, and now we are out sharing the Word. We are the preachers, teachers, gift-givers, and missionaries getting the message out to the lost and dying world."

The testimony of Bez and others like him has changed our perspective as to the most effective approach to church ministry. If you are not reaching the children, you are not planting new seeds to replace the old plants that will soon wither. A preacher not reaching the children is a farmer going out of business. Children learn what to love and what to value by the example of others. Our 18-month-old grandson would rather be throwing knives at targets than any other type of play because it is what his brother and grandfather do for entertainment. This intense interest is called mirroring—the tendency to adopt what you see, as when a yawn becomes contagious—and is instigated and controlled by mirror neurons. Separating little ones into "children's church" deprives them of the opportunity to mirror their parents in a context of worship.

Bez's three-year-old brain was absorbing the message. Today, he can stand at a pulpit and quote scripture after scripture that he never intentionally memorized. As a child, his synapses were connecting and memories were being formed. An adult would need to work and work to build such a reserve of knowledge, but a child, though he may not be able to quote the scripture at six years of age, has formed the brain network that will be awakened and utilized—with very little effort—later in life.

SMALL BIG THINGS

This past Sunday, I was part of a small home-church meeting. The teacher's message was directed at adults, in no way captivating the mind of a child. I glanced over to the other side of the room and noticed a sweet three-year-old girl sitting by her father. She sat staring straight ahead, twisting just a little in her chair. At that moment, her dad looked down at his sweet little girl. She must have felt his gaze, for she turned her face to him. His eyes lit up as he scrunched up his nose in a slight, silly smile. Her reaction was priceless. Her whole body scrunched up much like his nose, her eyes shone brighter than his, and her radiant smile instantly brought tears to my eyes. There are no richer moments in life than when two hearts and souls merge into oneness. I have seen moments like this before between this dad and his children. I was so profoundly moved, I had to resist the urge to run over and kiss the balding head of that 40ish-year-old father. That would really rock the church!

Don't hide your children away in the nursery; let them sit through the teaching of the Word. Let their minds be drenched with beautiful, old hymns. Let their souls be filled with GOD. Let their earliest memories of church be connected with you, with love, security, quality music, and all things good. Look into their eyes and smile dozens of times during the meetings so that the feelings and memory of love are connected to church and worship.

DONALD'S SYNAPSES

It is time to meet little Donald. Little Donald is a masterpiece in the making—or not. If Donald's parents use this time to the fullest and he is given many opportunities for connections, then he will have the brain wished for by many. Brain connections are being made as baby Donald is sitting on the floor, playing with toy trucks. He unconsciously hears his dad discussing stocks and bonds or maybe engines and transmissions and, at another time, politics, stock trading, or Bible doctrine. Though the tot seems to be oblivious to adult conversation, his brain is responding to the words, trying to decipher the meaning, and he is forming all manner of new connections. It is not necessary that he have a grasp of what he is hearing. The bits and pieces will be available later in life to be quickly assembled into meaningful thought. Someday, someone will ask little Donald, "Who taught you to read?" and the four-year-old will say, "I don't know, I just know." And he is correct. At four years old, Donald will pipe up at an opportune time and spout facts well beyond most men in the room. They will ask, "Who told you that?" and little Donald will respond, "I don't know, I just know stuff." And he does. The fact is, at four years of age, Donald had so many synapses making connections that he is creating a network for future excellence.

This little man was fortunate that his dad kept him at his side when conducting business. When the day came that Donald could articulate his thoughts, he did just seem to suddenly know the ins and outs of business, Bible teaching, stock trading, auto mechanics, and math. It is generally thought that Donald was born with extraordinary gifts, but the fact is, his gifts were imparted one sentence, one smile, and one experience at a time, starting when he was yet an infant and proceeding through his early years. The most formative and determinative time of a person's life is the first six years.

DOWNSIDE OF TOO MANY SYNAPSES

The brains of young children are supercharged with an overabundance of synapses. This provides for accelerated learning but also a high level of mental and emotional sensitivity. You have seen children who seem electrically charged; well, in a manner of speaking, this is true. Loud music, flashing lights, piercing motor sounds, too many people vying for the child's attention, blaring TV, or like disturbances should be avoided. This is especially important if a child shows evidence that his brain is under stress.

TV DAMAGE

A recent study of more than 2,600 toddlers showed that for every hour of TV the toddlers watched each day, their chances of developing serious attentional difficulties by age seven increased by ten percent. Psychologist Joel T. Nigg suggested TV watching correlates with brain problems.

Small children startle easily, become fearful when left alone, and scream for unknown reasons. Knowing little ones possess an overabundance of synapses, parents need to make an effort to protect their psyches from overstimulation or from anything nerve-wracking. Take note of what provokes them to anxiety. A simple rule of thumb is to make sure your children always have a sense of safety by your near presence. They may be in another room, but the normal sounds of you and the other members of the family going about your routine are reassuring to them. Children, and even tiny infants, who wake up in an empty room are prone to panic. You can see from what you have learned in our study of synapses that it is not wise to attempt to discipline them by leaving them to sort out their own emotions or deal with their panic alone. Time-outs can be cop-outs that impart isolation rather than discipline. You are contributing to the over-electrification of their brains. Rejection is not a training tool, it is a contributing factor. Your goal is to help your child learn to regulate his feelings. This does not mean you are to give in to his fits (that would exacerbate the situation), nor does it mean you are going to force him to get control. Small children need to be gently wooed into learning to self-regulate. Be an example. Be wise. Ask God for wisdom. He promises to give wisdom to those who ask. Raising children is not for the unwise.

Children should be disciplined for foul attitudes and rebellion, but not for insecurity or emotional turmoil. Remember how Baby Sue was trained into security? You cannot effectively discipline a child if you do not have his heart, he must feel comfortable and secure. (If you want to pursue this line of thought further, read our bestseller, *To Train Up a Child*.)

PRUNING CLEARS THE WAY

Even when a wise father and mother give special attention to providing all possible brain stimulating experiences for their child, he will still have more synapses than he will ever use. What happens to the thousands of extras? Those that are not fired (not challenged to learn) do not connect, and so the day will come when the brain will eliminate them. This process is called pruning.

As the child ages, the unused synapses begin to be pruned away, which means they literally die off and are absorbed. At around six years old, this process is in full motion. Like a room filled with too many toys and excess clutter, efficiency is restored by throwing out unused items and organizing what remains. It is similar to doing a disk cleanup and defrag of the hard drive on your computer; it will then run faster and more efficiently. The brain reaches a point where it, too, must be purged of the unused and un-necessary. Pruning causes the child's mind to be less cluttered, allowing him to focus better. After pruning, children will seem more mature and calmer. The neurons that control the eyes, ears, and speech have had a heyday and the connections will last a lifetime. The child's memory bank is chock-full of bits and pieces that will be connected to other neurons in years to come. The thousands of bits of information he has learned and the connections formed will now be easier to access when called upon in the future.

I cannot help remembering these verses:

"I will praise thee; for I am fearfully and wonderfully made: marvellous are thy works; and that my soul knoweth right well. My substance was not hid from thee, when I was made in secret, and curiously wrought in the lowest parts of the earth. Thine eyes did see my substance, yet being unper-fect; and in thy book all my members were written, which in continuance were fashioned, when as yet there was none of them" (Psalm 139:14-16).

How amazingly appropriate to the science of neuroplasticity! You see, the science is nothing more than a discovery of what God created.

Think of the experience of the preacher Bez. He now looks back and re-alizes that his Bible foundation was laid when he was a child. When he be-came an adult, and gave attention to learning the Bible, the new neurons made connections with the network that was formed when he was playing on the floor and competing for attention during a Bible study.

Remember the herb story and how my infant daughter rode around on my hip as I experimented with herbs? I never even considered the possibility that she might be learning. But research has demonstrated that as she experienced smells, textures, and concepts, her synapses were indeed making connections, instilling in her the knowledge of things I have long since forgotten. She was one of those children who, when asked how she knows the chemical properties of certain herbs, and how they are used to treat illnesses, she would answer, "Oh, I just always knew. I can smell them and know."

After the first pruning, the number of synapses seeking connections is greatly diminished. After pruning, the child's mind will not grasp new things as easily, but the things the child has learned will be readily available for his use. With the removal of clutter, the brain can now process the useful information it has stored. All the sounds of the alphabet will suddenly become words. The numbers will translate into math.

Pruning plays a major role in a child's brain. Take Roger for example, the little fellow who refused to make eye contact. His overcrowded and supercharged brain will be calmer after he is purged of unnecessary synapses. Without the overabundance of synapses all firing, he will not feel the need to retreat from stimuli. He will settle down and take notice of things around him. Due to the poor habits he learned during his period of overload, his parents may have to give extra attention to training him. He will appear to have suddenly grown up and become so much more mature and sociable. All the things he seemed unwilling to grasp, he will suddenly know. The stubborn little bugger will not seem so stubborn anymore.

HELP PRUNING

Sometimes the normal pruning process gets derailed. The root cause of many of the brain and/or behavioral problems seen in younger children is the failure of the brain to prune synapses at the appointed time. Small things can produce serious problems—things that affect both the mind and body of the child.

The lack of proper pruning can cause a child's brain to become overly active and excited. Children hide in the dark, crawl into small spaces, turn their eyes away, avoid being touched, and rock back and forth to cope with the overstimulation. And much to their parents' alarm, some children bang their heads. The pain or repetitive motion produces endorphins that provide temporary, drug-like soothing to counter the stress. When the synapses do not prune away, many children will have mannerisms or reactions that seem abnormal. Roger's inability to make direct eye contact is a clear indication of an overload of synapses.

Neuroscientists are discovering the reasons why some children prune right on schedule and others do not. The emotional trauma of moving to a new location, parents' divorce, or fear of someone in their life can disrupt the process. A big change in the child's diet, sickness, chemicals, and many similar causes can temporarily disrupt a child's system, and thus, inhibit pruning at the proper time. Take note that stress in the child's life is a big trigger. Stress releases an overabundance of chemicals/hormones which have an extremely negative effect on the gut and the immune system. Antibiotics and household chemicals also affect the gut negatively.

GUT–BRAIN CONNECTION FOR LITTLE ONES

The brain and the gut are closely linked. The gut houses an astonishing 80% of our immune system. Parents need to make sure their child's gut stays healthy and balanced. When a child exhibits symptoms of an electrified brain (like Roger), it is a signal that there may be problems in the gut–brain relationship. In Chapter 9, we discuss the brain-gut connection and consider many avenues for healing.

If there seems to be an escalating problem with your child's health or emotional state, seriously consider starting the healing process by rebuilding their immune system. Sometimes, antibiotics are necessary for a child's immediate health, but it is common knowledge that antibiotics destroy the natural flora in the intestines, leaving the body's immune system defenseless. When antibiotics are taken too often or incorrectly, it can leave your child's health—both physical and mental—in jeopardy. Vaccinations can also adversely affect your child's immune system, especially if the immune system has already been compromised.

With care, the immune system can be rebuilt, but it takes much diligence and time. Our daily lives are filled with toxins from food additives, GMO fruit and vegetables, plastic wrap, polluted drinking water, and air pollutants. They are also detrimental to the gut microbiome. Mold can also cause extreme health problems. You need to be conscientious and well read on these issues to make sure your child grows up in a wholesome environment. Keep in mind that dirt is actually beneficial to your child because it introduces beneficial bacteria to the microbiome. However, cleaning chemicals left in trace amounts on the bathtub or in clothes can be extremely toxic. A good working knowledge of this subject is critical to maintaining a healthy gut, which makes a bigger difference in the brain than you could ever imagine.

Many previously unexplained, odd behaviors are now becoming understandable and, best of all, correctable. There are YouTube videos that display the workings of the brain, demonstrating what appear to be millions of organic robots doing all kinds of constant building and repairing. I would encourage parents to watch some of these videos with their children and marvel at God's handiwork. Look for a YouTube video entitled, "Your Body's Molecular Machines" and it will get you started. Also, I highly encourage you to read *The Mind-Gut Connection* by Dr. Emeran Mayer.

THE LONG PROCESS

Brain pruning starts in the back of the brain where motor skills are controlled and gradually moves forward. The neural connections that survive the pruning process become more adept at transmitting information through a process called myelination. Myelin is a fatty cell material wrapped around neuronal axons and acts like insulation for the neural connections. It allows nerve impulses to travel throughout the brain more quickly and efficiently. Myelin reminds me of the insulation that is around electric wires in my house. The insulation keeps the hot wires safe and the current running undisturbed. The completed process of myelination (insulation) takes many years. The process starts in the back of the brain and slowly moves toward the prefrontal cortex in the front of the brain. The prefrontal cortex is where weighty decisions are made, and it is the last part of the brain to complete the insulating process. Scans reveal that this process is finally complete when a person is about 25 years of age. Until the myelination process is complete, a person doesn't have mature processing abilities, which explains why wise decision-making comes with age.

I CHARGE YOU

Start training your children to learn Bible verses. Have the children watch you print a simple Bible verse on a large card. Make sure they see and hear you as you spell the letters while printing them. Read each word slowly as you follow along with your finger. Let each child move their finger along the word as you read it. Move their finger for them as needed. Now turn on music so you can sing the verse or just make up a tune. Dance and hop around as you sing/speak the verse. Laugh, sing, read, trace over, and generally make learning the new verse a lot of fun. This is storing the new information into many areas of the brain. Do not test them or seek to measure their progress. It is all for fun and only fun.

"When I was a child, I spake as a child, I understood as a child, I thought as a child: but when I became a man, I put away childish things." (1 Corinthians 13:11).

Executive Function and Mindset

CHAPTER 7

Neuroplasticity has taught us that we can train our children to practice self-control in every area. This self-control translates over to a happier, healthier, and more successful life.

In measuring how "smart" someone may be, we tend to think in terms of intelligence and knowledge. This is generally referred to as IQ. But research and life have taught us that IQ does not necessarily translate into achievement. What really sets a child up for success and happiness is a set of acquired skills psychologists call "executive function." I call the process of building executive function "grooming the brain." Research has shown these skills to be the most important aspect of early brain development. Training your children to excel in executive function will make the biggest difference in their success. These acquired skills, unrelated to IQ, are grooved into a child's brain through the things they see, experience, practice, and value.

Executive function skills include:

- Paying attention
- Organizing and planning

- Initiating tasks and staying focused on them
- Regulating emotions
- Self-monitoring (keeping track of what you are doing)

Adele Diamond, PhD, professor of developmental cognitive neuroscience at the University of British Columbia, says, "Various studies have shown that executive function skills are more important to school readiness than is their IQ. Executive function is much more influenced by nurture, experience, and interaction than intelligence. It is possible to influence a child's ability to focus, to exert effort on learning a task, to practice self-control, and to relate one idea to another."[63]

According to Daniel Goleman, author of *Emotional Intelligence: Why It Can Matter More Than IQ*, one of the five important aspects of emotional intelligence is the ability to handle relationships. In his words, "Interpersonal effectiveness is dependent on our ability to manage the emotions of others. Brilliant projects and innovative insights are often never realized because of a lack of social competence and leadership skills.[64]

ATTITUDE FACTOR

Experience shows that success is often based more on attitude and less on ability.

The strength of this teaching is simple. Parents and teachers need to teach the child how to regulate his feelings. When a child pitches a fit, he is not regulating his feelings. When your son doesn't want to sit quietly during church and he cries to get his way, he has not been trained to regulate his feelings. When a child wants the candy, or doesn't want to be left behind, or any other "I want it now" and she falls apart emotionally, that is a child that has not been trained to regulate her feelings. When a child goes into a fit and the parent responds with a fit of his own, screaming, "Shut up!" or something similar, the parent is then mirroring the child's immaturity and reinforcing the brain pattern all around. More is caught than taught. Learning to regulate your feelings when things don't go your way is one of the most critical elements to success in life. Schools are

63 Hoffman, John. (2016). "6 surprising brain-builders for preschoolers." *Today's Parent.* Retrieved from: www.todaysparent.com/kids/preschool/10-surprising-brain-builders-for-preschoolers/

64 Winchester Hospital Health Library. (n.d.). "Emotional Intelligence: More Important Than IQ?" Retrieved from: www.winchesterhospital.org/health-library/article?id=14208

> ### INFLUENCE
>
> People will live up or down to the expectation of the people they care most about. You may not realize whom you are important to, or who is looking up at you, so treat others kindly and expect good from them. In this way, we help mold those around us.

full of children who have never been taught to regulate. Educators have to find a way to help children learn this vital character trait.

Christians are regulated by Christ dwelling within. The goal of neuroscientists seeking to impart redemptive traits in children is a psychological alternative to the Christian life. The Apostle Peter said, **"And beside this, giving all diligence, add to your faith virtue; and to virtue knowledge; And to knowledge temperance; and to temperance patience; and to patience godliness; And to godliness brotherly kindness; and to brotherly kindness charity. For if these things be in you, and abound, they make you that ye shall neither be barren nor unfruitful in the knowledge of our Lord Jesus Christ"** (2 Peter 1:5–8).

You, as a parent, have the opportunity to equip your children for happiness and success by grooming them to excel in these learned skills.

GROOMING FOCUS

The Schimmel Theorem Special Five

A group of brain researchers went to a first-grade teacher and asked her to allow her 30 students to take part in their research. The researchers told Miss Teacher that she had been chosen to be a part of this study due to her excellence, but to participate, she must agree to abide by the guidelines. She signed papers stating that she would follow their curriculum exactly. She understood that she would be videoed every day to make sure she was being a quality teacher and keeping to the curriculum. She also signed papers stating she would not speak of the research, the children's work, or anything about the program, until the experiment was over. Initially, the researchers tested the children and came back to Miss Teacher, identifying five students out of the thirty whom the test revealed had high IQs. She was cautioned to teach all students equally, showing no favor, irrespective of the test results, since a lack of bias was essential to their research.

Miss Teacher did her best, and the researchers checked in on her regularly, confirming that she was an excellent teacher and did her best to relate to all students equally. At the end of the school year, the researchers came back to test the students. They laid the results before the teacher for her to view. "Are you surprised at the results of the testing, especially the high test results of the five students with the high IQs?"

> **SELF-RESPECT**
>
> Every act of self-control leads to a sense of self-respect.

Miss Teacher smiled, "Not at all. Those five are truly brilliant, so I would expect these results."

The researchers then revealed the true nature of the experiment. "Miss Teacher, we lied to you. At the beginning of the year, those five students' tests were pulled out of the stack at random. They had the same results and the same basic IQ as all the other first graders we tested. You, Miss Teacher, were our research experiment. We wanted to prove that the mindset of a teacher could bring up the testing grade of the average student."

The brain has a system of neural pathways dedicated to attention. Due to her positive expectation, communicated through eye contact the teacher unconsciously caused the children to be totally focused. She enabled their executive function to develop to the fullest, resulting in self-confidence—the root of unhindered learning.

The reverse is also true. Teachers or parents can diminish learning ability by means of their criticism and low expectations accompanied by high demand. Instead of opening neural pathways, criticism and irritation actually close them down—making the child appear to have learning disabilities. A nervous, distracted child who knows you are irritated with him because he can't remember how to spell the new word, or do his math properly is learning nothing except that he is a failure. As a result, the brain does not develop the executive skill of self-confidence, it develops an expectation of failure.

When a child is effectively engaged in learning, the brain releases neurotransmitters to the synapses, helping them create connections to other synapses. Remember, every connection enhances learning.

Miss Teacher had unknowingly communicated a positive expectation to the five average students, and it had captured their attention and affected their self-image in a way that caused them to excel.

The goal: executive function—self-confidence, focus, and attention.

GROOMING SELF-CONTROL

Another executive function is learning to control impulses. If you are taught self-control as a child, it becomes so much a part of you that you come to love it. Deciding to exercise can be a challenge, but the person with the more highly developed executive function of self-control will meet the challenge head-on. Laying down that extra donut isn't a struggle for the child who has developed self-control, and he will not succumb to addiction. He will find it difficult to understand why another person does not simply make a wise choice. We are less likely to achieve any measure of success or happiness without developing this function. It is also critical to maintaining good health.

What two-year-old knows that he should not pull away and run into traffic? What five-year-old understands that it is time to turn off the TV and go to bed at 7pm? A parent's good habits are the starting point for young children to learn to self-regulate. When children are yet undeveloped in those areas, parents must function as the child's conscience, will, and preference. In the process, the child develops his own reasoning and will to practice delayed gratification. Children's brains are molded by our expectations, attitudes, and especially by our fellowship. There is more to this than just conditioning. It is important that we focus on grooving their brains in a way that will make their journey through life much easier.

It may be harder for us as adults, but it is never too late to retool the brain to accept self-control or self-regulation. There are many videos on YouTube that train adults how to develop self-control. Individuals and corporations are finding them quite useful. These experts teach people who want to develop executive function skills to use deep breathing and relaxation to improve self-control. The more I learn about adults seeking self-control, the more I value child training.

> **GRATIFICATION**
>
> Delayed gratification is one aspect of self-control.

> ## SELF-CONTROL
>
> How does learning delayed gratification translate to adulthood? Self-control helps the cigarette smoker lay down his habit because he knows it is bad for him. It causes compulsive shoppers to stop sooner, rather than later. It means gambling, over-spending, and poor eating habits will not be a problem in their lives. It plays a role in controlling anger, lust, and depression.

The Marshmallow Mania

For forty years now, children have been teasing their younger brothers and sisters with a reenactment of the famous marshmallow study led by psychologist Walter Mischel, PhD. This study is one of the most famous pieces of social-science research and is also among the most revealing. It is interesting to note that the research being done today using our current preschoolers is coming up with totally different conclusions. Few children that are raised in this generation are trained to resist the desire for immediate gratification. Regardless of parents' education, today's children have little self-restraint. So researchers assume that the older studies were not done correctly. The reality they are unwilling to admit is that today's culture and parenting are failing to instill impulse control in children.

The Marshmallow Study—Over Forty Years Ago

A researcher walked into a room of thirty preschool children with a plate of marshmallows. After all the children became aware of the marshmallows, she told them she had to leave the room for just a few minutes but would return shortly. She explained that each of them could have two marshmallows when she came back. But those who simply couldn't wait for their two marshmallows could ring the bell, and she would come back immediately to give them one marshmallow only. But those who waited would get two marshmallows later.

As was expected, some of the children rang the bell almost immediately, and some of the other children watched them eat the yummy treat and then rang the bell. Others sat stoically (and some anxiously), watching and waiting until the teacher returned. They then received their promised two marshmallows.

Are you wondering what your child would do?

Children do just as their parents and caretakers have conditioned them to do. Children are born without any propensity to exercise self-control. They are either allowed to mature as would an animal, with no self-regulating boundaries, or they are groomed to practice self-denial during their earliest years. What 12-month-old baby will choose to avoid sweets?

The follow-up on these children is fascinating. In a study that took place ten years later, Mischel found that the children who had delayed gratification had higher SAT scores.

But that wasn't the end of the follow-up. The marshmallow study has been duplicated hundreds of times. The website for the American Psychological Association had this to say: "As it turns out, the marshmallow study didn't end there. Recently, B.J. Casey, PhD, of Weill Cornell Medical College, along with Mischel, PhD, Yuichi Shoda, PhD, of the University of Washington, and other colleagues tracked down 59 subjects, now in their 40s, who had participated in the marshmallow experiments as children. The researchers tested the subjects' willpower with a laboratory task known to demonstrate self-control in adults. Amazingly, the strength of the subjects' willpower had largely remained constant over four decades. In general, children who were less successful at resisting the marshmallow all those years ago performed more poorly on the self-control task as adults. An individual's sensitivity to so-called hot stimuli, it seems, may persist throughout his or her lifetime. Additionally, Casey and colleagues examined brain activity in some subjects using functional magnetic resonance imaging (fMRI). When presented with tempting stimuli, individuals with low self-control showed brain patterns that differed from those with high self-control. The researchers found that the prefrontal cortex (a region that controls executive functions such as making choices) was more active in subjects with higher self-control. And the ventral striatum (a region thought to process desires and rewards) showed boosted activity in those with lower self-control."[65]

Self-control or self-regulation crosses over to every area of our lives. Failure to develop the ability to exercise delayed gratification, and thus,

65 "Delaying Gratification." *American Psychological Association*. Retrieved from: www.apa.org/helpcenter/willpower-gratification.pdf

self-control, can wreak havoc on a person's health, welfare, relationships, wealth, and emotional well-being. Self-control, self-discipline, and delayed gratification are learned skills that parents can groom into their children.

GROOMING SELF-RESTRAINT

Moms Are Special

Children, as a whole, desire their mom to be above reproach, to be a loving princess who is kind, honest, and giving. This need for Mom to be virtuous is as universal as mankind. No child wants a coarse-talking mother.

Most adults dismiss their road rage responses as, "I'm a good driver, and people who can't drive correctly should get off the road." Children are embarrassed when Mother displays this selfish anger. Observing their mother act nasty creates an image in the child's mind that is exactly that—nasty. A child knows in his heart and soul that what he is seeing is unkind, mean, and rude. He feels the hurtfulness of it. He may think, "Is that the way Mom feels about me when I am bad?"

Regulate by Example

The easiest way to teach children to regulate their feelings and responses is by example. When a parent never shows anger, overt frustration, selfishness, or dishonesty, children will grow up feeling their parent's temperament is the norm. They will practice regulating their responses through a process of osmosis. Researchers have learned that much of this is due to mirror neurons—brain cells that do nothing but mimic what we see and hear. I step into an elevator and do a big, old, noisy yawn. Before the elevator comes to the next stop, more than half of those riding with me will be fighting to stop their own yawn. Their mirror neurons make it almost impossible to resist. I do it every chance I get—for research, of course!

BELIEVE

We are what we believe we are.

It was only in 1992 that a researcher discovered mirror neurons. With additional research, scientists have discovered that these neurons are much more powerful in controlling our behavior than previously thought, even the behavior of an entire nation.

> ## STRENGTHENED BY MISTAKES
>
> Correcting a mistake creates a stronger synaptic connection than if you had done it right the first time. This same principle is seen when a bone is broken, and it heals back reinforced, making it stronger than it was before.

Mirror neurons are described by their name. When I smile, countless neurons in my brain are firing. You see me and, without a thought, corresponding neurons in your brain begin to fire as if you are the one smiling. When an infant is confronted with a smile, his smile neurons fire involuntarily, creating a corresponding happiness. He has mirrored your feelings.

But mirror neurons are not limited to happy smiles. All emotions and actions are mirrored. When we exhibit anger, unthankfulness, dishonor, or overeating in front of our children, their mirror neurons fire in kind. They can't help but be a reflection of what they see. Maybe that is how it came to be that the prophet said **"...visiting the iniquity of the fathers upon the children, and upon the children's children, unto the third and to the fourth generation" (Exodus 34:7).**

Research has shown that the four people with whom you most closely associate will be your mirror. Whether you like it or not, whether you believe it or not, and whether you resist it or not, your neurons will link up with your close associates. You will come to think like they do, react like they do, and develop habits equivalent to theirs. And even more amazing, according to research, the people they hang out with will also have a strong influence upon your life, even if you never meet them. It is like a hidden disease they carry that no one expects to catch. The psalmist must have known that when he said, **"Blessed is the man that walketh not in the counsel of the ungodly, nor standeth in the way of sinners, nor sitteth in the seat of the scornful" (Psalm 1:1).**

GROOMING MEMORY

Most of us feel that we are deficient in the area of memory. Memory is one of the executive function skills that can be instilled in children or, with effort, developed in adults. Researchers have outlined several methods to develop the skills of initiating a task, staying focused to completion, and building memory. To do this, they involve children in the age-old child's play of telling stories and play-pretend.

Storytelling

Through the prophets, God employs storytelling as his preferred means of communication. Likewise, to teach his precepts, Jesus used parables—stories—based on common events. The Bible is a book of stories. God makes himself known to us by telling us the stories of his relationship with people down through history. He introduces real characters and reveals their fears, victories, struggles, and defeats. Also revealed is his joy when they learn to trust him and become his friend. The Apostle Paul acknowledges this when he says, **"Now all these things happened unto them for ensamples: and they are written for our admonition, upon whom the ends of the world are come" (1 Corinthians 10:11).** See also Romans 15:4.

If you want to deeply groove your brain or that of your children with the thoughts of God, there is a very simple technique. Acquire a means to listen to the King James Bible being read. Alexander Scourby is the very best by a country mile, and you can download the audio file to your phone. This is a great way for children to go to sleep at night or naptime. It will improve their diction and infuse them with the words of God. It is a fantastic way to increase their executive function while you have some downtime.

"Thy word is a...light unto my path" (Psalm 119:105).

"So then faith cometh by hearing, and hearing by the word of God" (Romans 10:17).

Read or watch the Good and Evil *comic book Bible for free at www.goodandevilbook.com. Your children will enjoy following the pictures while they learn Bible stories and truth.*

One Eye, Two Eye, and Three Eye

I have few memories of my father's mother (Mama Granny, as we called her). She lived nearly a day's drive from our home, so we did not see her often. When we did, she was busy operating her store, which was the largest in the small town where she lived. It was her livelihood, so it came first. But I do remember that during my entire youth, she shared one bedtime story that never ended—adding to it with each telling. We looked forward to the "rest of the story" at each visit. She said it was the story her mama told her. Her story was strange, maybe over-the-top and quirky, but it mystified me with its outlandish impossibilities. It was the story of three little girls: one with a single eye right in the middle of her forehead, one with the normal two eyes, and the other with three eyes across her forehead. She called the girls Little One Eye, Little Two Eyes, and Little Three Eyes. In Mama Granny's ongoing story, she told how the three little girls dealt with issues of rejection, anxiety about how the sisters looked, bullies making fun of them, and the camaraderie of the sisters as they stuck together and taught others to be kind. We heard stories of how Little Three Eyes helped poor Little Two Eyes when a situation came up that required three eyes. I can't recall just how that came about, but as a child, I could clearly appreciate the wonder of three eyes in times of need. The same held true for Little One Eye being the hero.

We children always slept with Mama Granny when we visited, so it was our nighttime story for several years, starting when I was about three years old. Can you imagine telling a three-year-old about a three-eyed kid? Back then, we weren't as squeamish as people are today. Mama Granny would start out by having us recount the previous story from three months earlier. I now realize it was so she could recall where she was in the storyline and maintain continuity.

I am nearing 70 years old, but I can still recount pieces of her story as if they were told to me just yesterday. She did not know that she was increasing my executive function skills—my ability to pay attention, organize and plan, initiate tasks and remain focused on them, regulate emotions, and self-monitor.

Their Turn to Tell One

Now here we are, 65 years later, and my grandchildren love my "homemade" stories as well. They especially love it when I weave into the story their own parent as my little boy or girl. I always end the story by asking them to tell a story. Some children, reluctant to talk, require a little boost, such as asking them what they did that was funny, or how they scared a parent by jumping out and saying, "Boo!", or about an animal they found, etc. Storytelling uses working memory to keep track of events, and it opens up memories to weave into their homemade story.

Play-Pretend

Play-pretend has been a childhood pastime forever. Dreaming up make-believe plots and learning to stay in character builds concepts and ideas in children's brains and causes them to think flexibly.

Research has revealed that children develop higher executive function ability when their toys are not store-bought. Remember our discussion of loose parts? When children are given access to things like cardboard boxes, paper, sticks, dirt, rocks and sand, clay, rope, and all kinds of junk that ends up dumped under the porch of a country home, it encourages unlimited imagination and expression. Their brains develop many more interconnected pathways, and the play significantly increases their executive function. In other words, imaginative play makes kids smarter and more capable academically and socially.

These suggestions are not on the authority of a wise, old grandma, although I have practiced this all my life, they come straight from the research labs of scientists studying executive function and how it is best developed in children.

My second daughter, Shalom, tells of her childhood make-believe:

The Flower House

by Shalom (Pearl) Brand

When I was a little girl, my younger sister and I played house all day, every day. We built pretend houses everywhere we went.

I remember days when Dad would come home from work and stop in shock at the mess Shoshanna and I had made in the sunroom. We took every book, chair, cushion, bit of cardboard, or blanket that Mom would let us use and built ourselves a fancy home.

One time, we found a pile of old faded flowers the graveyard keeper had tossed over the fence onto our farm. In great excitement, we took them to our yard and stuck them in the ground to create flower walls for our house. We thought it was so wonderful. We ran to find Dad and Mom so they could come and see our magnificent new house. With great pleasure and pride, we showed it off. Like the fine parents they are, they smiled and sat at a makeshift table in our splendid flower kitchen and pretended to eat with us.

I look back to my childhood and realize that when my parents saw the plastic flowers all over the front lawn, they must have been thinking, "Oh, no! What a mess!" But as a child, I never had a clue that our flower play-house was anything but beautiful. Their "smart little girls" only filled their hearts with gladness.

The first year of my marriage, I lived in a magical world of making a real house become a special home. A pleasure and pride very akin to what I knew as a child filled my heart daily. When Dad and Mom came over to visit, I fed them real food at a real table, and it was so much fun!

Last night, my good husband brought home some short pieces of wood from his job. My two little girls found them and right now, as I am writing this, they are outside gleefully making a new playhouse with the wood and some fake flowers left over from a party. When they are finished making their playhouse, like my mother before me, I will go out and sit with them in their kitchen and pretend to eat dirt cake. Then someday, when my daughters are married, with the same pride of feeding me dirt cake, they will feed me fine foods at their real table. They will, as I have done, reflect on the glorious days of their childhood, remembering that Mama took time to play-pretend with them.

GROOMING RESOURCEFULNESS & COURAGE

Another area of executive function that needs to be grooved in your child's brain is the ability to plan and carry out a sequence of actions in order to achieve a goal or solve a problem, and then adjust those plans if the situation changes. Researchers offer ideas as to how parents can develop these skills in their children.

- Camping with a parent and learning to build a fire and cook a simple meal builds brain cells. This can be just as effective when it takes place in your own backyard.

- Planning a party by making a list of things to buy, selecting gifts, preparing the site, and cleaning up afterwards is excellent in developing executive function skills. It also teaches children the rewards of hospitality.

- Playing games like Monopoly® or Scrabble® helps build neural connections that enable thinking ahead.

- Studies show that playing chess raises all other academic scores by improving critical thinking.

- Using Legos® to build vehicles, farms, factories, and even cities can broaden a child's imagination, but dirt, mud, sticks, and waterways are even better!

My friend Laura Newman tells this story of how she is training her children to plan and carry out a sequence of actions so they can achieve a goal or solve a problem, and then adjust those plans if the situation changes. It is fascinating to see how she has trained her children to regulate their feelings in regard to something that could cause fear due to the potential for pain. She has also taught them to appreciate the opportunity, regardless of the discomfort. I give Laura Newman an A+ in motherhood.

Queen Emilie Visits the Dentist

"Emilie held her head high like a queen yesterday at her first dentist visit; she had been waiting until she was old enough, and that has been a while! The whole office staff got such a kick out of her excitement at coming to the dentist! This was a real big-girl opportunity.

We have been encouraging her by talking up her plans to produce her very first video on this occasion. With the help of her older siblings (and Mama), she had carefully planned and laid out exactly what she wanted to do and had assigned tasks to her helpers!

> **"**Whether you think you can, or think you can't, you're right.**"**
>
> Henry Ford

She was not dreading this visit.

I am often asked how I "get" my kids to swallow pills, take strong-tasting medicine, eat food that isn't normally popular with kids, or other normal life challenges that we all face with our children. It's not just what I say in that moment, but how we live in the day to day. It is easy to transfer our fears or anxieties to our children through our words and reactions. In our efforts to reassure our kids, we cause them to look for why they need reassurance.

Fear is a thought of uncertainty or negative assumption about a future moment. Confidence is an important key to success in life. Instead of fear, we choose to celebrate the future and face new experiences as an adventure, living in faith. We cheer one another on when trying something new, whether it's swallowing a capsule or visiting the dentist for the first time."

Well done, Queen Emilie, and her wise mother.

Mirror Neurons

Remember mirror neurons? In early child-hood, your child's brain mirrors your emotions. They begin to learn about pleasure by reflecting your delighted smile. A toddler learns who and what is interesting by observing your responses. The emotional signals you emit are your child's cue as to how

> **SELF-IMAGE**
>
> Our self-image, strongly held, essentially determines what we become.

he should act, respond, feel, and what he should like. Your cheerful resolve, rather than alarming response to something that could be stressful or painful will cause the child to be able to temper his fears. You can manage your child's feelings for him. Hugs of reassurance and a smile will dispel possible panic. A smile or a giggle will wash away a pout and tag it as an unwanted mood. You are modeling what your children will become.

GROOMING CONFIDENCE

Being a Giver and Doer

Our office is usually a quiet place of mental attentiveness. Due to the type and the amount of work that is being done, everyone must be focused on their tasks without distraction. We write, publish, advertise, and ship books in fifty languages. The Bible says, **"And further, by these, my son, be admonished: of making many books there is no end; and much study is a weariness of the flesh" (Ecclesiastes 12:12).**

Many days, I get to work when it is still dark because working alone keeps me focused. So by ten in the morning, my weary brain hits a wall. About that time, Ellen, our office manager's wife, shows up wearing her baby in a sling and leading her two toddlers as they deliver a plate of gifts. As a general rule, these two tots are shy, but when they are delivering gifts to the office personnel, the joy and sparkle in their eyes speaks of something lasting and good that is being groomed in their souls. Sometimes on their plate I find a single cookie, a tiny piece of cake, or a sliver of apple. Once they brought each of the office family a thick strip of bacon, still warm, individually wrapped in a greasy paper towel. It smelled wonderful and tasted even better.

My wearied spirit and brain are always quickened and amused by the

> " Ever tried. Ever failed. No Matter. Try again. Fail again. Fail better. "
>
> Samuel Beckett

thrilled givers. But much more importantly, the two tots are developing a spirit of giving and blessing others. They are stepping out of their shy, emotional norm by having something in their hands. Their focus is on others instead of themselves. They have confidence that what they are offering is going to be pleasing all around.

As they mature, this confidence will extend to other areas of life—a most critical element to success. Mama Ellen is building in her children a deep pleasure in giving to others, and she is instilling confidence in service. She is gift-grooming their brains. They are developing executive function skills that will last a lifetime. The children are being grooved with the knowledge that giving and blessing others is a blessed thing. Go and do likewise.

Developing Confidence Naturally

Researchers studying mindset and executive function wanted to understand how these skills affected neurons in the brain. Their goal was to find ways to equip and train a child to grow up to be naturally self-disciplined, self-confident, and with leadership abilities. *Naturally* is the significant word: the child's brain is grooved so deeply that he takes the wiser course naturally—without making a deliberate decision to do so. This does not mean that children who were not intentionally trained grow up sadly lacking all these good habits. But in varying degrees it means they will have to put in more effort and make conscious choices to achieve the same level as those who were groomed to practice these traits naturally.

Long before brain scans were developed, God instructed parents on training their children. **"Train up a child in the way he should go: and when he is old, he will not depart from it" (Proverbs 22:6).** My husband and I have always called it child training.

To the distinguished professors of psychology and philosophy and the TV talking heads, the term "child training" invokes images of oppression and manipulation. But the science of neuroplasticity supports the historical and biblical approach to raising children. Parents taking care to instill the executive function skills of attention, self-control, memory, planning, and creating are accomplished in biblical child training.

One leading researcher in the field of executive function, who obviously opposes what she thinks of as biblical child training, strongly denied that this scientific approach to teaching had anything to do with "child obedience." She conceded that delayed gratification and paying attention did make a child "look" well-behaved, but it was not obedience; it was simply teaching a child to solve problems and accomplish goals. But we Bible believers have always known and taught that obedience to higher standards is achieved through a heart and mind change, not through intimidation or threat. It is refreshing to see that science has caught up with, and now acknowledges, biblical principles.

A Sweet Reward

Thankfully, children are not doomed in life if they get a lousy start. Some abused or ignored children will rise above their unfortunate youth by taking charge and re-grooving their brains. It may be that a kind teacher or relative sees the need and responds with time and energy. Often-times, a little light shining against the backdrop of so much darkness has a disproportionately positive impact in retooling the child's brain. When just one person believes in you, the impact they make becomes more powerful by grooving the brain deeper than the painful memories themselves. Remember the Schimmel Theorem Special Five story where the teacher made such an amazing difference in the lives of those five children simply because she thought they were special? How many children in this world feel they are special in our eyes?

It was of great encouragement to me to read psychologist Jason Moser's 2011 study[66] of the neural mechanisms that operate in people's brains when they make mistakes. Moser found that when people are aware they have made a mistake and give attention to correcting it, the brain responds with electrical activity called Pe—the error positivity component. It is a brain signal thought to reflect conscious attention to mistakes. What is interesting is that when people make mistakes, the brain sparks and grows. A growing

66 Moser, J.S., et al. (2011). "Mind your errors: evidence for a neural mechanism linking growth mind-set to adaptive post-error adjustments." *Psychological Science*. Retrieved from: www.ncbi. nlm.nih.gov/pubmed/22042726

brain is good. Amazingly, researchers found that making a mistake and then struggling to correct it builds stronger synapse connections than doing it right the first time! Think about it this way: a broken bone heals stronger than before the break. The gospel message is that we cannot let a single failure or a whole life of failure cause us to give up and surrender to our weakest self. Jesus said to the fallen woman, **"...Neither do I condemn thee: go, and sin no more" (John 8:11).**

Another passage says, **"Now no chastening for the present seemeth to be joyous, but grievous: nevertheless afterward it yieldeth the peaceable fruit of righteousness unto them which are exercised thereby. Wherefore lift up the hands which hang down, and the feeble knees; And make straight paths for your feet, lest that which is lame be turned out of the way; but let it rather be healed" (Hebrews 12:11–13).**

GROOMING LOVE

Teaching children how to love has not yet been added to the list of executive function skills but it should be, because knowing how to love covers a multitude of deficit. Love needs to be more than "I will love you because you do good things for me." The following is an example of how pure love is grooved deeply into the hearts and minds of children.

A Wise Daughter

For several years, my daughter Shalom and her family lived on our farm in my mom and dad's old house. Several times each day, Mike and I had occasion to drive down the lane past their house. Shalom's children are outside creatures, so they would usually be out playing when we drove by in our ATV buggy. If they were not outside, we would see them lined up looking out the window when they heard our buggy coming. I could feel their love through the windowpane. Sometimes, when we were too busy to stop, we would wave and throw kisses. But most days, we could stop and visit at least once. Sometimes we would take the kids for a thrilling ride down the lane. Mike yells when he gives the kids rides and somehow makes a fifteen-mile-per-hour ride feel daring. The five children always saw us as FUN. "Here comes Mama Pearl and Big Papa! This will be fun!" They love us, and we love them by virtue of the sweet fellowship and often communion. It was

> **"** Control over consciousness is not simply a cognitive skill. At least as much as intelligence, it requires the commitment of emotions and will. It is not enough to know how to do it; one must do it, consistently, in the same way as athletes or musicians who must keep practicing what they know in theory. **"**
>
> Mihaly Csikszentmihalyi

amazingly satisfying sharing those quick, loving moments and seeing their joy in spending a few minutes with us. Every grandparent should be so blessed. This past year, Shalom and Justin found their own special homestead. It is only about seven miles down the road, but it is far enough away that we only see the kids once or twice a week now.

A new, little man joined the clan the year after they moved. We have not had the pleasure of connecting with our new grandson, Ryder, nor he with us, like we did with the other children. He has not come to know us like his brothers and sisters. But Shalom, his mama, goes above and beyond to make sure he knows he loves us better than anything. I am honored and amazed at how effective her love grooming is.

Every time Shalom's family comes to The DOOR[67] on Thursday night to hear Big Papa teach the Bible, as she enters the door with Ryder on her hip and he sees me, she says to Ryder as she lifts him half off her hip in excitement, "MAMA PEARL!!! Ryder, here is Mama Pearl!" The other kids take the cue and rush in for hugs; even the teenager needs no prompting. Ryder's eyes light up; he knows something wonderful is happening, although he doesn't quite know what. Shalom doesn't stop there. She moves in to give me a hug, which basically forces him into an embrace, while saying in a most excited voice, "Ryder, hug Mama Pearl. We love Mama Pearl." Ryder half grins and complies like it is big fun. Although I am not in his life like I was with the other grandchildren, he still knows they all love Mama Pearl and Big Papa. I have not earned his love. I have not won his heart. His mama made sure the love we have is just as dear as the love we shared with the other children.

My heart is full of thanksgiving for this precious gift, a gift to me and to

67 You can watch Bible teaching at: TheDOOR.studio

the kids. I know that true satisfaction in life comes from just what Shalom is instilling in her children: love, appreciation, family, honor, and respect.

But know that her grooming has ramifications far beyond the bond she is creating. The brain of the child is being formed to favor love and honor. In molding him to a single issue, she is grooving his brain to have broad pathways of love and fellowship.

GROOMING LEADERSHIP

Strong, quality leadership is a skill that can be built into a person. Most people don't see leadership as a sacrifice, but it is. It is much easier to sit on the sidelines and let someone else take charge, and bear the burden of planning and overseeing. Leadership is a skill dependent upon the development of all executive function skills: self-confidence, self-restraint, self-motivation, focus, follow-through, memory, resourcefulness, and love. No one chooses to follow a leader that can't regulate his own moods, feelings, responses, and desires.

The Good Librarian

I clearly remember a few teachers in my grammar school and junior high years. Some were sweet, some were mean, some were lazy, and a scant few were really interested in pouring into my life and helping me learn. One such bright star was the school librarian. She was the only teacher in all my years that noticed my lack of hearing as well as my need for glasses. That is a remarkable oversight on the part of all my teachers, since I am stone deaf in the right ear and have some hearing loss in the left. Plus, I couldn't see well. Think about that fact! All those years, and not a single teacher ever noticed I had difficulty hearing or seeing except for the librarian, and she wasn't even one of my regular teachers. I wonder how many children in our public schools are just put through the assembly line and no one ever wonders why they have a learning disability. I am thankful for the librarian.

Since she was so old, she needed help putting books on the shelves. She offered me a job as her assistant librarian, which meant I could skip a couple classes each day. I was eager to help, and I wanted to please her because she believed I was smart—I could tell by the way she talked to me. She looked *at* me when she talked, not *over* me. She regularly asked my opinion on what books the other children would be interested in reading and how we could display the books so they would be easier to find. We worked together changing the library to reflect the shifting themes at school. She obviously appreciated my input. She was developing in me confidence that my opinion mattered, that my creative style was good, and that I could do this job by myself, if needed.

During this one hour a day, five days a week, for one school year of my life, this woman grooved executive function skills into my brain. Each day when I finished my library chores, she would choose a book and we would sit, one on one, and discuss the information we read. It was only twenty minutes or so a day, and she was often interrupted by other students, but those minutes were the highlight of my junior high years and most likely the turning point in my education.

It was her mindset toward me that won the day. Just like the teacher in the Schimmel Theorem Special Five study, she made me believe that I was above and beyond simply by the way she treated me, the way she looked into my eyes and discussed subjects with me.

I was not using library time to finish my classwork, nor were we going through any curriculum that would improve my performance. The things we read were of no consequence to a formal education. Yet, when I look back to my real learning, it was in the library, discussing subjects such as shoeing horses, how to write, ocean currents, why opossums hang by their tails and carry their babies on their backs, and what can be found in mud puddles. She was my teacher supreme.

Due to my lack of hearing, I was behind in all my classes until she entered my life. Reading was a struggle, math was just a confusion of numbers, history and science were a waste of time, but she opened the door to my curiosity. Through her I learned the executive function skills that research has shown to be so central to success in life. She taught me how to focus. She built in me a working memory, taught me to carry through with planning by teaching me the duties of the library, and she taught me how to help others. She gave me confidence to speak to my other teachers and tell of my need to sit closer to the front rather than where I was assigned. She opened up the magic of books and, through them, a world of things I didn't know existed. Her greatest gift was that of confidence. I was worth her time, therefore, I was worth a lot.

As parents, we hold in our hands a glorious opportunity. Scientific research PROVES that true intelligence is not found in rote learning, memorization, or being able to pass a test. Yet this is what educators have insisted is proper learning. Repetition might shove some facts into the hippocampus, but most of the grueling hours spent temporarily ingraining the information do not make a wide web of neuronal connections or produce emotional intelligence so needful for life. For your child to excel, it takes ideas, concepts, and challenges. The child must feel he can do, learn, climb, and be anything he wants to be. He must learn to value self-control, creativity, and resourcefulness.

EMOTIONAL INTELLIGENCE MATTERS

Executive function skills develop emotional intelligence, which is established as more important for happiness and success than IQ. What you have just read concerning the marshmallow story, the flower house, young Emilie having courage when she went to the dentist, and the two tots learning to love serving others are examples of how we can help our children develop strong executive function skills. These character traits are key to emotional intelligence. Strong emotional intelligence is the stuff that makes us happy, content, confident, successful, and resourceful. Emotional intelligence is not a personality trait inherent from birth. It is developed in children by parents, siblings, and close associates. Someone in the child's life will have to make a concentrated effort to train him to highly value these life skills and be willing to sacrifice to make it happen. You can understand why God says in Proverbs 22:6, **"Train up a child in the way he should go: and when he is old, he will not depart from it."** It does not say discipline up, fuss up, or work up; it says train up...in the way he should go. Cause the child to desire self-control, self-confidence, and self-motivation until those things become part of his character.

Daniel Goleman, in his seminal work *Emotional Intelligence: Why It Can Matter More Than IQ*,[68] reasoned that "...in a sense, we have two brains, two minds, and two different kinds of intelligence: rational and emotional." He also maintained that our use of emotional intelligence is as important in life as our intellectual capability.

68 Goleman, Daniel. (1996). *Emotional Intelligence: Why It Can Matter More Than IQ*. London: Bloomsbury.

Goleman delineates four expressions of emotional intelligence.

- *Being self-aware* – The ability to recognize a feeling as it is happening is fundamental to emotional intelligence. If we are unable to notice our emotions, we can be overwhelmed and can flounder at the mercy of these strong feelings.

- *Managing emotions* – The ability to maintain an even keel or bounce back quickly from life's upsets builds on the preceding skill. We want to have a sense of control over our emotions so that we can deal with them appropriately.

- *Having self-motivation* – Underlying the accomplishment of any sort of goal is the ability to master our emotions in pursuit of that end. For creative tasks, focus and mastery (learning to delay gratification and stifle inappropriate desires) are important skills, and emotional control is essential.

- *Recognizing the emotions of others* – "People skills" are based on a capacity for empathy and the ability to stay tuned to the emotions of others. Empathy kindles altruism and lies at the basis of professions that deal with caring for others.

What really sets a child up for success and happiness is the acquisition of these executive function skills. **"If any of you lack wisdom, let him ask of God, that giveth to all men liberally, and upbraideth not; and it shall be given him" (James 1:5).**

I CHARGE YOU

Tell your children the marshmallow story and ask them if they could wait two minutes and not eat a marshmallow. Talk about how cool the children are that can wait, and reassure them that you could wait ten minutes or maybe even a whole day. Then have the children plan their own research study where they choose the temptation and decide on how long they will have to wait to have it and what they get if they wait. Do this project once a week. Study the other executive function examples, and help the children create their own research. Involve other families to make it more fun.

"For the Lord giveth wisdom: out of his mouth cometh knowledge and understanding" (Proverbs 2:6).

Sacrificing Our Brains to the Screen

CHAPTER 8

Neuroplasticity has taught us through a multitude of brain scans that most cartoons are damaging to the brain. Be wise.

Introduction: Great Wasting of Life

Introduction by Debi Pearl

Brain researchers assert that the great dumbing-down of this generation is primarily due to the digital playground consuming children. It is not so much the influence of bad content (though in many cases that is a serious problem), it is what the brain is not doing when held captive by a screen. If, instead of being exposed to games and movies, children were held in isolation for the same period of time, the dumbing-down results would be pretty much the same. There is very little positive effect on the brain when kids watch someone else do pretend-life. There are exceptions, as in limited exposure to educational material, but how many parents limit their children to occasional science and history videos? No doubt there is educational and brain-building power in watching a YouTube video to learn how to perform a task. The difference is in seeking media support for a hands-on approach to life versus

ENDANGERED MINDS

In *Endangered Minds*, author Jane Healy speculates the odd, restless behavior seen in young children today is the product of "plastic" changes in the children's brains due to TV exposure. College professors complain of having to "dumb down" their teaching due to students' inability to think deeply.

living life vicariously on a screen. Media can be useful, like the little four-page sheet of instructions found in the box of something that needs assembling, but when kids just sit around reading the directions, never assembling the parts that construct a well-rounded life, their brains develop along very narrow and limited veins. Most parents are confident that their children have limited exposure to media, but most children are being dumbed-down as never before and it is revealed in the emotional state of young adults.

During that time in a child's life when the brain is being developed and needs a broad range of sensory experiences to reach its full potential, it is held captive by the two-dimensional world of "screentopia." The brain is designed by God to develop in an active, changing, three-dimensional environment. In two dimensions, it is unable to complete its development. Research reveals the brain cells that control eye coordination are being lost so that people no longer react to what is happening in their peripheral vision, resulting in car accidents and other coordination oddities.

Furthermore, a barrage of "noise" coming from unnatural sources confuses and overloads the brain, causing it to release chemicals that destroy, rather than build. This is a recently proven source of damage to the brain, and, at this point, few are aware of it. Screened electronics are inflicting serious mental impairment on this generation of children. Here in the good old USA, one in six children are testing as mentally and/or emotionally delayed. In the next section, Dr. Nicole Dawson explains how media disrupt natural brain development. As parents, we can make wise, educated decisions about how to raise our children to become all that God intended, or we can take the easy road and end up with—you guessed it—the one in six. That is not to say that five out of six are escaping damage; it is just that the kind of damage they are suffering is not so blatant as to be catalogued by behaviorists.

Until this study, I had no idea what could be done through media to manipulate entire nations. The mechanics of how they retard development are bad enough, but when you add the hidden agenda of the producers of children's content, it takes on a whole new level of sinister. I will not explore that side of the entertainment world in this book, our purpose here is to gain an understanding of the brain and neuroplasticity.

Set extreme limits on electronics and stick to them. You will never regret the effort. Don't allow your children to be raised by the all-consuming world of Silicon Valley and the twisted minds of media producers.

SACRIFICING OUR BRAINS TO THE SCREEN
by Dr. Nicole Dawson, DC (Doctor of Chiropractic)

The concept of brain grooving has fascinated me for many years, not only as a mother, but also as a prenatal and pediatric chiropractor. I have spent hundreds of hours studying complex neurology, working in the cadaver lab, and ultimately, have gone on to care for thousands of patients. Applying this knowledge to a child's development has been a very rewarding experience, both as a parent and a healer.

Having a basic understanding of how the brain works can be a wonderful tool for parents. It allows us to appreciate the symphony of life being intricately composed as our children form their own network of neurons. Each child is a masterpiece in the making. As parents, it's our job to facilitate the full expression of their God-given potential. We have more influence in guiding their development than we realize.

> **MEDIA TRADEOFF**
>
> Each type of media—whether it be radio, internet or TV—changes the balance of our individual senses, increasing some at the expense of others.

As with most things in life, where there is great potential for good, there also lies the possibility to do great harm. There are many ways we can influence positive brain grooving in our children, and there are equally as many ways we can derail those efforts. One of the biggest factors is the impact of television and other screen media on our little ones. Simply put, digital media and the developing mind do not mix.

The official guidelines set forth by the American Academy of Pediatrics

ACCLIMATIZING TO THE TV

Sudden change causes a physiological response: the heart rate decreases for four to six seconds. TV triggers this response at a much more rapid rate than we experience in real life. Our brains change to accommodate the new speed. The cost is that slower activities, such as reading, complex conversation, and other intellectual pursuits become a struggle.

(AAP) advocate that children under 24 months have no exposure to media and children 2–5 should be limited to only one hour per day. The AAP also submitted a research review in October 2016 titled *Children and Adolescents and Digital Media*[69] in which they cite "that most 2-year-olds used mobile devices on a daily basis and that most of the 1-year-olds assessed (92.2%) had already used a mobile device." In exploring the risks of media exposure, the AAP paper goes on to explain, "Risks of such media include negative health effects on sleep, attention, and learning, a higher incidence of obesity and depression, exposure to inaccurate, inappropriate, or unsafe content..."

Neural Pathways versus Reading a Book

The AAP and other leading experts in the field of pediatric neurology all agree that infants and young children should not be exposed to television or other digital media. This includes television that may be running in the background. In the 2016 article titled "Inside the Human Brain: How Watching TV Changes Neural Pathways versus Reading a Book"[70] posted on medicaldaily.com, Samantha Olson explains:

"In 2013, a team of researchers from Ohio State University interviewed and tested 107 preschoolers and their parents to see how television impacted a child's theory of mind. The more a child watched television or was

69 Chassiakos, Yolanda, et al. (2016). "Children and Adolescents and Digital Media." *Pediatrics*. Accessed from: pediatrics.aappublications.org/content/early/2016/10/19/peds.2016-2593?versioned=true

70 Olson, Samantha. (2016). "Inside the Human Brain: How Watching TV Changes Neural Pathways versus Reading a Book." *Medical Daily*. Retrieved from: www.medicaldaily.com/neural-pathways-watching-tv-human-brain-reading-book-389744

exposed to television, even if it was playing in the background, the weaker their understanding of their parents' mental state. Ultimately, if the television was on in the vicinity of the child, it impaired their theory of mind, which is defined as the ability to recognize another person's beliefs, intents, desires, and knowledge, as well as their own."

"Children with more developed theories of mind are better able to participate in social relationships," said the study's lead researcher, Amy Nathanson, a communications professor at Ohio State University. "These children can engage in more sensitive, cooperative interactions with other children and are less likely to resort to aggression as a means of achieving goals."

A more recent study from 2015 published in the journal *Cerebral Cortex* revealed watching too much TV could actually change the brain. Researchers studied 276 children between the ages of five and eighteen. They found that as the children spent more time watching TV, the areas of the brain responsible for processing visual and emotional stimuli became larger, harming the language centers of the brain.

This may be why increased TV exposure for children under the age of three is linked to delayed language acquisition, which sets them up for years of playing catch-up in school. When it comes to school, children who sit in front of the TV for two or more hours a day are more likely to have greater psychological difficulties, which include hyperactivity, emotional and behavioral problems, and social conflicts with peers in the classroom.[71]

Clinical Experience

In my own experience in observing children, it is not difficult to tell whether or not they have been exposed to media in their formative years. When children are exposed to television early in their development, it has a dulling effect. Their eyes appear glossy, they are often withdrawn, and they are slower to respond to changes in their environment. Children who have grown up playing outdoors and who have had far less exposure to television, are more alive, alert, and attentive.

The reason television affects the brain so profoundly during this critical time of growth is because it sets the child's brain up to be in receiving

71 Olson, Samantha. (2016). "Inside the Human Brain: How Watching TV Changes Neural Pathways versus Reading a Book." *Medical Daily.* Retrieved from: www.medicaldaily.com/neural-pathways-watching-tv-human-brain-reading-book-389744

mode only. As the child sits sedentary and stares, he is downloading an overwhelming amount of information without the physical or kinesthetic interaction of his body. Children are not ready to process stimuli in this way. Learning builds upon itself through association. The young brain craves a more intimate interaction with the environment. Real-life experiences and interactions are the building blocks used to develop a child's understanding of self. This is crucial! Little ones do not have enough life experience to relate to the type of information they are being exposed to in media.

Young children also do not view media the same way adults do. They do not understand plots, nuances, or jokes. What they see are flashes and frames lighting up at a dizzying speed with no context with which to understand the information. The flicker rate of television runs typically between 60 and 300 light images per second. That amount of light flashing at a child literally shocks his brain and puts him into a trance-like state that dumbs down the mind.

To really understand the impact of this, we need to look at three primary ways digital media physically affect and alter the developing brain.

Brain Networks

Our brains are divided into two primary sides: the left hemisphere and the right hemisphere. The two sides look alike physically, but they have very different roles. The hemispheres connect through a dense fiber of neurons located in the center region called the corpus callosum. This center region acts like a mediator and helps to pull the hemispheres together for greater processing ability and improved comprehension.

The corpus callosum needs the child to move, engage, experiment, and relate to his environment in order to activate and build different areas of the brain at the same time. This cooperation between the hemispheres is crucial for the brain to work as a unit, using multiple areas at once and in harmony with each other. Unfortunately, when children watch TV, their brains are robbed of that experience.

Electronic media primarily interact with the frontal lobes of the brain, especially the right side, so the brain develops in an unbalanced way, reducing communication between the hemispheres. This creates a less functional neural network. The right frontal lobe becomes enlarged through hyper-excitation. This hinders processing and communication with other areas of the brain.

The frontal lobes are where we learn to interpret social interactions, but this learning needs to happen through interaction with real people. That is how the child learns tone, meaning, and empathy via feedback from his environment. The child needs authentic human interaction to properly groove the frontal lobes and help them intricately link to other portions of the brain.

When we integrate the brain from side to side via strong cross-connections, we see exceptional intelligence. A famous example of this is physicist Albert Einstein. In a 2013 article on the website Accelerating Intelligence titled "Well-connected hemispheres of Einstein's brain may have contributed to his brilliance," Ray Kurzweil reviews a scientific article from the journal *Brain* and concludes: "The left and right hemispheres of Albert Einstein's brain were unusually well connected to each other and this may have contributed to his brilliance, according to a new study, the first to detail Einstein's corpus callosum."[72]

Final thought: When we put our children in front of media, the information is not grooving their brain in wholesome or healthy ways. The input is jumbled to a child and lacks meaning and context. It is also causing hyper-excitation of the frontal lobes, thereby shocking the brain. This hinders the brain from integrating and stunts their intelligence, both emotionally and cognitively.

The Conscious versus Subconscious Mind

Our alert and aware state of mind is called the conscious mind. When we are conscious, we can intentionally direct our thoughts and behaviors. Adults have over 60,000 thoughts per day that we are consciously aware of, but this only accounts for 5% of our thoughts!

The other 95% of our thoughts are silently running in the background, called our subconscious mind. The majority of our body processes—how we feel about things and other important information processing—are all happening without our direct awareness.

Throughout those first few years of life, a child's subconscious mind is wide open, especially at birth. It is a dream-like, hypnotic state, and young children are being programmed by their environment until 6–7 years old.

72 Kurzweil, Ray. (2013). "Well-connected hemispheres of Einstein's brain may have contributed to his brilliance." *Kurzweil Accelerating Intelligence*. Retrieved from: www.kurzweilai.net/well-connected-hemispheres-of-einsteins-brain-may-have-contributed-to-his-brilliance

Young minds in this state are not having analytical, critical thoughts. They are going with the flow, as if they are floating down a river and accepting the experience for what it is.

This means their minds are being programmed by what is put in front of them. Their minds are wide open and ready for learning. Young children accept what is presented as truth without question, regardless of the source.

Much of a child's personality—how he sees the world and how he sees himself in the world—gets imprinted in these first few years of life via the development of the silent, subconscious mind. It is like a sponge. The results of this time period will seep out and show their hand later in life, but much of what children are exposed to during this time will determine whether they are well-adjusted or ill-adjusted adults.

Final thought: Be very sensitive to the environment your child is developing in during these crucial years from age 0–7. His subconscious mind is running the show. This is a time of super-learning, especially the silent, deep thoughts and attitudes that will color his world. This is an essential time to instill positive connections he will carry with him for a lifetime. When we put these impressionable minds in front of media, children are drawn away from the real-life experiences they need to shape life skills. Media viewing trains them to be passive witnesses to artificial stimulation. This dulls their ability to engage and develop their whole person.

BRAIN WAVES

The brain communicates via chemical exchanges and electrical impulses. The electrical impulses are measured and grouped according to their tone and intensity into wave patterns. The main brain wave patterns are beta, alpha, theta, and delta. Having some basic information on brain waves is important because it highlights the significant dangers of media's effect on the developing mind. Children's minds are humming at a different frequency than adults, and we need to be sensitive to that in our brain grooving efforts. Here, we will explore how media put our children into a dangerous and hypnotic trance that negatively affects their growth.

Delta waves are the slowest. They are found in infants and young children, as well as adults while they are asleep. Babies need to sleep so often because they live in a delta wave state. Their daily experience of life is similar to when an adult is dreaming.

Theta waves are the next to slowest pattern. They are found in children from 2–5 years old, a period when they are starting to differentiate self from non-self. "You took my toy and I want it back." This is a time of connecting to their inner world of feelings and imagination. They still do not possess the ability for critical or rational thought.

Alpha waves are the next to highest level. They are found in children from 5-9 years old. This is the time when the conscious and analytical mind begins to form. Children at this age are beginning to interpret and make judgments about their environment. Exposure to digital media pushes our brains into the alpha wave state.

Beta waves are the most active state of mind and the one in which adults usually operate. Beta waves show up in children at 9+ years old. This is the world of conscious, alert, and focused thinking that allows us to keep pace and function in society.

Since our adult brains are typically in high beta mode, we often assume our young children should keep pace and think as we do. When we understand that their brains are humming in the dreamy delta or theta wave mode, we can begin to appreciate their needs are much different than our own.

Delta and theta brain waves are where we find deep healing. They are also where brilliant ideas or concepts are produced, some of which have gifted humanity in amazing ways. Here are some examples: Albert Einstein was in a dream-like state when he formed the theory of relativity. In 1965, Paul McCartney of The Beatles composed his famous song "Yesterday" when he awoke from a dream and quickly wrote it down. Niels Bohr was the father of quantum mechanics and he often talks about the dream that inspired his discovery of the atom. Even Larry Page had a dream that led to the creation of Google, and the list goes on.

As you can see, while our children's brains are developing in the delta and theta wave state, a lot is happening. It is a time of potential and possibility when the soul and body are merging into reality. It is a dreamy, magical place that should not be rushed or curtailed in your child's development. He needs this time to fully form the inner workings that lay the foundation for exceptionally high intelligence later in life.

When we put our children in front of digital media, we are disrupting their budding genius by pulling them out of the delta and theta wave state and pushing them to absorb alpha wave frequencies they are not ready to process.

The famous psychologist, Thomas Mulholland, *found that after just 30 seconds of watching television, the brain begins to produce alpha waves, which lulls children into a comatose-like state.* Mulholland performed an experiment in which ten children were asked to watch their favorite television programs. His assumption was that since these programs were their favorite shows, the kids would be involved in them and there would be an oscillation between alpha and beta wave activity. As they studied the children's brain waves while watching media, they observed that this did not happen. While they watched, the children were not reacting, orienting, or focusing, and maintained an alpha wave state.

Final thought: As well-meaning parents, we go to great lengths to guard our children's welfare. Yet instead of protecting their developing minds, we invite technology into our homes. Parents who hand their children over to electronics for educational benefits could be doing more harm than good. We must be mindful that technology is designed to make money. The vast majority of programming was created with the intention of selling your family products or services and most is designed with a worldview that is not Christian. These companies hire the best psychologists and marketing experts in the world to study how to get around parents and target children. Don't believe me? See the 2006 article in *USA Today* titled "Six Strategies Marketers Use to Make Kids Want Things Bad" by Bruce Horovitz.[73] According to the website for the Campaign for a Commercial-Free Childhood, "...companies spend about $17 billion annually marketing to children."[74]

If you want to nurture the healthy development of your child's brain, turn off the TV and turn on their mind.

—Dr. Nicole

73 Horovitz, Bruce. (2006). "Six strategies marketers use to get kids to want stuff bad." *USA Today.* Retrieved from: usatoday30.usatoday.com/money/advertising/2006-11-21-toy-strategies-usat_x.htm

74 "Marketing to Children Overview." *Campaign for a Commercial-Free Childhood.* Retrieved from: commercialfreechildhood.org/resource/marketing-children-overview

Debi concludes: The young brain comes into the world clean, like a book not yet written—thousands of white pages ready to receive good information. We parents must be diligent in what we allow to be printed on the pages of their developing brains.

There will come a day when harmful things are poured into our children's minds and hearts, but our job is to stave this off as long as possible, thus giving them time to gain the strength to make wise choices.

I CHARGE YOU

Set aside two days a week where there will be no screen time. Show the children where you have marked it on the calendar so when they whine, you can put their finger on the red circle that marks the date. Any time you take away something that is so consuming, you MUST fill that empty spot with something just as stimulating. Have others over for a book reading or visit the park and read to the children there.

Visit the library one of those days and have each child select books for reading. You could have some audio books that you listen to together during this time. Make sure some of the books you get from the library are fun stories, a few are science or history, and be sure to include project books such as how to do arts and crafts. Crafts are a great exchange for screen time, especially if Mama does a craft, too. Gradually add more craft days and limit the number of days for screens. Be SURE that you read aloud to your children at least one or two books each day.

"I will set no wicked thing before mine eyes: I hate the work of them that turn aside; it shall not cleave to me" (Psalm 101:3).

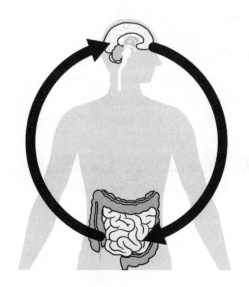

The Brain-Gut Connection

CHAPTER 9

*Neuroplasticity has taught us that the gut is the second brain
and thus extremely important in our mental well-being.*

ONE SMART GIRL

Laila-Bug is nine years old and a skinny little runt. She knows all about the microbes in her gut. Mama Pearl told her. The brain in her head is called the Big Brain. Her tummy is called the Little Brain. The Big Brain and the Little Brain are actually connected and must work together very closely, otherwise, neither will function correctly. On occasion, Laila fondly pats her belly and tells her microbes "Hi." She knows that there is a big glob of them right under her skin. Laila holds out her hands and pretends to hold the glob of microbes. Mama Pearl told her they are about the size of her kitten. Again, Laila pats her flat, skinny tummy, wondering how so many could fit inside of her. She knows that her microbes are not actually part of her body but are very welcome visitors, busily breaking down her food and facilitating the function of her immune system. Laila knows it is her job to keep them healthy so they can keep her healthy because if they get sick, she can be attacked by all kinds of terrible diseases. Plus, if they are in trouble, it will make her Big Brain act weird and then she will act weird.

Even though Laila-Bug is just a child, she has made up her mind to choose healthy foods whenever she has a choice. She started eating an avocado and a boiled egg for breakfast instead of sweet cereal. She asked her mom to buy her some sardines to eat for lunch. She bathes her sardines in mustard because that is good for her too. She snacks on carrots, celery, and homemade pickles. Knowing about the function of her microbes, Laila has developed a taste for healthy foods that most kids can't stand. She also eats cake and other sweet stuff when it is available to her, but it isn't something she begs to have.

Laila-Bug is an outside creature even when it is cold or roasting hot in the summer. She likes to build forts and high-jumps for her bike and all kinds of fun stuff. Lying on the trampoline in the late afternoon with the sunshine beating down on her is her favorite place to take a nap or just to lollygag. She tells her brothers that lollygagging is proven to be an important part of

MICROBIOME DIVERSITY

"By analyzing the gut microbes of 77 toddlers, ages 18 to 27 months, scientists were able to correlate certain behavioral traits with specific bacterial species. In general, kids with more diverse microbiomes tended to be more curious, positive, social, extroverted, and impulsive. Those toddlers with lower overall microbial diversity showed more fear, cuddliness, and self-restraint.

Researchers hypothesize that gut microbes, by modulating stress hormones like cortisol, could be having an effect on how children interact with people or react in new situations. An outgoing, social, and confident child may have a more diverse microbiome. A shy, reserved kid, who is hesitant and scared, has fewer microbes. Research shows that digestive flora does have a role in childhood behaviors."[1]

1 Christian, L. M. et al. (2015). "Gut microbiome composition is associated with temperament during early childhood." Brain, Behavior, and Immunity. Retrieved from: www.ncbi.nlm.nih.gov/pubmed/25449582

THE VAGUS NERVE - The brain's super-highway connecting all major body organs

Stress overstimulates the vagus nerve which damages it and disrupts the gut microbes resulting in:

1. Gastrointestinal tract issues such as:

   Irritable bowel syndrome (IBS) and inflammatory bowel disease (IBD)

2. Neurodegenerative disorders such as:

   Parkinson's, Alzheimer's, and Huntington's disease. Also, can lead to depression, anxiety, and forgetfulness

3. Inflammation, which affects the immune system, can lead to an autoimmune disorder

4. Chronic fatigue can stem from an exhausted vagus nerve

5. Can negatively affect any organ

Healing the vagus nerve:

1. Stop stressing

2. Heal the gut

3. Take quality micronutrients

4. Practice deep breathing

5. Learn how live a mindful life (chapter 15)

6. Accupuncture

7. Electric stimulus

Two-way communication

Known as the "6th Sense"

https://www.ncbi.nlm.nih.gov/pmc/articles/PMC5808284/
https://www.healthline.com/nutrition/gut-brain-connection#section1

goodbrain health because it gives her Big Brain a chance to chill out. Laila knows that the sunshine feeds her body with vitamin D, which helps build her immune system.

Laila-Bug will not struggle with her weight as an adult. Her microbes are a wiggling pile of happy as they digest her food and turn it into high energy for her developing Big Brain. She doesn't have brain fog or days when she feels depressed. The neurotransmitters in her Little Brain—her tummy—are working in concert with the Big Brain in her head to keep her alert and feeling happy.

Basically, her Big Brain and Little Brain are dancing together undisturbed. Due to their cherished relationship, Laila-Bug is one healthy little girl. When it comes to good gut health, she is smarter than most adults.

> *II* As your weight goes up, the actual physical size and function of your brain goes down. *II*
>
> Dr. Daniel Amen,
> Amen Clinics Program

PARTNERS FOR LIFE

The brain has a partner, a very needful partner, and that partner is called the gut. Science refers to the brain in the head as the Big Brain and refers to the gut as the Little Brain. The connection between the Little Brain in our gut and the Big Brain in our skull has a significant influence on our mental state and plays key roles in combating certain diseases throughout the body. In many cases, healing the mind can only occur by healing the gut.

Technically known as the enteric nervous system, the gut consists of neurons embedded in the walls of the tube that begins at the esophagus, runs about 30 feet through the stomach and the small intestine, through the large intestine, and ends at the anus. The Little Brain contains some 100 million neurons, more than either the spinal cord or the peripheral nervous system.

This mass of neural tissue filled with important neurotransmitters does much more than merely handle digestion or inflict the occasional nervous pang. An important role of the gut is communicating with the brain. For several reasons, it is critical that this communication between the brain and gut is working in top form. The neurotransmitters that are housed in the gut play a key role in regulating your mental state. Without your gut being able to function in this capacity, you will have serious emotional issues. Your immune system, which is vital to your overall health, is also found in the gut.

Without the gut-driven immune system, your body is more susceptible to colds, flu, and other viral or bacterial infections. Also, you are more vulnerable to cancer and autoimmune diseases. Of course, the gut controls your digestive system, which supplies fuel to keep the brain functioning. Have you heard the term "brain fog?" It is the result of a malfunctioning digestive system that is unable to supply your brain with the proper fuel. The gut earned the name Little Brain for two reasons: 1. It is critical to the function of the Big Brain and 2. The gut is the only system in the body that functions independently of commands from the Big Brain.

> **KEY**
>
> A healthy gut is the key to a healthy brain.

Recent scientific findings have thrown light on a biblical concept that seemed to have arisen in a prescientific culture. How wrong we were. Two thousand years ago the Apostle Paul said, **"If there be therefore any consolation in Christ, if any comfort of love, if any fellowship of the Spirit, if any bowels and mercies, Fulfil ye my joy, that ye be likeminded, having the same love, being of one accord, of one mind"** **(Philippians 2:1–2)**. Many passages reference the bowels as the source of affection and mercy, similar to how we use the word *heart* today. But with what we now know of the bowels as the Little Brain, it is obvious that it is more anatomically accurate to say, "I love you with all my bowels." But that sounds too weird to be well received. In love, who cares about scientific accuracy? Furthermore, a heart looks better on a greeting card than a rendering of the bowels.

In learning about neuroplasticity, we were introduced to the concept of the brain being like a map of many roads—the greater our web of intersecting roads, the greater our capacity to remember based on associations. In the next section, we will use several illustrations to describe the gut-brain connection and function: gardening, relationships, eating habits, nutrition, and combating disease. I use story form because it helps groove the brain in a broader way. Let's look at how the gut affects the brain.

DEAR OLD GEORGE

Unknowingly, dear old George has been treating his gut guests rather poorly. He can't understand why he always feels as if he is walking through a fog and doesn't feel like doing anything.

George has always eaten a lot of processed foods. When they get to his gut, the microbes don't like what they are being fed because they can't turn it into needful nutrients to produce serotonin. Without serotonin, George lives in the doldrums. The milkshake he drank had lots of sugar, but George already had a stored surplus of sugar, so the microbes just sent the sugar overload to the fat storage room, expanding it more and more.

The hamburger had a little magnesium that the microbes could pull out, but not enough to keep George's brain from feeling lousy. Most of the other food had nothing in it that the body could use for fuel, so out it went to the backed-up dump pile. The microbes sent a message to George's neurons asking for more nutrient-rich foods so they would have something with which to create fuel for his brain and body. So George moseyed into his kitchen to see if there was anything ready for him to eat. He was out of luck. Furthermore, his wife Sue Ann was mad at him again, so it was a good time to get out of the house. He jumped in his truck and went to town to get something to eat. Poor old George ate more microbe-killing food, so the starving microbes didn't have the ability to help George's brain work properly. The gut cannot do its job without good food to nourish its friendly visitors. The unfed microbes are feeling weak, and over time, some of the toxic food has damaged the microbe work force, reducing their number and completely eliminating some colonies. Because of the total absence of some kinds of microbes, much of the food George eats is now partially indigestible. So it is rotting instead of being digested, which explains why George stinks and has skin rashes.

SUE ANN, SUE ANN, WHAT WILL YOU DO?

Sue Ann eats well and wishes George would do likewise.

The microbes in Sue Ann's bowels receive a lot of healthy nutrients from the good food she eats, yet she is chronically ill. She suffers from diarrhea, constipation, bloating, constant headaches, and extreme anxiety. She goes to the doctor often and is sure she has an autoimmune disease. Why is Sue Ann always sick? Maybe she's just wearing out her vagus nerve with all the stress.

Sue Ann is irate with George because he is lazy and misses a lot of work. She is nervous about bills not getting paid on time, and she wishes George would just pay attention to what he is supposed to do! She takes it as a personal insult. She is right, of course, but being correct does not mean that her attitude is doing her any favors. Sadly, Sue Ann's attitude is slowly but surely

MICRONUTRIENT BUILDING BLOCKS:
AKA, FISH TO THE RESCUE!

Julia Rucklidge, a clinical psychologist from the University of Canterbury in New Zealand, has been researching since the late 1990s how micronutrients affect the brain. Researchers all over the world have conducted study after study, concluding that taking high-quality micronutrients is much more effective for long-term mental health than using any of the medications available today.

Research has established that whether you are a 4-year-old boy with ADHD, or a 27-year-old with bipolar disorder, or a 55-year-old who has developed Parkinson's, or even an 80-year-old with Alzheimer's, your chances of long-term improvement are much greater with the use of micronutrients rather than prescription medications.

All their studies overwhelmingly prove that using tryptophan, methylated B vitamins (especially B-12), magnesium (every cell of your body NEEDS this), essential fatty acids in the form of omega-3 fish oil, and choline (similar to B vitamins) makes a big difference in mental health. They are the building blocks for your brain. Of course, eating raw, steamed, and fermented vegetables is also critical for a healthy brain, for they are the foods that produce healthy microbes. Eleven epidemiological studies from all over the world have proven that a clean, fresh diet lowers the risk for depression, whereas a diet of processed and nutrient-deficient foods significantly increases the risk.

On the subject of prevention, Julia Rucklidge recounts in a lecture she gave through TED: "One interesting study looked at 81 adolescents who were at risk for psychosis. Half received omega-3 fatty acids in the form of fish oils, which is an essential nutrient for brain health; the other half of the subjects received a placebo (a fake pill) for 12 weeks. One year later, 5% of those who received the fish oil developed psychosis versus 28% of those on placebo. That is an 80% reduction in the chances of getting psychosis by simply taking fish oil." It is interesting that the positive effects remained an entire year after they stopped taking the fish oil.

destroying her important little microbial helpers. Her constant bitterness is producing chemicals in her stomach and her brain that are responsible for this destruction. Without her microbes, she cannot produce serotonin or any other important hormone. Her immune system is breaking down, which is why she has the flu again.

Bitterness is more damaging to microbes than bad food. It is like poison to the tiny microbes, and no amount of nutritious food can save them if poison is dumped on them. Bitterness is like a microbe pesticide.

Sue Ann has a choice. She can continue to focus on George's failures, or she can get on with her life in a happy, thankful manner. If she understood the processes going on in their bodies, she could take steps to reverse this downward spiral. She could provide good, tasty meals and snacks for George and he might start feeling better. He might also start doing what needs to be done. If George and Sue Ann worked together as partners, both their Little Brains and Big Brains would benefit and they could help each other function at optimum levels. They would be happier and certainly healthier.

Even though science is just now discovering how the body and brain are best served by righteousness and that stinking thinking (sin) is destructive, God made that announcement long ago:

"**Trust in the LORD with all thine heart; and lean not unto thine own understanding. In all thy ways acknowledge him, and he shall direct thy paths. Be not wise in thine own eyes: fear the LORD, and depart from evil. It shall be health to thy navel (belly), and marrow to thy bones (blood and immune system)**" (Proverbs 3:5–8).

"**A merry heart doeth good like a medicine: but a broken spirit drieth the bones**" (Proverbs 17:22).

"**Pleasant words are as an honeycomb, sweet to the soul, and health to the bones**" (Proverbs 16:24).

Neuroplasticity researchers have identified the human attitudes that produce optimum physical and mental well-being. They strive to create programs that will impart these human traits—all to no avail. **Yet he who knows nothing of neurons or synapses, but walks in the light of God's love and goodness, will bear that sweet fruit to its optimum. God admonishes us: "My son, forget not my law; but let thine heart keep my commandments: For length of days, and long life, and peace, shall they add to thee" (Proverbs 3:1–2).**

None of us will live in this flesh forever. We all get sick. We all die. But he who loves most, lives best, and his days will pass like poetry, rather than a trail of misery.

VIDEO GAME WINNER, JERRY

Jerry is 13 years old.

He likes sweets and gets his feelings hurt if he doesn't get what he wants. He tends toward depression, which scares his mother, Sue Ann. He eats the meals his mom prepares, so he is getting sufficient nutrition. He loves playing video games and can do it for hours without getting tired, but taking the trash out makes him feel weak. He seldom gets any exercise. Mom and Dad say he is just not the athletic type. He's had antibiotics twice this year due to a cold or cough. There was no infection, but Mom was worried it could become an infection, so she insisted the doctor prescribe antibiotics just in case. But antibiotics don't discriminate between bad bacteria and friendly microbes. They just rush in, killing them all. Jerry's health is being compromised with every dose. Mom knows this, but opted for the drug because she frets over her son since his immune system doesn't seem to be very strong. And when he is sick, he is prone to more depression. It is quite obvious that Jerry's friendly microbes are dying off. Neither Jerry nor his mom ever heard of the marshmallow study, neither do they know anything about executive function skills like self-control, self-restraint, and impulse control. Mom doesn't know about gut microbes and their link to brain neurons. If she knew, she would take steps to make her son healthy.

GARDEN JOYS

It is a well-established fact that the root of many mental and physical maladies ranging from ADHD to skin rashes is a poorly functioning gut. As we have seen, a good, healthy gut translates into overall health. Your gut is a delicate ecosystem. It depends on you to take good care of it so it can take good care of you.

The gut is a microcosm, a miniature counterpart of the larger ecosystem of nature. We find definitive parallels in organic gardening models.

Some gardens are green and lush and resist bugs and disease. Other gardens look like a cartoon of morbid plant death with tomato leaves covered in yellow spots and the tomatoes with large, rotten patches. Gardens can

BRAIN GARDEN

The brain is our garden and its roots are nurtured by what you eat. Everything you do that affects the gut also affects the brain.

produce drastically different results depending on the soil. The difference is found in the balance of ecological factors, including plant food and beneficial microbes.

The weirdest stuff goes into creating good dirt: animal poop being the number-one ingredient, along with rotten organic matter like leaves and grass clippings. The worms come next to feed on the rich, organic matter. You don't have to herd them in or buy worms; they are just drawn to the place where the eating is good and there they multiply like crazy. A truly successful, healthy garden full of delicious vegetables is determined by the number of worms present. Worm poop is the finished product that provides food for the plants. Enzymes abound in that rich environment. It is said that the worm is the most important creature on earth.

Another benefit of an organically balanced ecosystem is that the plants are so healthy. The bad bugs will not dine on them. Bugs search for sickly plants grown in soil where the worms have been killed off by neglect or by added chemicals. A healthy garden, like a healthy body, must have a good pH balance. If the soil is too acidic, the plants will burn up. If it is too alkaline, they will be weak and yellow, struggling until they waste away.

Your gut is the most amazing garden of all. Like the soil, it is an ecosystem that works on the same principles as a garden. All living things flourish with optimum micronutrients, and without them, your body and brain will not be able to function properly. Your worms (microbes) are your best friends.

FEED YOUR BRAIN—NUTRITION MATTERS

Every neuroscientist knows the human brain to be the most complex, organic entity on earth. It requires a careful balance of minerals and vitamins to function properly. Nutrition matters. Poor nutrition is a significant contributor to mental illness. The rates of mental illness are on the rise as the quality of food we eat declines. Usually, when a person is suffering mental illness, they will be found to have serious gut issues as well. A person might look well fed and yet still be in a state of starvation for want of critical micronutrients (vitamins and minerals) that allow the body and the brain to thrive.

Dr. Emeran Mayer is a gastroenterologist, neuroscientist, and UCLA professor in the departments of medicine, physiology, and psychiatry, and author of *The Mind-Gut Connection*. He is doing work on how the trillions of bacteria in the gut "communicate" with enteric nervous system cells. His work has led him to think that psychiatry needs to incorporate treatment of the Little Brain (gut) along with therapy for the Big Brain that is housed in the skull.

> **FAT BRAIN**
>
> The brain is comprised of 60% fat. Eating a lot of good fats from nuts, seeds, and fish is necessary for good brain function. Olive oil preserves memory.

MORE ON GUT CONNECTIONS

The gastrointestinal (GI) tract includes the salivary glands, mouth, esophagus, liver, pancreas, gallbladder, small and large intestines, and rectum. The GI tract is made to handle toxic material, and, with the help of our microbes, it does a good job breaking down some pretty lethal stuff. But it is critical that there be no leakage from the GI tube into the body cavity. Stress causes peculiar irritations inside the gut that can damage the tract to the point where it weakens and allows undigested food or waste to leak into the body cavity. When this happens, the immune system goes into overdrive, resulting in food allergies and a host of other symptoms such as: joint pain, fatigue, depression, odd emotional disorders, deep stomach aches, chest pain, muscle soreness, cognitive dysfunction (foggy brain), asthma, and skin problems like eczema, which most people don't associate with digestive issues.

At this point, the symptoms are labeled as a known disease. In addition, the immune system is being drained, which means the victim will be more susceptible to colds, flu, cancer, and a host of other maladies. Children who are being raised in a household full of stress are particularly vulnerable. Children caught between two estranged and angry parents are highly susceptible to gut issues. Kids need to be planted in a garden of peace.

FOCUSING ON WHAT IS IMMEDIATELY AROUND YOU

Due to the extreme stress in today's lifestyles, researchers have developed a new science they call *mindfulness*. On brain scans, it is quite astonishing to see how effective this deliberate focus can be in bringing peace and quiet to the mind. Mindfulness, as taught by health practitioners, is learning to live in the moment rather than stressing about what has happened or what needs to happen. Mindfulness is focusing on the breeze coming through the window, the height of your chair, the color of the plate—the things that are there with you at the moment. Later, I will discuss mindfulness further.

Much of what is being taught by doctors on the subject of mindfulness is surprisingly similar to biblical principles. Practicing thankfulness is at the top of scientists' lists. Amazingly, for many people, this simple mind awareness has proven to help start the process of healing their gut. Mindfulness is also used in recovering from profound grief, violence, trauma, and other emotionally devastating events.

> ### OXYGEN
>
> By taking slow, deep breaths, you can boost oxygen to your brain. This will help you overcome fear or anxiety. Brain cells are particularly sensitive to oxygen.

CREATING AN ENVIRONMENT OF MINDFULNESS

Indulgence in electronic entertainment prevents children from establishing an environment conducive to mindfulness. If kids are left in an entertainment vacuum, they will invent entertainment that can be called mindful. They will color, play with simple toys, dig in the dirt, and excavate water puddles. These things provide contemplative quiet to the soul and bring healing to the body and mind. Help your children find peace by shooing them out the door to play.

When I was young, from spring to late fall, most families sat on their porch every evening. It was a restful downtime when people connected with family members and neighbors. It was mindfulness in its natural form. We were mindful of the flies or the mosquitoes, the heat or the cold, the fireflies or the stars. We shared tales of the day's events or the same old stories we had heard a hundred times that got bigger with each telling. Stress of the day was washed away in the fellowship of the moment. Today, people are too busy, too entertained, and too upset. They find it easier to tune life out with music or media.

"Thou wilt keep him in perfect peace, whose mind is stayed on thee: because he trusteth in thee" (Isaiah 26:3).

Medication usually doesn't help relieve the busyness of life or self-induced stress. Counseling can sometimes actually make it worse. Researchers, seeing the brain's need for rest and restorative focus, coined the term *mindfulness* to describe the state of mind one must achieve to be physically and mentally healthy.

JUST LEAVE IT ALONE AND EVERYTHING WILL BE FINE

When I was a teenager, a dear friend came to live with us. She came because she was losing a lot of weight and was depressed. Obviously, her gut was under assault. But 55 years ago, no one knew how the gut worked or what to do about it. At that time there were no probiotics at the local drug store. No one had a clue as to the cause, but she was under 100 pounds and shrinking fast. She didn't like to eat because "it hurt her belly." She was an anxious, nervous wreck, but she was my friend, so we were going to do something about it.

Her mother was continually fussing over her to eat, which made matters worse. Her health, as well as other daily issues, made living at home uncomfortable. So we offered her a home away from home to see if maybe that would help. My mom talked to me before my friend moved in. She told me that she remembered seeing someone in this condition some years earlier, and the worst thing to do was notice what the gut-patient was or was not eating. My mama was from the old school, and often she would say, "Just leave it alone and everything will work out."

When you are chronically stressed, the composition of gut microbes is altered, causing the gut to begin functioning like a completely different organ. When Dr. Emeran Mayer was interviewed by Tom Bilyeu on a program called *Quest Nutrition and Impact Theory*, Dr. Mayer said, "Negative emotions are never good for anything."

Our house was typically very relaxed due to my mama's philosophy. When my dad yelled, which he did often, she just grinned and winked at us where he couldn't see. It was her way of saying, "Oh, he will come around, just wait and see." He always did. I can never remember him actually saying he was sorry, but he would try to do something real sweet to make up for his bad attitude. It was obvious he was ashamed. His contriteness always brought on another of my mama's "I told you so" winks, which were a little funnier than her regular winks.

I look back and realize she was incredibly wise. It wasn't only my daddy she handled; she was lowering stress for the whole family. If we had extra people drop in for dinner, which happened often at our house, she would just open a can or two of pork 'n' beans and pour them unheated into a pretty serving bowl. She had previously convinced my little brother, who ate the bulk of our food, that pork 'n' beans were the best thing on the planet. The little guzzler would eat the beans, so now there was food left for our visitor.

Like my mama said, things had a way of working out without drama if you used a little common sense. With her technique of reducing the fight-or-flight chemicals, I believe my mama saved the lives of more microbes in all our guts than anyone on the planet. Obviously, she added a few to my friend's gut as well.

When my nerve-racked friend moved into our house, she joined the contest against the little guzzler, which involved besting him on who would get the rest of the mashed potatoes or meatloaf. Within a week, she was eating; within a month, she was obviously gaining weight, and in a few more

❝ The enteric nervous system doesn't seem capable of thought as we know it, but it communicates back and forth with our big brain—with profound results.[1] ❞

Dr. Jay Pasricha, director of the Johns Hopkins
Center for Neurogastroenterology

1 (n.d.). *Johns Hopkins Medicine*. Retrieved from: www.hopkinsmedicine.org/health/wellness-and-prevention/the-brain-gut-connection

months, she was back to normal. Depression, anxiety, and weight loss never plagued her again. A change of philosophy could reduce the tension in a lot of people if they would just learn from the real-life experts like my mama. If my friend's gut can be fixed, so can yours.

MINDFULNESS

I would not say my friend was practicing "scientific" mindfulness, but it would certainly have been a natural form of it. I think she was forced into mindfulness because we were *there,* in her face, being a family. She didn't have time to think about herself or her woes, so healing came quickly. And then, of course, at my mama's table were regular dishes of sauerkraut and homemade pickles, along with organically grown cabbage slaw and sweet potatoes. Also, our garden dirt was made of naturally composted animal poop, so the circle was made complete. I am sure my friend's microbes were delighted to come and dine. It is likely that the whole ecological habitat in her gut was not fully recovered, but it was the beginning of a comeback.

FAST-TRACK HEALING

On YouTube, you can find several different interviews with microbiome specialist Summer Bock. Summer was first a certified master herbalist, then she went back to medical school. In her last term, her health began to seriously fail. It was obvious to her that her decline started with her digestive system. This health crisis led to her becoming a fermentation guru.

Her videos demonstrate a very simple method of making sauerkraut. When sauerkraut is made naturally, without heat or canning, it introduces some very important, friendly microbes into your gut.

She suggests one cup of sauerkraut per day until healed. It would be an easy fix for some of my readers. Make your brain happy and eat more sauerkraut. Start slowly, with just a teaspoon a day for the first three days, as it can really cause a lot of gas if you're not accustomed to it.

TRADING POOP IS FOR THE DESPERATE

When your microbes are suffering, you will physically suffer as well. Your stomach will hurt so badly and your digestive system will be so nasty that you will be willing to do most anything to get well. You will become sensitive to mold, chemicals, and other environmental infractions. You will become one of the "afflicted."

Often, people who have lost too many of their microbes and become desperate will opt for a fecal transplant. Yes, you read correctly! Fecal transplant is just a medical way of saying the doctors are putting someone else's poop into your colon. A person would have to be in pretty sorry shape to opt for that treatment, or at least I would. But it works like a charm if all the conditions are met. Like you read, microbes work tightly as a community, like a colony of bees. They will attack foreign microbes and perpetuate their own survival and replication. Therefore, when a fecal transplant is done, it will not work unless the ENTIRE community of microbes in the host has been destroyed so the new colony is able to thrive as a unit.

Parents of autistic children have been known to use round after round of antibiotics to kill their child's microbes, so that when they introduce fecal matter into their child's gut, they have a greater chance of establishing a new ecosystem. The greater the need, the greater the chance you are willing to take. Hope is eternal.

THE 4RS

Dr. Amy Myers' primary practice is working with patients who have gut issues. She, along with thousands of other practitioners, use the well-known method called the *4R Plan* to help her patients recover. You can find her videos on YouTube as well.

My 5R plan is even more complete:

Remove: Clean your gut. Several times throughout the years, I have used the naturopath Richard Schulze's products for cleaning up the gut. You can find him on the internet.

Restore: This means change your diet to be mostly raw or steamed organic vegetables so your microbes will want to come and dine at your table.

Reinoculate: This is where you need to find a truly great probiotic. There are a number of companies that excel in providing this type of product and a greater number of companies that sell trash in the name of probiotics. For years, I have used Life Extension's FlorAssist. If you're dealing with autism or another brain disorder, you might consider looking for probiotics that contain the bacterium *L. reuteri*. And eat organic sauerkraut.

135

Repair: We have already discussed many ways of repairing the gut. Most methods begin with eliminating the bad stuff from your diet and then reintroducing healthy microbes through foods. If you look on the Web, you will notice organic bone broth is getting a lot of attention. Health practitioners are advocating bone broth as a proposed means to temporarily seal leaks in the junctions of the gut. It is not a scientifically proven method, but I know several people who are using it with apparent success. You will need to find a good organic source or make your own bone broth. You can learn from YouTube videos.

Repent: Until you change your attitude and/or lifestyle, no amount of cleaning your gut and eating good food will bring healing.

This is just an introduction to the subject of gut health. I hope I've made you aware of the possibilities for healing, but you must be your own healer. Do your research and take control of your health and that of your children. You might even be able to help your husband if you can introduce him to the subject without judgment and offer hope for a healthier life.

I CHARGE YOU

Go to the library and get picture books on the gut. Let the children help you buy three foods that will make the gut healthier. Talk about these foods, the bad foods, and what they are doing to your microbiomes. Read aloud to your small children the stories in this section about Laila Bug. Make Jell-O, and let them hold three pounds of it in a plastic bag. Tell them this is how many tiny, worm-like creatures are in their tummy, making their food into blood, bone, muscle, and brain so they can grow and be smart.

"Drink no longer water, but use a little wine for thy stomach's sake and thine often infirmities" (1 Timothy 5:23).

Autism

Neuroplasticity has taught us that we need to make educated, wise decisions in order to give our child the best chance of a healthy body and mind.

In a 1990 study tracking 10,000 children, it was found that three out of 10,000 manifested clear symptoms of autism. Six years later in 1996, the CDC began tracking and found that 34 out of 10,000 children showed clear symptoms of autism. Eight years after that, in 2004 something provoked an alarming increase in the rate of autism. One out of every 150 eight-year-old children was autistic. Few scientists or researchers agree on the cause. Some suggested that the increase could be accounted for by better detection and reporting. Most researchers consider that to be ridiculous, as do I. A child with clear traits of autism is easy to identify.

Just ten years later, in 2014 one child in 59 tested positive for autism. According to these statistics, in 2019 we will reach a rate of one out of every 46. Look at the numbers again...it is tragic and scary. Usually, autism doesn't become apparent until a child is three years old. If the trend continues at this pace, in 2024 children will have a one in 23 chance of being diagnosed with autism. Autism is a plague that is receiving too little attention, likely because of the global impact of disagreeing on the cause. Major institutional, environmental, and possibly cultural changes would be mandated. [75]

Researchers do not agree as to the cause of this rapid increase. But as numbers continue to rise, we can see that something horrific and new to our environment is causing our children to suffer brain damage.

What has changed since the 1990s that is causing such statistically high numbers of brain damaged babies? What can we do to stop it? Discovering the answers is like putting a complicated, solid white puzzle together. There are many rabbit holes, possible roots, and likely complicit evils. Whatever it is, it is something we are doing today as a society that we did not do fifty years ago.

This explosion of statistics has researchers all over the world desperately seeking to know WHY. What exactly is autism? What does it do to the brain? What can we do to stop the growing numbers? And once a child is diagnosed with autism, what can be done to help the child overcome some of the difficulties associated with it?

The research is a new science with many different voices vying to be heard. I have plowed through a mountain of information and will give you the best I have found. There are many side issues that predispose a child to autism such as premature birth, low birth weight, genetics, drugs, etc. We will not be discussing any of these in depth.

A SPECTRUM

Autism is considered a "spectrum": a word describing a wide range of symptoms with many possible causes. It appears that autistic children do not prune their synapses properly. If you need a brief refresher on pruning, you can find the information in the section titled "Pruning Clears the Way." When pruning fails, the child's brain is electrically overcharged, resulting in a great deal of stress. To function normally, neurons in the child's brain need the unused synapses to be pruned away.

In a healthy brain, the neurons actually eat the unused synapses. For some reason, this process doesn't happen in some children. What interferes

75 Boyles, Salynn. (2002). "CDC: Autism Rates Higher Than Thought." *WebMD*. Retrieved from: www.webmd.com/mental-health/news/20021231/cdc-autism-rates-higher-than-thought#1

with the pruning? Poor gut health in the mother and the child has proven to interfere in the pruning process. But that is not new, so it cannot be the sole cause. Environmental toxins, vaccinations, genetics, and even emotional trauma have been shown to be tied to stalling or totally stopping the brain's pruning. But again, some of those things have always been part of the human experience. Why are we seeing problems only now, in the past 25 years? Many scientists believe the issues that disturb pruning are just the tipping point of a delicate state with a much more crippling cause.

ON A PERSONAL NOTE

I would never advise anyone to have their children vaccinated. It took a lot to wake me up to this decision. When my first two children were babies, I kept their vaccination cards carefully up to date. Every few months, like a dumb lamb to the slaughter, I stood in line waiting for the free government handout in the form of vaccinations. I shiver with anxiety when I reflect on that day, 42 years ago, when my neighbor and I drove to town together to have our 3-month-old baby boys receive their shots. Within hours after the shot, my son was very sick, and during the night his fever spiked. I bathed him in wet washcloths, gave him the meds the clinic advised us to give in the event there was a fever, and I prayed. Still his fever raged. Sometime during the night, I was sitting in the bed trying to comfort my sick baby when I felt death in the room. I knew the death angel had come for my son. I know this is weird, and if I heard you say it, I would roll my eyes. But it was my experience. I woke up my husband and said, "Pray! The angel of death is in the room, and he has come for our baby." He was too tired to even wonder what was wrong with me. I slapped him on his bare back as hard as I could and shouted, "You wake up and YOU pray for our son...NOW!" He clearly didn't believe me, but he started to pray. Instantly, I could feel death leaving the room. Within minutes, my son's fever broke and he slept peacefully in my arms as I sat in tense fear, leaning against the headboard. I was still sitting there at daybreak when I saw the ambulance's flashing lights next door. The angel of death had come, and he took my neighbors baby home where he is even at this moment, looking into the face of the heavenly Father (Matthew 18:10). It could have been my baby, as well.

Now, you would think this would have scared me into NEVER considering another vaccination, but I was schooled to believe that the government and doctors knew best. My daughter was three years old before I took her in for her shots. Just a few hours after her vaccinations, she broke out all over her body in a large, four-leaf-clover rash. I immediately took her back to the clinic and was shocked at the nervous and speedy reaction of the nurses. One pulled me out of the room to speak to me privately. "Have any of your other children ever had a bad reaction?" I told her about my son. I will never forget the expression on her face when she whispered, "Don't come back here, ever. Don't let anyone give any of your children another vaccination." When she walked out of the room, I was suddenly a wiser mother.

ALUMINUM[76]

All of this happened over 35 years ago. Vaccinations were simple back then and a whole lot safer. Aluminum, a critical component of most vaccines, is added to act as an adjuvant. This means the aluminum serves to wake up the immune system, provoking it to recognize the antigen in the vaccine. In the 1980s when my children received their vaccines, they would have received 1,250 micrograms of aluminum by their 18-month birthday. Today, that number is 4,925 micrograms.

Canadian scientists Chris Shaw, PhD and Lucija Tomljenovic, PhD, addressed this subject in a critical study they published in 2011 in *Current Medicinal Chemistry* titled "Aluminum Vaccine Adjuvants: Are They Safe?"[77] They wrote:

"Aluminum is an experimentally demonstrated neurotoxin and the most commonly used vaccine adjuvant. Despite almost 90 years of widespread use of aluminum adjuvants, medical science's understanding about their mechanisms of action is still remarkably poor. There is also a concerning scarcity of data on toxicology and pharmacokinetics of these compounds. In spite of this, the notion that aluminum in vaccines is safe appears to be widely accepted. Experimental research, however, clearly shows that aluminum adjuvants have a potential to induce serious immunological

76 Information in this and subsequent sections can be found here: Handley, J.B. (2018). "International scientists have found autism's cause. What will Americans do?" *J.B. Handley Blog.* Retrieved from: https://jbhandleyblog.com/home/2018/4/1/international2018?fbclid=IwAR2sTbjlZzQQb7LgY-hZQWf0W_WrYXNut4xcRRwuvhtjdIzQ9Iaesk2zzvCg

77 Tomljenovic, L., and Shaw, C. (2011). "Aluminum vaccine adjuvants: Are they safe?" *Current Medicinal Chemistry.* Retrieved from: www.ncbi.nlm.nih.gov/pubmed/21568886

disorders in humans. In particular, aluminum in adjuvant form carries a risk for autoimmunity, long-term brain inflammation, and associated neurological complications and may, thus, have profound and widespread adverse health consequences."

Here is a transcript (edited for clarity) from a YouTube video of the speech given by Robert Kennedy, Jr., director of Children's Health Defense at the New York Rally & Lobbying Day for Vaccine Injury, on May 14, 2019:

> I have six kids. I had eleven brothers and sisters. I had over fifty cousins. I didn't know a single person with a peanut allergy. Why do my kids all have food allergies? Is it because they were born after 1989? If you were born prior to 1989, your chance of having a chronic disease, according to HHS, is 12.8%. If you were born after 1989, your chance of having a chronic disease is 54%. What are they? They're the neurodevelopmental diseases: ADD, ADHD, speech delay, language delay, tics, Tourette's syndrome, ASD/autism. The autoimmune diseases: Guillain-Barre, multiple sclerosis, juvenile diabetes, rheumatoid arthritis. The anaphylactic diseases: food allergies, rhinitis, asthma, eczema. All of these exploded in 1989. Congress ordered the EPA to do a study to find out what year the disease epidemic started, and the EPA did that study. They said it started in 1989.

> There are lots of culprits, many new things. We have cell phones, PFOA, ultrasound, glyphosate, etc. Our kids are swimming around in a toxic soup. We're not saying all of those illnesses came from vaccines. But there is no intervention that is so exquisitely and precisely timed as what happened in 1989, when the vaccine schedule was changed. This raised the levels of aluminum and mercury—tripling and quadrupling them—and went from the three vaccines I had as a child, to the 72 my kids received. Next year, it will be raised again to 75.

AMISH ARE BLESSED NO MORE

For years, many people have thought Amish children do not have autism because they do not vaccinate. For the last 30-plus years, I have lived in what the Amish/Mennonite folks refer to as a "Plain people community." As a midwife, I have helped birth their babies and read their local news bulletins. I have heard the latest interesting family tidbits coming from their many colonies, including those in Mexico, Belize, South America, Canada, and further afield. My neighbors use horse and buggies and outhouses (bathrooms outside with a hole in the ground) and, for the most part, grow their fruits and vegetables organically (at least what they use for their own family). In recent years, they have started eating more processed foods, but as a rule, what their children eat is far better than the average American school child.

My children grew up with their children. My son married a sweet little Amish girl. These Plain people are more educated and smarter than the regular citizen. They are more skilled on the latest and most advanced information concerning herbs, natural healing, GMOs, companion planting, and a thousand other practical subjects. It is not unusual for a son or daughter with an 8th-grade, Amish-type education to leave the fold, work their way through college, and become a neurosurgeon or space engineer. As a group, they have made a very educated decision not to vaccinate, and up until the last ten years or so, I never heard of a single case of autism among their hundreds of thousands of children. But in recent years, still eating organic foods for the most part, and adhering to their stand against vaccinations, that has changed. The number of cases of children being diagnosed with autism is still lower than the general population, but autism is becoming more common in their ranks.[78]

So with what we have learned from the Amish, it appears that the culprit is not limited to diet or vaccinations; although, clearly, vaccinations are part of the equation. Then what is the cause—the root of this abrupt rise in autism among the Plain people? Why now, and what can be done to reverse the trend?

CELL PHONE LINK

New research has determined that "fathers pass on the cause of 80% of autism cases."[79] Many scientists in this field think that cell phone radiation could be what is affecting men's sperm. Cell phones were introduced to the general public around 1995 and thus, could be responsible for the spike in

---

78 (2010). "Prevalence Rates of Autism Spectrum Disorders among the Old Order Amish." *Left Brain Right Brain.* Retrieved from: leftbrainrightbrain.co.uk/2010/05/17/prevalence-rates-of-autism-spectrum-disorders-among-the-old-order-amish-2

79 Sample, Ian. (2017). "Fathers pass on four times as many new genetic mutations as mothers – study." *Genetics.* Retrieved from: www.theguardian.com/science/2017/sep/20/fathers-pass-on-four-times-as-many-new-genetic-mutations-as-mothers-study

autism cases since that time, as well as the epidemic levels seen today.[80]

Many pediatric neuroscientists are beginning to believe that the failure of the brain to prune is due to damage done to the man's sperm.[81] The cell phone is generally carried only three or four inches away from where   sperm are produced. Scary!

For me, this idea is a pivotal point because among the strict Plain people, worldly things have been shunned (not allowed). They have no cars and no electricity, meaning no electric washing machines or dryers, lights, or TVs. They use wood for cooking and heating. BUT in every Plain community in the world, you will find that many—maybe even MOST—of the men have the latest and best cell phones in their pants pockets. Many families use solar power to provide charging for the phones.

> **AUTISM / GUT**
>
> Interestingly enough, over 70% of people with autism also have gastrointestinal problems and issues related to their gut.

The Environmental Health Trust published the "Top 10 Facts about Cell Phones and Wi-Fi." Here are a few highlights:

> Every wireless device is actually a two-way microwave radio that sends and receives a type of non-ionizing electromagnetic radiation called radio frequency radiation (RF–EMF). This machine-made radiation is millions of times higher than the natural electromagnetic fields (EMFs) our grandparents were exposed to.
>
> Numerous peer-reviewed and published research studies show that these man-made, pulsed electromagnetic frequencies cause adverse biological effects and are very different than the natural electromagnetic fields that have always existed in the environment. Research on humans has found an association between cell phone use and brain cancer, headaches, and damage to the brain and immune system. Yale studies found that cellular radiation exposure during pregnancy led to increased hyperactivity and memory problems in the offspring.

80 "Probability: Sperm fragmented by cell phone radiation behind 60–80% of autism spectrum disorders." *RF Safe*. Retrieved from: www.rfsafe.com/fathers-sperm-fragmented-by-cell-phone-radiation-behind-60-80-pecent-of-autism-spectrum-disorders

81 Preidt, Robert. (2015). "Father's Sperm May Hold Clues to Autism Risk." *WebMD*. Retrieved from: www.webmd.com/brain/autism/news/20150415/fathers-sperm-may-hold-clues-to-autism-risk

Multiple research studies report cell phone radiation penetrates more deeply into children's brains in comparison to adults (Fernandez-Rodriguez 2015, Fernández 2015, Mohammed 2017).[82]

A 2018 study found that teens who held cell phones up to their head had decreased memory performance on researchers' tests.[83]

THE MIRROR NEURONS LINK

Autism is a major disorder, likely caused by several different neural factors. Neurologist V.S. Ramachandran says evidence suggests mirror neurons being damaged are in some way responsible for autism. When you smile at a baby who is four or five months old, he should automatically smile back because healthy mirror neurons automatically fire in reflection of a smile.

This will sound like a tall tale, but it is the absolute truth. When one of my babies was being born, as his head came out of the birth canal, even before the rest of his body was delivered, the first thing he saw was his daddy's smiling face. Between contractions, this half-born child mirrored his daddy's big smile. Nathan is now in his 40s, and we are still wowed by the event. His mirror neurons were responding before he was completely born. What an indictment on those who are responsible for aborting babies. The rest of our children were a few days or weeks old before they had such a reaction, but they all had mirror neurons that provoked them to mimic us. If we yawned, they yawned.

Mirror neurons are what allow us to "read" people. Females are usually much better at deciphering what a person is feeling. As you might expect, the average female has more mirror neurons than the average male.[84]

Dr. Ramachandran says that if a child doesn't return a smile, it could be a sign the child will become autistic when he is two or three years of age. When you consider that boys have fewer mirror neurons than girls, it is not

82 (n.d.). "Scientific Imaging Of Cell Phone And Wi-Fi Radiation Exposures Into The HumanBody" *Environmental Health Trust*. Retrieved from: ehtrust.org/science/scientific-imaging-cell-phone-wi-fi-radiation-exposures-human-body/

83 (2019). "Top 10 Facts about Cell Phones and Wi-Fi." *Environmental Health Trust*. Retrieved from: ehtrust.org/take-action/educate-yourself/top-10-facts-about-cell-phones-and-wi-fi-2

84 Ramachandran, Vilayanur S., and Oberman, Lindsay M. (2006). "Broken Mirrors: A Theory of Autism." *Scientific American*. Retrieved from: www.utdallas.edu/~otoole/CGS_CV_S08/R10_broken_mirror.pdf

a surprise that boys have a much higher rate of autism than girls (4.2 boys to every girl).[85]

Autistic children don't appear to be capable of empathy. Empathy is made possible by active mirror neurons, which are also needed for a child to be capable of pretend play. For a child to put himself in the shoes of an action figure like Superman, mirror neurons are necessary. Scientists are speculating that in the absence of mirror neurons, there are ways to employ biofeedback and drugs to enhance the function of neurotransmitters. Research is also being done employing dogs to develop empathy and sympathy in autistic children. Results are nothing short of miraculous.

A WORD TO THE WISE

Neuroscientists are advising men to keep their cell phones out of their pants pockets. Keep them away from your young children. Better to be safe than sorry. Turn your Wi-Fi off at night when you are not using it. Being overly cautious could save you a lot of grief.

Many countries have banned the use of cell phones in or around schools due to overwhelming evidence of possible harm. The mayor of Haifa, Israel, Yona Yahav, called for the removal of Wi-Fi from all schools. Yahav said, "When there is a doubt, when it comes to our children, there is no doubt."

GUT ISSUES

Many brain issues in children appear to have their source in the mother's gut. Scientists do know that autism, bipolar disorder, and schizophrenia have things in common, and the gut and the brain have a very close connection. The lack of proper digestive enzymes and microbes can cause inflammation in the gut, resulting in serious emotional disorders. This may play a major role in autism. We learned about this in the previous chapter.

Remember, the body produces the neurotransmitter cortisol in response to anxiety, stress, fear, or any negative emotion. Autism causes a lot of stress. Too much cortisol in the gut destroys good microbes, which inhibits the body's ability to extract essential minerals and vitamins from food. This then causes the digestive tract to be extremely inflamed. Gut microbes

85 Zeliadt, Nicholette. (2018). "Autism's sex ratio: explained." *Spectrum News*. Retrieved from: www.spectrumnews.org/news/autisms-sex-ratio-explained

also produce the chemicals and hormones that are necessary for emotional balance. It is the principle of cause and effect.

Dr. Norman Doidge has written on this subject and has several videos on YouTube that will direct you to discover more about it. In his book, *The Brain's Way of Healing* he discusses amazing revelations being made by neuro-researchers to aid those who suffer from autism, chronic pain, Parkinson's, and a host of other debilitating diseases. He offers lasting hope based on science recognized around the world. Seek and find, but YOU need to be proactive.

Autism and other brain disorders come in shades. Some children's brains seem to fluctuate with odd peculiarities. One day the child seems relatively normal, and the next day he is raving and wild. Is it bad food, red dye, black mold, a knock on the head, or maybe stress that causes these terrible swings in behavior? Obviously, something is going on in his brain that is driving him bonkers.

Autism is a diagnosis that petrifies parents. It can be akin to a jail sentence for the child. But it doesn't have to be if the parent knows how to avoid the worst of it and how to bring healing when it hits. This next story began years ago. I never met the lady—I only read her cries for help. I told her to record her story in a book. I have watched for it over the years, but, regretfully, it has not come forth. I will share with you what my neurons recorded. Edith stumbled on different ways to bring healing to her Benny.

I CHARGE YOU

Children need to understand what autism is so they can have more compassion for children who are struggling with it. Depending on the age of your children, get library books that have pictures of autistic children. If your children are older, you can find books on how cell phones work and their potential negative effects on the body. You might even open up the subject of vaccinations—pro and con. This can be a research project for older, school age children and for you as well.

"Behold, I send you forth as sheep in the midst of wolves: be ye therefore wise as serpents, and harmless as doves" (Matthew 10:16).

Benny's Story

CHAPTER 11

Neuroplasticity has taught us that there is hope for everyone.

Edith's son was full-spectrum autistic. This was around 1990, before the internet was available to us. The library was our only source of information and there were scant few books on autism. Most people had no clue what the word even meant. Edith needed someone to talk to who would not judge her for having such a "weird, mean child." At the time of her second letter, I had started fostering an extremely brain damaged baby whom we affectionately called "Peanut." Even though I was told there was no hope for Peanut due to her tiny skull, I thought someone, somewhere might have discovered something that could help the child. I was constantly ordering books from every library across the country, trying to research everything I could find on the brain. Healing her brain was on my front burner, so the letters from this mama-bear concerned for her autistic son were enthralling. She stirred both my heart and my mind.

In a very raw way, Edith's letters introduced me into her private world of dealing with autism. She drew a picture of her brokenness, the marital strain, and her husband's distancing himself from both his wife and son. Her intense love and protection were coupled with her revulsion and desire to just be done with the drama and send Benny to an institution. Edith's story kept me riveted.

In the midst of her horrible life, through every letter she wrote, there was a tiny ray of hope still burning somewhere in the recesses of this mother's heart. She wrote of high fences that her husband had covered with used roofing tin to keep people from seeing into their yard. The fences kept the neighbors from seeing, but they were unable to keep Benny Boy confined. She wrote of being overrun by mice and rats because he slopped food all over the house and of his nasty diapers, which he continually dug in, smearing the contents all over the walls. Edith wove her ghastly life story as only one who is truly suffering can. She told and retold of the never-ending, high-pitched screaming that caused the neighbors to call the police. At that time, most of the police had never heard of autism, so they didn't know what to think. Sometimes even I wondered. It was an endless list of sad tortures for both her and the boy, but the constant sleepless nights were the worst part of it.

I sent to her every scrap of information I could find, much of it on diet: no red dyes, no sugar, and low carb. Eat fermented foods like sauerkraut, lots of fiber, and only organic. I told her to feed him lots of fresh fish, nuts, and seeds, and the most important thing was to pour good quality olive oil on everything he ate. I had her test her house for mold and make sure to get rid of all cleaning toxins as well as air fresheners, which she used in extreme. I told her to use vinegar and baking soda as cleaners. She added key natural supplements to his diet, especially the B-vitamins and magnesium. She did everything I suggested and more. She started keeping charts of Benny's behaviors so we could document any improvement. I knew I was her one escape from her world of torment, someone who heard her voice crying in her wilderness. It was so sad.

Fearing the neighbors and police, she started videoing her son. This proved to be very helpful to her, for she was able to look back at the videos and see that Benny did make regular improvements over several months.

AND THEN THERE WAS FLOP

The first miracle to come into Benny's life was in the form of a dog. His dad brought a lazy mutt home to see if his son would take to it. Edith was not

pleased when her husband phoned saying he was bringing the dog because she didn't think she could deal with any extra work or stress. But she
changed her mind the instant she saw Benny respond to the dog. Edith said
it was miraculous. Almost as if he were a normal child, Benny ran to the
dog and threw his arms around it. Benny, as is typical with autistic children,
didn't tolerate being touched by people, but with the dog he was different.

The couple had no idea that in years to come, dogs would receive highly
specialized training to help bring healing to those suffering from autism. Babies who show a lack of mirror neurons might avoid developing the bizarre
symptoms of autism if they have a gentle breed of dog in their lives at an
early age.

None of this information was available to Edith, yet God had intervened
to send them this dog named Flop. It seemed this lazy dog was born trained
just for Benny. Every step Benny made, the dog made. When Benny slept,
the dog slept, lying across the child. The first night Flop came to be Benny's
friend, Edith slept all night. She called it a miracle, and in a way, it was. She
sent me a picture of Benny hugging Flop. He was a mutt that had the long
body of a wiener dog. He was overweight, not young, and refused to go outside to pee when it was raining. He was not the breed, age, or type that would
later be chosen to work with autistic children. But Flop didn't know he was
unsuitable; he did his job well. Today, dog trainers often choose golden doo-
dles for autistic children because they are smart, gentle, loyal, and can track
the child if he wanders off. Oh yes, and they don't shed.

Autistic children are able to develop the missing empathy and sympathy
through their relationship with the dog. There are many heart-warming videos on YouTube showing the amazing benefits of a dog for an autistic child.
Twenty-five years ago, Edith only knew that cleaning up after Flop was not
such a bad job.

Benny had stopped his high-pitched screams since Flop had come into
his life. Flop was most likely not responsible for this miracle, but Edith gave
him the credit. Pruning had probably started in Benny's brain. With the natural raw foods, sauerkraut, and vitamins and minerals, the pruning of Benny's synapses was likely more complete than it had been when his first pruning should have taken place, at around six years of age. The pruning would
greatly reduce the amount of stimulation to Benny's brain. Now lights would
not seem so bright, sounds would not be so loud, and people would not be
as scary. Benny's life was improving, and so was Edith's.

THEN CAME THE TRAMPOLINE

Benny and his family lived up north, so all their winter months were spent inside a dark house. (That would be enough to give me brain damage.) It was also a part of the equation that I had not considered since I live in sunshine almost all year (and I plan to do so until my dying day). Edith wrote that she had read in a book that jumping on a trampoline might help, so in the late fall, they bought a trampoline. She had developed the habit of rarely letting Benny outdoors because she didn't want him chilled. With Flop to keep him company, she had a lot more peace that Benny would not try to escape the fence. Flop was too fat and old to run away.

Spring came to the cold north and sunshine came calling. Now Edith had discovered that music helped calm Benny. If Edith had known how effective music would be, she would have started it the very first day he showed autistic symptoms. Dad rigged up a sound system outdoors. On the very first day of Spring, Edith turned it on so Benny could bounce to the music. Neuroplasticity has proven that music therapy plays a major role in helping autistic children. It is beneficial for many brain issues.

Benny's mom bundled him up tightly and helped him onto the trampoline. She tried to help Flop onto the trampoline, but he was too fat for her to lift. She was busy setting up the camera and didn't notice her son's activity, but she could hear over the beat of the music her son's laughter; a new, beautiful sound for her Benny Boy. When Edith stepped behind the camera, you can imagine her shock to see her skinny 11-year-old son's, stark white, naked boy parts bouncing up and down. His pants were wadded up around his boots and his coat and shirt were lying on the ground.

Did I mention that Benny Boy's mama was really fat? Edith didn't mention that fact to me until she wrote to tell me of that day's events. For a short, fat, 48-year-old mama who had spent the entire winter sitting in an easy chair, getting on the trampoline to contain a wild, naked boy took considerable time and effort. In the end, it proved impossible. Her retelling of the event was the first really funny thing she had ever written to me. After more than 25 years, it still makes me laugh.

While the camera continued to roll and the music played, Benny Boy made the most of his pleasurable, naked occasion. Mama finally gave up her begging and pleading and went to call Benny's daddy. She knew he would dread coming home and drag his butt the whole way. She was right, it took him an unconscionable amount of time to travel the short distance. But all the while, naked Benny Boy jumped and danced to the music. The perturbed mama did think to turn the camera off and take it inside just in case the police were called again, as her videoing his naked play would have been suspect indeed.

Edith had no idea that vitamin D3 is crucial for autistic children. Benny had been shut up all winter in a dark house, so his body was probably soaking in the sun's healing rays and filling him with needful vitamin D. Nature finds a way.

When Benny's emotionally distant daddy came home, the most remarkable thing happened. He saw his son happily engaged and hysterically laughing while Flop barked with newfound energy. Except for the boy's appreciation for Flop, the father had never seen his son really joyful. Dad just broke down and wept. Then Benny's daddy crawled on the trampoline and jumped with his cheerful son. The picture Edith had painted in my mind of her husband was one of a broken and sad man. He was soft spoken, with no authority, and he worked at a factory. But on this day, he had an opinion. At the father's command, rain or shine Benny was to be turned loose on the trampoline every day to jump until he was totally worn out. And every day, Benny stripped down to his birthday suit. Dad said, "That's okay. He knows something we don't."

> **PROBIOTIC**
>
> One Harvard study suggests using probiotics that contain the bacterium *Lactobacillus reuteri* for autistic children.

Benny's overall improvement was greatly accelerated from that day forward. A high level of vitamin D3, which comes from exposure to sunlight, has now been proven to significantly improve the well-being of those with autism. You can find many great resources concerning vitamin D from Rhonda Patrick, PhD. She is one of the best I have ever heard speak on this subject. Up to 80% of Americans are deficient in vitamin D—scary, because it is so important to prevent early aging. Exercise does wonders for the brain as you read in Dr. Ellen's chapter, "Bring Back PLAY," so the vigorous play on the trampoline was helping Benny's brain.

Good nutrition over the previous months had made a drastic difference in Benny's life. Getting his gut teeming with good bacteria helped bring peace to his brain by calming the inflammation. All the good fats were critical in helping restore Benny's brain. And there was Flop, the wonder dog that taught Benny how to love.

Autism is the brain screaming for help. Benny's brain had found help.

AUTISM IS NOT A LIFE SENTENCE

Benny would be middle-aged now. I have often wondered how he fared in the many years since Edith and I corresponded. After you watch videos on autism on YouTube, scroll down through the comments and read testimonies from many autistic adults. They tell stories of their struggles and their wonderful life successes. Sometimes it is a mama telling how proud she is of her son, now serving in the military or graduating from college. I read one mama bragging about her autistic son who is now a trial lawyer. Every comment I have ever read was written to say, "See? I made it! Life threw me a curve ball, but now I have peace and success." I always scroll down looking for one signed *Benny*.

Autism is not a life sentence. Think about that statement. Bipolar disorder is not a life sentence. Depression is not a life sentence. Brain trauma is not the end. You are not a victim. You have a choice. Those with Parkinson's disease can live again, dancing and laughing. Now researchers know that even Alzheimer's—the old-people's rotten-brain disease—can be helped.

Micronutrients can be the significant turning point in many people's lives. Brains need a lot of nourishment to stay healthy. Exercise is a major component of a healthy brain. The right kind of music is an important piece of brain healing we all need to explore. Learning forgiveness, thankfulness, appreciation, joy, love, and peace is God's way of maintaining a healthy brain. Living in the moment is so important. Sunshine, hard work, study, and creativity are all growing us and making our brains better. And, of course, every child needs a dog like Flop.

SUGGESTIONS

If you have noticed that your baby lacks mirror neurons, then to be proactive in preventing a possible lapse into autism, here are some suggestions.

1. Avoid vaccinations and any medication that is not absolutely necessary.

2. Maintain a low-stress and regimented lifestyle so there is predictibility and little emotional stress to your child.

3. Eat organic, clean food.

4. Get a gentle family dog.

5. Play gentle, high-quality music during the day.

6. Turn on Bible reading at night to play softly for 30 minutes as your baby falls to sleep (I recommend the KJV as read by Alexander Scourby).

I CHARGE YOU

If your children are old enough to understand, you should read this story to them. Find books that they can look through on training dogs to assist children with autism. You could find YouTube videos on autistic children. YouTube also has plenty of videos on how to train dogs which could open up a whole new area of learning. If you know of a child with autism, have your children pray for them and their families. You might even consider buying another copy of this book as a gift for the mama with an autistic child.

"Be of good courage, and he shall strengthen your heart, all ye that hope in the Lord" (Psalm 31:24).

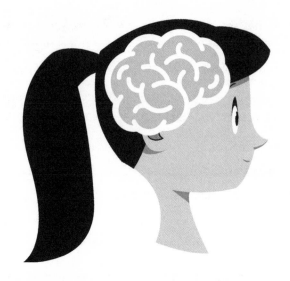

The Brain of Young Adults

CHAPTER 12

Neuroplasticity has taught us that the brain of a young adult is not yet completely developed so it is critical that our teens trust us to guide them.

BRAIN ANATOMY 101

The brain is composed of three major parts: the brain stem, the cerebellum, and the cerebrum. The **brain stem**, shaped like a widening stalk, links the spinal cord to the brain. It controls reflexes and involuntary processes like breathing, heart rate, and the gastrointestinal tract. The brain stem is the communication portal from the brain to the body. Without a functioning brain stem, there is no life.

Behind the brain stem in the back of the head and below the upper brain is the **cerebellum**, which controls balance and coordination. It has two hemispheres. In Latin, *cerebellum* means "little brain", for it is smaller than the **cerebrum,** just above it.

The **cerebrum** is the largest part of the brain and is also divided into two hemispheres. The **cerebrum** is responsible for higher processes like memory and learning. It is composed of several sections, but in this chapter, we will discuss the **prefrontal cortex**, which is the outer layer (like a skin) and is about ½ centimeter thick. It is the very wrinkled "gray matter" you see in brain pictures. The deep wrinkles or folds in the cerebrum increase the overall surface area, providing for more processing neurons. We need this extra processing area because that is where consciousness is regulated.

PREFRONTAL CORTEX

The prefrontal cortex (PFC) is the area of the brain where executive functions are housed—things like organizing our thoughts, strategizing, staying vigilant, and establishing mindfulness. It is also responsible for checking impulse behavior, which helps us see the wisdom of exercising caution. Undeniably, the PFC is important. It is the part of the brain that cautions us, "If you say it, eat it, do it...what's next? Is that what you want?"

The thing that is rather disconcerting about this impulse control area of the brain is the timing of its completion. Who would have guessed it? Your highly intelligent, over-confident, demanding teenager has an incomplete brain. His PFC is not all there until he is at least 25 years old. These half-brained teenagers with full-grown bodies and overgrown sex drives also have loads of neurotransmitters screaming their self-importance. This results in them truly thinking they have the insight to judge the adults in their lives. They actually believe they know everything and can reason better than any adult. I still remember when I knew everything. It is scary now to know that I was a half-brained dimwit, riding a horse named Know-It-All to a battle against the forces of ignorance and complacency. The ranks of all revolutions are filled with young people under the age of 25.

You might want to educate your teenager on the developmental delays of his PFC. You could start each morning by having him repeat: "As a young adult under the age of 25, I do not have a complete prefrontal cortex, which means I might be inclined to make poor decisions, exercise poor judgment, misunderstand someone or something, or just don't know for sure if I am right about something. I am really very stupid. I must listen to my parents and those in authority even more than when I was four years old if I hope to come through in good form and without regrets." I should warn you, he won't believe you. If he gets to be 15 years of age and he does not have faith in you, he will pilot his own ship despite any adult interference. It is a dangerous period in life, but we survived it; maybe he will too.

As it were, the PFC is the place where your soul finds expression in the brain and body. Now you can see why it is so important for parents to help their teenager process life until he has his whole brain.

MRI SCANS PROVE THE POINT

In 2011, Deborah Yurgelun-Todd, PhD, director of neuropsychology and cognitive neuroimaging at McLean Hospital in Belmont, Massachusetts did a study using MRI imaging to see just what is happening in young adult brains compared to the brains of fully mature adults.[86] She put young adults, under the age of 25, in an MRI and monitored how their brains responded to various pictures of faces with extreme expressions. The object was to see how they interpreted the emotion of the person in the picture and what parts of their brain were activated when making the decision. They put adults through an identical test and documented their brain responses and answers, as well.

In response to one picture, 100% of the adults quickly identified the expression as fear. The scans also revealed that all of the adults used the same area of their brain to come to that conclusion—the PFC. The teens and young adults, however, had a variety of opinions as to the emotion expressed in the picture. Some thought it expressed sadness, others were sure it was confusion or shock, and some simply couldn't decide. Surprisingly, even the more mature and sophisticated young adults did not correctly identify fear. These intelligent students had no ability to make a judgment on how a person might be feeling or responding to them. This is an important piece of information for parents raising half-brained teenagers. It might help us to take their aberrant behavior less personally.

These results help us to better understand how a teenager can so misrepresent our motives and words. They might be told to clean up after the dog and relate a big story of humiliation, for their brain interpreted the event as rejection. Knowing this, parents need to be careful when their young people come to them with tales of being ill-treated or rejected by others, or when they come with a bad report on the motives of others. As their brains are developing, they need to have their interpretations of reality filtered through the wisdom of mature adults.

86 "Interview: Deborah Yurgelun-Todd." *PBS Frontline*. Retrieved from: www.pbs.org/wgbh/pages/frontline/shows/teenbrain/interviews/todd.html

CORTEX

The prefrontal cortex is involved with focus, fore-thought, judgment, organization, planning, impulse control, empathy, and learning from mistakes.

Most revealing through the scans, Yurgelun-Todd was able to identify which area of the young adults' brains processed the emotional information. It was not the higher functioning PFC, as in adults; it was the **amygdala**, which is responsible for immediate reactions including fear and aggressive behavior. This region develops early. Because young adults must resort to making decisions from the **amygdala,** it is possible that their conclusion can be distorted or totally wrong. What seems an easy choice or judgment for an adult might not be so simple for the younger generation. The problem is they "think" they are correct because the judgment part of their brain has yet to be fully developed.

A 2005 National Youth Risk Behavior Survey[87] suggests that adolescents are more likely to drive under the influence of alcohol, disregard seat belts, use drugs, and take part in unprotected sex. There are over 16,000 adolescent deaths in the United States each year, 70% of which occur from vehicle crashes, homicide, and suicide. Adolescents' spur-of-the-moment decision-making behavior, as well as lack of experience, accounts for much of this tragedy. It is young people who fall off of cliffs taking selfies or jump into shallow water and break their necks.

FINALLY MATURE AT 25

Most young people would scoff at the idea that they lack a mature brain. You can't tell them anything—that is, unless they have learned to trust you more than they trust their own perceptions. If you have won your child's heart when he is young, then in his early twenties, he will give extra weight to your advice and counsel. Our goal as parents is to lead our children to continue to walk by the principles we have instilled in them and to seek counsel before making any life-changing decisions. When they know from science that

87 Eaton, Danice K., et al. (2005). "Youth Risk Behavior Surveillance – United States, 2005." *CDC Morbidity and Mortality Weekly Report.* Retrieved from: www.cdc.gov/mmwr/PDF/SS/SS5505.pdf

their brains have not completed the process of what is referred to as **insulating**, they will exercise caution according to our advice.

Next is the story of a friend—a good Christian boy who lacked mature, executive function skills and failed to consider the consequences of driving too fast.

"JOHNNY ANGEL"

This afternoon as I drove down the road, one gnarled old tree awakened thousands of memory neurons that are over 52 years old. "Johnny Angel" was the song that was playing on the radio when I glanced in the mirror and saw the ambulance coming up behind me. Tommy could sing that song better than the voice coming over the radio.

As I write this, I feel the same tightness in my stomach as I did then. The Little Brain (my gut) is reacting to the dread. This physiological response has caused some researchers to speculate that the millions of neurons found in the gut have conscious thought. Amazing!

My old body feels a chill with the memory of Tommy's last ride. He didn't die that day, but in a way, he did. His '65 Chevy was wrapped around an old gnarled tree much like the one I just passed. Today, my brain's "feeling memories" are washing over my synapses, bringing dread, fretfulness, and anxiety, even though my "thought memories" can barely remember any details. But I clearly recall seeing him three years after the crash, so changed in manner that I hardly recognized him. Clearly, he would not need a girlfriend now.

Not a millisecond has passed, yet thousands of childish memories are recovered as my marvelous brain guides me down a busy, two-lane highway at 65 miles per hour. My wired-together neurons, old and new, are firing away, connecting, reconnecting, and creating. I can almost hear Tommy's mocking, delightful laughter again when we girls complained about his fast driving. We were all careless, but he more than most. We called it daring, crazy, wild. I now know that his

> **PROCESSING**
>
> Most information processing occurs in the cerebral cortex.

behavior was due to his PFC not being fully developed, as well as the fact that he had not been taught to regulate his life. Tommy was the coolest guy in school and at church. He played the guitar and led the youth group. He was so handsome, dressed so fine, had such cute dimples, and he gave all us girls a thrill with his songs. But the Tommy we knew vanished that day, never to return. He didn't have the opportunity to finish developing his brain. My foot eases off the gas pedal, although I don't notice, it is an automatic neural reaction. I drive like an old lady because...well...of memories like this one.

I feel a new flickering sense as I remember that Tommy had just started dating the not-so-nice Belinda. She was known for sleeping around, and the whole youth group was shocked and totally disappointed in him. We were all a little mad that he had chosen a girl outside our youth group. He had always been our leader and had such strong convictions. So why choose her? Looking back, I can see this rocked our little world.

My gut contracts again as I remember seeing Tommy just a few years after his wreck. He was sitting on the front row at church, rocking back and forth, clapping his hands and slapping his knees like a six-year-old. When he had the wreck, we were told that he had brain damage and had lost his manhood. At the time, I had no idea what that meant, but when I saw him sitting there in church, I just somehow knew. I can't stop my brain from wondering if his new relationship with Belinda had anything to do with his wreck. It sure sobered us kids up when it happened.

As I drive along reminiscing, old feelings make new neural connections with the new feelings. At an unfathomable speed, the neurotransmitter cortisol bathes both the old and the new connections. I become tensely alert and stay that way for my entire journey. The neurotransmitter cortisol is making a difference in how I am driving as well as how I am feeling. It is also making me burp because my gut has responded. I know that Tommy's wreck changed my life in many ways, and today the memories are affecting my driving, my mood, and my physical body.

As my car slows, my mind turns to a local "Mr. Cool" young man, and I wonder if he drives recklessly and what girl has his eye. I silently pray for him to have wisdom. In some way, the neurons in my brain have made a connection between the local boy and Tommy. I have unconsciously judged the local young man for being foolish. Even now, as I write this, I catch my own thoughts continuing along this same vein. He probably is foolish. Tommy is still shaping my mind.

My synapses have been busy—they are always this busy. My brain never stops, for when I sleep, it rehearses what I have covered during the day, which reinforces my memory. My brain—the actual organ—grew more neuronal connections by simply seeing the old tree, thus, it became a tiny bit larger. I am reminded that things that fire together, wire together, and if you don't use it, you lose it. Most likely, it was that sad love song, "Johnny Angel", that Tommy could sing so well. It is a tear-jerker, so it deeply grooved my emotional network, as well as the network made by music and lyrics. By humming it hundreds of times over the last 50 plus years, the whole network involving much of my brain is still alive.

The intricate system of brain wiring has done its job. I am bone-weary when I get home and I really can't say why.

My brain is "fearfully and wonderfully made."

TEEN HORMONES

A teenager's hormones affect his emotions and impulses and have a way of taking control of all other faculties. Hormones, like estrogen, progesterone, and testosterone—the sex hormones—fluctuate greatly, causing mood swings. It is hard to catch them at a point where they are balanced. An imbalance in hormones can cause extreme agitation and even depression. It can diminish a teen's ability to think and concentrate. And the newly experienced thrill of desire can cause feelings of guilt. But hormones can also motivate a kid to learn at an accelerated rate. The key is to fill his life with challenging opportunities—things that will burn hormones in constructive pursuits.

TOTAL CHANGE IN TACTICS

You can't continue to raise a teenager like you raise a pre-pubescent child. The combination of a brain in high gear and a body in high gear accelerates everything, and if that energy is not directed toward productive ends, you are going to see an explosion in the wrong direction. A teen's brain and body are searching for stimulation and craving input. Hormones are the drivers, the force that motivates the kid to want to do great things, to accomplish something, to succeed. Hormones grease the wheels and demand engagement in life experiences. They motivate teens to go to extremes while ignoring pain or risk for hope of achievement. Olympic gold medalists are mostly teenagers. Rank-and-file military personnel are primarily 18- to 22-year-olds. A boy can be a total loser and voluntarily go to boot camp, relishing the hardship and even abuse from his drill sergeant, and come out a proud and confident man. A 19-year-old will charge an enemy position when a 30-year-old

160

will cower. Teenagers are looking for a challenge, a cause, something to give their lives meaning and purpose. They are an arrow fired by hormones seeking a target. Provide the target.

Parents don't usually see teen years as a great opportunity—rather, as something to be endured until the kid is cured. One moment, we see a distracted child that is looking straight at us yet doesn't hear a word we are saying, and the next day we see runaway emotion and passion directed at things that don't seem worth the effort. Suddenly, the teenager is a wise guru or prophet capable of great professed wisdom, able to pass judgment upon the world and family with the certainty of John the Baptist himself. Protests and political movements are made up of teenagers and those in their early twenties.

> ### TEENAGERS
>
> Teenagers have the body of an adult and the hormones of an animal, but sadly, not the brain of a grown-up. This can really cause some trouble.

You cannot tell your child what he is going to be passionate about. He will choose, and there is nothing you can do to change his preference. So you must prepare him mentally and spiritually from infancy, instilling the tools of wisdom and discernment at an early age. A young child who was trained in the executive functions of self-restraint and self-discipline (remember the marshmallow study?) will have developed an appreciation for being motivated by reason rather than impulse.

PRACTICAL

There are some practical things you can do to minimize the hormonal impact and aid your teen in making wise choices rather than being swept along by feelings and impulses.

It is during the awakening age from puberty to late teens that young men need to actually be doing something rather than sitting in a classroom with a flock of girls surrounding them. Both boys and girls need to be handed a hammer and, by example, shown how to build something. They need to be handed a wrench and shown how to fix something. They need to chop firewood for their grandparents or fix an old lady's automobile tire. They need to be taken hunting, fishing, camping, and engaged in outside activities. Kids love survival camps because they want to feel like conquerors. They need to be heavily engaged in activities that allow them to be developing both the body and brain together. This is why sports resonate with many teenagers who are confined to the concrete and asphalt of city life. However, activities in nature and on the farm are far superior to sports.

Girls have the same need to learn how to be productive human beings. Young women need to be doing things that interest them—music, art, growing and gathering herbs, cooking, sewing, training animals, or any pursuit that involves both the brain and the body. Every young person needs to be able to step back from a hard challenge and say, "I did it. I knew I could. Look what I did." And you need to be there with a delighted expression on your face saying, "Wow! That is amazing. YOU are amazing. I am so blessed to have you as my kid. I am proud of you."

We know of one family that has thirteen children. Can you imagine having to be diligent and attentive to every child over a period of 35 years? It is demanding enough if you live on a farm, but if not, it is a very big job indeed. Some families do well with their older children because the kids are raised when the parents are still young and have energy to meet the needs of the kids. But as the years pass and responsibilities increase, they have less energy and maybe get a little bored, so they are not as proactive in the lives of the younger children by the time they reach their teen years.

This couple with 13 children set into motion a lifetime event so that all their children, from the youngest to the oldest, could participate. As a family, they began sponsoring World War II remembrance events. The kids did research, made clothes of that era, refurbished old war vehicles, contacted old vets and listened to their stories, and a multitude of other activities. Over time, they got the entire town involved in their project featuring the old war vets, many dressed in uniform. They call it "Remembering World War II." Their project grew as their older children became adults, and it is still going strong as the last of their clan are maturing.

Our family did mission outreaches. During their teenage years, our children traveled all over the world aiding missionary families. Our first daughter went to Papua New Guinea when she was just 17 to help a missionary family. One teenage son was needed in a war zone to assist a missionary in the evacuation of his wife and six young daughters. The next son was sent at age 17 to aid his sister in Papua New Guinea where she was doing translation work in an unreached tribe. You can read her story in *Rebekah's Diary*.[88] It is an astounding read which could direct the heart of your teenage daughter toward the things of God.

Rebekah's songs, written from the top of a mountain in a tiny primitive hut, are recorded on the CD *From the End of the Earth*. Your children will love to sing along. There is a free download of her story that could change the direction of your teenagers (*www.ngj.org/gami-akij*). There is nothing so sobering as traveling into third-world countries and seeing the needs of people. Just making missionary books available could be life changing. In the back of this book, we have included a list of resources that have been a blessing to many.

You, as parents, must expose your teenagers to a variety of wholesome and worthy opportunities that are physically and mentally challenging and you must provide the means to achieve them. If you don't, your teens will by default be directed by the culture around them.

SUGGESTIONS
Good reading on missions

In My Father's House - Corrie Ten Boom

Commandos for Christ - Bruce Porterfield

Through Gates of Splendor - Elizabeth Elliott

They Called Me Mama - Margaret Nicholl Laird

Mrs. C. H. Spurgeon - Charles Ray

The Man Who Moved a Mountain - Richard Davids

One Shall Chase a Thousand - Mabel Francis with Gerald B. Smith

Susanna Wesley - Arnold Dallimore

Hudson Taylor's Spiritual Secret - Dr. and Mrs. Howard Taylor

By Searching : My Journey Through Doubt Into Faith- Isobel Kuhn

Behind the Ranges: The Life-Changing Story of J.O. Fraser - Geraldine Taylor

Goforth of China - Rosalind Goforth

Climbing - Rosalind Goforth

How I Know God Answers Prayer - Rosalind Goforth

88 *From the End of the Earth* and *Rebekah's Diary* are both available at www.nogreaterjoy.org/shop

Amy Carmichael: Let the Little Children Come - Lois Dick

C.T. Studd: Cricketer and Pioneer - Norman Grubb

John and Betty Stam - Kathleen White

Created for Commitment - A. Weatherell Johnson

Fanny J. Crosby: An Autobiography

Evidence Not Seen: A Woman's Miraculous Faith in the Jungles of World War II - Darlene Rose

The Last of the Giants - How Christ Came to the Lumberjacks - Harry Rimmer, LL.D.

Henrietta Mears and How She Did It! - Ethel May Baldwin

Mover of Men and Mountains – R.G. LeTourneau

I CHARGE YOU

If you have tweens or teenagers in the house, you should read to them Dr. Yurgelun-Todd's picture study proving that young adults use the amygdala area of the brain in making judgments. Talk about teens you know or have read about that have made really poor choices which resulted in tragedy, such as texting and driving. Talk about small decisions teens make every day, which they think are okay, but without their prefrontal cortex functioning, the teens might actually be making really bad choices. Look at pictures of the brain and discuss it. Also, talk about how insulation works in the world of electricity and how that relates to the brain being insulated. If you don't know, then look it up on YouTube and learn together. Learning anything together will enhance learning for all. Knowledge and understanding of how the brain works could save the life of your teen. Share this chapter once a month with your teen so he or she will be refreshed on the value of wise decisions and being open to instruction. Have the older children write a project paper on this aspect of the brain.

"And that from a child thou hast known the holy scriptures, which are able to make thee wise..." (2 Timothy 3:15)

Big Brains

CHAPTER 13

Neuroplasticity has taught us if you don't use it, you will lose it.

CONNECTIONS ARE GOOD

Using a brain grows a brain. Up to 700 more neurons can develop in a day if we use our brain, and each neuron means thousands of additional synapses that can form connections. The wider the range of things we learn, the greater the number of connections, and increased connections translate into more extensive mental, emotional, and social intelligences. The more experiences we have and the more life we live, the more connections our synapses make with various parts of the brain responsible for reason, imagination, retention, taste, color, emotion, creativity, etc. With all of these new connections, our brain structure actually grows.

The reverse is true as well. When the brain is not challenged with ideas and experiences, it diminishes in capacity. As exercising the body makes it stronger, exercising the brain makes us more intellectually capable. As your body is what you eat, your brain is what you think.

Throughout history (and even today to a lesser extent), it has been common in every culture to believe that some strata of society are born more intelligent and more gifted than are the commoners that make up the majority. Consider India with its caste system, or Charles Darwin's "scientific" conclusion that some people groups like the Aboriginals of Australia were sub-human, as seen by their "lack of intelligence." Slavery was justified on the grounds that Africans were an "inferior race."

But when Darwin reported that he had found a sub-human tribe in Patagonia, missionaries made contact with the unreached savages. Within a generation, the test scores of Patagonian children exceeded many of their European counterparts.

So why has it been a universally accepted axiom that some groups—the ones at the top of the food chain—are of superior intellect? Any group of people who struggle from day to day for their survival and are not engaging the brain in a wide variety of disciplines will have less-developed neural networks. This will cause them to appear less intellectual when compared to more sophisticated cultures that provide a greater variety of mental stimulation. But when their young children are exposed to more extensive learning opportunities, their brains develop the same capabilities as those who have had long histories of academic achievement.

THE RENAISSANCE PERIOD—BLUE BLOODS

Europe, and especially England, was divided into the "blue bloods" and the "commoners." Even the common people—farmers and tradesmen—could see the obvious superiority of the blue bloods. I often think of the amazing Renaissance period—the magnificent music, the remarkable literature, the glorious art, and the outstanding architecture that remains unrivaled to this day. And they did not have the internet from which to draw accumulated knowledge and experience.

The common tradesman developed his skills to a highly refined state, but he had very little knowledge or experience outside his particular craft. The blue bloods were raised with tutors in a great variety of fields.

It would have been tough to be born into a time and place where you knew you were just dumb compared to those who had rule over you. The peasants all through the Dark Ages and Renaissance suffered scarcity of quality food, lived in unsanitary conditions, had little opportunity for education, and had very poor self-images. Their worlds were small and occupied with survival, with no time or incentive to learn anything beyond their single trade.

It takes nutritious food to feed the brain and the body, including lots of quality fats. Up until the last few hundred years, good fats were hard to find. The lack of wholesome food affected the basic building blocks of DNA, causing physical and mental weakening. The lack of sanitary conditions resulted in all kinds of intestinal worms and gut issues, which would greatly magnify brain fog. Plus, the lack of opportunity meant there were very few neurons being wired together compared to those who had a wider range of experiences. The brain sat idle generation after generation. The environment of limited opportunity led to a dumbing down in DNA, giving way to low expectations. The lower class appeared to be quite dimwitted. Clearly, they were at a disadvantage.

Blue bloods, on the other hand, had quality organic foods, clean housing, excellent schooling, and the finest books written throughout the centuries by the very best minds. Their extensive training began at a young age.

They learned several languages, math, music, art, fencing, horsemanship, shooting, archery, wrestling and boxing, business, politics, and finance. The boys were even taught the history and tactics of war. Their children were challenged and stimulated in a way that caused them to develop a wide range of neural connections, increasing their capabilities in every way. The young ladies were schooled in needlework, music, singing, dancing, poetry, world travel, and elite conversation. Both boys and girls were well schooled in the fundamentals of animal and land husbandry, as well as being steeped in leadership responsibilities, all of which were critical for continued prosperity. Their education was hands-on. All these mental, social, and physical challenges developed the neurons that caused their eyes, ears, feet, hands, memory, and mindset to operate in high gear. From their youth, they had well-nourished, well-connected brains with plenty of the critical fats needed for optimal functioning. Their superb training would have greatly expanded the synapse connections to the neurons in many different areas of the brain. They had a wide net of communication all across the brain.

" Other things equal, a life filled with more complex flow activities is more worth living than one spent consuming passive entertainment. *"*

Mihaly Csikszentmihalyi

To this culture, it would appear that the blue bloods were not only born with a silver spoon in their mouth, but also with better DNA, which at that time they called breeding. Surely, this stark difference in classes had a profound effect on science, lasting well into the twentieth century. You were either born smart or you were born lower class, which meant you were dumb. Even today, most everyone thinks that people are born with a fixed IQ.

Just think how the blue bloods expanded their brains, allowing them to have great ability to see things and do things that our generation appears incapable of doing. Inventions had to come out of nothing, there was no preexisting groundwork upon which our generation depends. Music, the creation of musical instruments, and the marvelous ability to craft them were all part of their creative endeavors. Researching the different dynasties shows the same superpower ability, the same advanced education, self-discipline, extreme training, and many varied subjects of learning in other people groups.

Researchers would love to see a brain scan like the blue bloods must have cultured. And to think, that same kind of well-connected brain can be ours! All it takes is work. Don't forget, big brains are made by many connections webbing out all over the brain and back again. The more experiences, the more thought in many directions, the more interest, the more activities, the more friends and acquaintances—the more our brain grows. And when it comes to brains, bigger is better.

As I write this book, I have millions of options at my fingertips. I find the latest research from all over the world, and even that which was done a hundred years ago. I can glean from any era and every culture in the world. I can quickly write, delete, rearrange, and consult the most extensive thesaurus ever in existence. My computer even spellchecks as I write, making many corrections automatically. Think about writers of old that wrote with a feather and homemade ink on expensive paper. Yet their writings are so complex, running several plots with many intrigues and perceived feelings. How did they do it? Were they smarter than we are now?

WHAT REALLY MADE A BLUE BLOOD?

If we could go back to that era and take our investigative tools to research the differences, we might conclude that the blue bloods were indeed smarter and stronger with better reasoning skills and higher IQs. But it was not their genetics that caused them to produce a higher culture of governance, music, art, architecture, and science; it was mental development that occurred as they engaged the brains of their children in a great variety of disciplines. This increased the synapse connections and broadened their neural network.

STUNTED MEDICAL HISTORY

Oddly enough, it was this mentality of a superior class that was in some way responsible for the lack of advances in brain science right up until the 1960s! It was just assumed for all these centuries that some people were born capable of advanced learning and others were not. It has been and is still assumed by most people that IQ is fixed and constant according to our DNA. Before the 1980s, only a small handful of doctors were big-minded enough to think the brain might actually continue to grow and develop—that it even had the capacity to heal itself. How could an educated doctor believe that the brain had the ability to detect abnormalities and take the proper steps to heal itself? Or that it is capable, through choice, of growing in intellectual capacity, actually increasing the IQ? That sounds far-fetched, but it is true.

Brain science was thwarted by the very blue bloods who thought themselves to be a superior breed. This is why it was such a shock to Paul Bach-y-Rita when he observed the brain of his deceased father and realized that it had found a way to carry out its function with only 3% of the brain stem intact.

Before brain scans could map the brain and see its internal function, no one knew that it could initiate its own rewiring so as to effect a radical change. No one knew that it could change for the worse under the influence of negative attitudes—unthankfulness, bitterness, and just general moodiness. With stinking thinking, the brain produces chemicals like cortisol that diminish mental and emotional capacity.

Given their presupposition of the constancy of the brain, the so-called

> **"**The brain Michael Merzenich describes is not an inanimate vessel that we fill; rather it is more like a living creature with an appetite, one that can grow and change itself with proper nourishment and exercise.**"**
>
> Dr. Norman Doidge, *The Brain That Changes Itself*

blue bloods had no reason to think they could take one of these beggarly, little street urchins into their homes, feed, clothe, and educate him, and have a child equal to their own bloodline. No one knew until the last few years that the brain is what you make it.

The teen years are God's gift for growing big brains. Teens are driven more than at any other time in life and that drive comes with an increased capacity to learn and develop brainpower. It is not a time to be wasted.

LIMITED BRILLIANCE

The brain reflects the soul of the individual. The narrower our interests, thought life, friend pool, and activities—basically, the less demand we place on the brain—the smaller it becomes, purging itself of unused connections, leaving the lights out in neurons that could have shone brightly with activity.

As we discussed before, the map concept clearly illustrates this. If you have one major interstate, ten lanes wide, going both directions, it would be an incredible transportation avenue, but it would not encompass a very large area of the country. A network of many roads is more efficient, both for the country and the brain. You might not have a superhighway—except in a narrow field such as music or coding—but you would have access to a much broader area.

> **"**Life is a matter of choices, and every choice you make makes you.**"**
>
> John C. Maxwell

People have a tendency to develop patterns of thought. You sleep on the same side of the bed, open the same drawers, eat the same foods, etc. You function without effort or thought, so your brain just keeps traveling down the same roads. As the mind travels the same familiar roads over and over, in time it makes a wide highway in the brain. It is so much easier to take familiar roads in the city, just as it is easier to do the same thing in the mind. But comfortable familiarity wrapped in routine keeps the brain from branching out to create a greater network.

If a memory or a bit of knowledge is connected to a multitude of different avenues reaching every area of the brain, that piece of knowledge can be readily accessed from many angles. If the brain suffers damage in one area, wiping out access to a memory or motor skill, the programming can be accessed in different areas of the brain that remain intact. A brain that has a wide range of networking is the most efficient.

Have you ever noted that often highly gifted people who have had a single focus all their life are fumble-bums in so many other ways? Exceptionally "smart" people who devote all their time to perfecting a single discipline are often clueless in other areas such as relationships because they never took the time to practice them. They have never formed those vital neural connections.

Incredibly intelligent scientists, musicians, or artists who have devoted their entire lives to one field are the superhighway people. They excel in their field but are noted for being socially inept, emotionally incapable of close relationships, or lacking in everyday life skills. Their executive functions are not in full sail. You might be willing to sacrifice your life for one of the arts, but real joy, love, and thanksgiving come from balance.

EBB AND FLOW

Over a lifetime, one's intelligence will ebb and flow. If we "think dumb" for an extended period of time, choosing amusement and entertainment, or avoiding social situations, eschewing challenges and intellectual engagement, our brain will begin to dim.

The smaller our life, the smaller our mind. But during times when we are highly engaged with study, people, reasoning, creativity, physical challenges, and great conversations, our brain chemicals flow, connections are made, and our brain thrives. This ebb and flow of brain growth and shrinking continues all through life

---

CEREBRAL CORTEX

The prefrontal cortex—the most advanced brain region—is also the most sensitive to the detrimental effects of stress exposure. Even quite mild, acute, uncontrollable stress can cause a rapid and dramatic loss. Research has provided clues as to why stress-signaling pathways can lead to symptoms of profound prefrontal cortical dysfunction in mental illness.[1]

1 Arnsten, Amy F. T. (2009). "Stress signaling pathways that impair prefrontal cortex structure and function." *Nature Reviews Neuroscience*. Retrieved from: www.ncbi.nlm.nih.gov/pmc/articles/PMC2907136/

OLD ROADS LEAD TO NOWHERE

Roads that are not used regularly become grown over with weeds and eventually become unusable, which is what often happens to people's brains as they age. It is well known that when older people stop working, they quickly deteriorate mentally, physically, and/or emotionally. Age slows us down physically and makes us want to sit and watch the world go by. What we don't use, we lose.

For that reason, older people are advised to take up a new sport, hobby, music, language, or other challenging activity. It is a way of opening up new areas in the brain, establishing a wider range of connections. In the process, old neurons link up to new ones, expanding the neural network. Young people are often locked into a "dead end" life because they choose passive entertainment over mental and physical growth, which allows their brain to waste away, just as it does for an elderly person.

I CHARGE YOU

Make a list of things to do with your children that will increase their brain power. Your list should include physical exercise, competition, music, animal care, memorization, art, social events, serving others, cooking, and many other activities that have nothing to do with school-books. After you make your list, read it aloud to your children and ask them what they would enjoy doing that would grow their brains. Give them some ideas, and if they are still coming up dry, take them to the library and help them find books that will stimulate ideas to grow big brains. Being a parent of a teen takes real sacrifice. We have to get up and get involved. Watching the screen is so much easier, but we lose when we snooze.

"Study to shew thyself approved unto God, a workman that needeth not to be ashamed, rightly dividing the word of truth" (2 Timothy 2:15).

Shrinking Our Brain

CHAPTER 14

Neuroplasticity has taught us that our emotions, reactions, and attitudes literally reshape the physical structure of our brain.

Through the research shown, we now know we can grow our brain, thus, our intelligence. However, we can also shrink our brain and actually diminish our IQ. One of the most amazing things scientists have learned through the study of neuroplasticity is the fact that stinking thinking actually shrinks our brains. This often results in emotional disorders, as well as diminished emotional and intellectual intelligence. Many people spend at least part of their lives actively shrinking the most important organ in their body—their own brain. It happens by dwelling on bitterness, anger, defeat, and blame. Here is how it worked for Lydia Rose.

WHO ATE LYDIA ROSE'S BRAIN?

In a prestigious music school set in one of the richest Jewish districts in New York, there was an opening for a music teacher for the beginners' cello class. Lydia Rose felt she was over-qualified, but she had heard that one of the finest musicians in the world occasionally volunteered to teach there. She knew he was scouting for new, upcoming talent, and she wanted to be that talent. He was part of an internationally acclaimed orchestra she aspired to join. Even though she was the youngest and had the least teaching experience, she was not surprised that she got the job over 27 other applicants.

At 21 years of age, Lydia Rose's prefrontal cortex (PFC) was not completely developed. Remember, this is the area of the brain crucial to reasoning, making wise decisions, and logic. It is also the area where judgments are formed. As we discussed, during this period up to about age 25, you are considered an adult yet the PFC is not completely insulated, so you lack the caution and judgment that will come later.[89]

TROUBLE IN PARADISE

After only two weeks of classes, Lydia Rose was called into the director's office. He spoke with obvious annoyance. "You were given the guidelines for the first two weeks of classes and were told to follow them explicitly. It has come to my notice that you did not follow the curriculum as directed."

Lydia Rose was expecting praise because she knew she had put together an amazing protocol and had thrown her whole heart and soul into her students. She was beyond shocked at the rebuke. She answered him somewhat huffily, yet with firm conviction: "In all good conscience, I could not use such silly guidelines. They were written just to make the students appear as if they were learning to play in the first few lessons, which is ridiculous. I came here to teach my students to excel, which means laying a solid foundation."

> *"* For every minute you are angry, you lose sixty seconds of happiness. *"*
>
> Ralph Waldo Emerson

Mr. Director stood, leaning forward with his hands open, fingertips resting on his desk. He looked down at the papers under his fingers, appearing to study them as if what was on his desk was of great importance. He finally asked, "Is that your final word?"

"Yes," Lydia Rose said firmly, if somewhat breathlessly.

Sighing, her employer glanced up briefly, meeting her eyes. "As you

89 Fetterman, Anne, et al (reviewers). (2019). "Understanding the Teen Brain." *URMC Health Encyclopedia*. Retrieved from: www.urmc.rochester.edu/encyclopedia/content.aspx?ContentType-ID=1&ContentID=3051

> " Of all the virtues we can learn, no trait is more useful, more essential for survival, and more likely to improve the quality of life than the ability to transform adversity into an enjoyable challenge. "
>
> Mihaly Csikszentmihalyi, *Flow: The Psychology of Happiness*

wish. I expect your resignation by the end of the day. You can use any excuse that will aid you in getting your next job. I would recommend that until you are the boss, you do as you are told." The director pulled out his chair and sat down. He put on his reading glasses and began shuffling through the papers on his desk. It was as if nothing much had just transpired.

Lydia Rose stood glued to the floor in utter, stunned bewilderment, unable to break the spell that gripped her. How could her entire world dissolve in less than two minutes? The director's second fleeting glance showed surprise that she was still in his office. He voiced a clipped, "You are dismissed."

Believing you are the best while still young can sometimes be detrimental. Being put in a position of authority where you feel superior is equally damaging when you are put down by those who do not value your "brilliance." Remember my friend Tommy, who wrapped his '65 Chevy around the old tree? In a manner of speaking this was Lydia Rose's car wreck. Depending on her response, Lydia Rose stood to lose pieces of her brain just as surely as Tommy did, only her loss would be slow, steady, and unseen.

The director had more on his mind than music. He was responsible for keeping the school financially viable, which meant encouraging donors. Many of the students were grandchildren of the school's supporters. To prevent discouragement, the children needed to see quick results, as did their families. This approach had worked well for many years. But he had too much to do to explain all his reasons to a new, easily replaced teacher.

THE WORKINGS OF LYDIA ROSE'S BRAIN

Lydia Rose's feeling of importance came from the hormone **serotonin** released by the confidence she acquired from her selection to a position of consequence. She felt she had earned the right to do things her way—the "right" way. The Scripture says in **1 Timothy 3:6, "Not a novice, lest being lifted up with pride he fall into the condemnation of the devil."** The pride of authority and excellence is a problem in the church as well. Men of God need to have the wisdom of years before being given rule of God's people.

Lydia Rose's initial shock caused her brain to overproduce the neurotransmitters **noradrenaline** and **adrenaline,** which put her in fight-or-flight mode. She could have responded in anger and resentment, or she could have fled in defeat. These chemicals would continue to be overproduced if she kept looping these aggravated thoughts. Instead of wisely holding her counsel, which she would do if her PFC were fully developed, she shared her hurt with others and proved through much drama that she was wrongly treated. Mirror neurons multiplied the hurt.

Lydia Rose did not have a rebellious heart or even a sense that she was bucking the system; she simply wanted to do what was best for the children—from her perspective.

It was hard to be blamed and then be dismissed for something when in her heart of hearts, she wanted to please. I feel her pain. Life is full of these situations: falling in love and being rejected, having a friend and sharing your heart, only to find they talked behind your back, or being overlooked for an important role when you know you are the best choice. All these disappointments, frustrations, and mistreatments can make or break you. Hopefully, this rejection will be the making of Lydia Rose. She will be wiser, stronger, more forgiving, and certainly more capable of seeing life from a wider perch than just her own. But according to research and experience, she will most likely stay agitated and continue to blame others for her dismissal.

> **MAKING IT WORSE**
>
> You can make yourself feel worse almost immediately by dwelling on the worst possible outcome of a situation.

If she had a fully developed PFC, she would have possessed the wisdom to weigh the issues from a broader perspective. In coming years, these types of issues will not arise because Lydia Rose will have developed the part of her brain that is responsible for weighing matters and considering consequences...unless she damages her PFC through bitterness or negative thinking, and then even as an adult she will lack the neurons that govern wisdom and judgment. In accordance with the nature of the brain, her negative thoughts actually bring physical changes to her brain and body.

If I could, I would counsel Lydia Rose to:

Stop your mind from dwelling on how mistreated you think you are. Just because your PFC is not fully developed until you are 25 doesn't mean you do not have some capacity for logical, reasoned thought. You have the power to overwrite your emotional responses, to reject the promptings of your brain patterns, and to exercise your God-given will to follow a higher calling.

Think about the fact that the director is older, wiser, and has nothing against you personally. He liked you. He hired you. He wanted you for the job. He told you what to do. He just met you, so it couldn't be anything personal.

Consider the fact that you are the one who violated the rules. Consider that this is not the time and place for your special lessons. Consider the director's fruits: they are good, they are many, and they are lasting. You are just getting started.

Learn from your mistakes. Wow, this is a big one! LEARN what not to do next time, learn there is a time and place for everything, learn there are a lot of people to consider other than those within your small circle.

Plan how to move forward and fix the situation as painlessly as possible.

Seek wise counsel. Turn to someone who has a good track record of joy and success. If their opinion differs, let them help you see things from their perspective.

The STOP, THINK, CONSIDER, LEARN, PLAN, and SEEK approach is the exercise of the PFC, and it is subject to the choices of Lydia Rose's soul. If she were to follow my advice, her brain would make exciting new connections that would boost her brain power and emotional stability. If not, she would shrink in brain and character.

At some point in life, we must be led by a calling higher than the promptings of past brain patterning. Christians are greatly advantaged in that we have the wisdom of the Word of God and the Spirit of God working in our spirit to prompt us to a higher calling. We are able to form our brains according to our convictions rather than be a slave to our past experiences.

You will remember earlier in the book, we saw that the brain becomes more fully connected when a person makes a mistake and corrects it rather than if they never made one.

WIRED TOO WELL

The big piece of information in Lydia Rose's story is that "things that fire together, wire together." This event was most likely linked with an old neural network defined by feelings of importance that Lydia Rose developed throughout her young life.

Feelings of importance are significant in a child's life, for they stimulate competition that leads to success. But as with all of life, we must find balance and develop wisdom to manage our impulses. When circumstances catch us by surprise and we are prompted to overreact, it is critical that we have learned in our youth to control our emotions. Yet even if we were never trained to exercise self-control and rely upon our reason rather than compulsions as young adults, we need not be victims of our neurotransmitters. We can control how we act, think, and feel. This is where knowing and practicing the executive function skills we studied in chapter 7 come into play.

The study of neuroplasticity has taught us that we are not born with psychosis; it develops through our constant looping of emotional trauma.

Christians have always known by experience that mental health issues can be managed, if not cured, by an infusion of God's forgiveness and obedience to the principles of Scripture. We have seen it over and over again. God gives us the courage and strength to seek the high road and not give in to bitterness, fear, anger, and self-loathing.

The world of mental health has assumed that no emotionally crippled person has the ability to simply reject the negativity and do the right thing. But even before neuroplasticity became a prominent science, one truly notable neuropsychiatrist named Abraham Low taught that if you want good mental health—to be happy and successful—you must, in defiance of your fears and insecurities, choose the preferred path one step at a time, one event at a time.

ABRAHAM LOW

Dr. Abraham Low[90] is one of my favorite neuropsychiatrists. He was surely one of the deepest thinkers, as revealed in his book *Mental Health Through Will-Training*.[91] His whole program was built on walking a person through

90 "Abraham Low." Wikipedia. Retrieved from: en.wikipedia.org/wiki/Abraham_Low

91 Low, Abraham A. (1984). *Mental Health Through Will-Training*. Glencoe, IL: Willett Publishing Co.

making positive choices, rather than being carried along by emotional responses and old brain patterns, which can lead to psychosis. In his book, he shares the methodology employed in a program in which he had classes for people with severe psychosis. His patients were angry, sad, scared, or housebound, with every form of phobia and destructive thinking you can imagine. Rather than viewing themselves as victims of someone else's mistreatment, whether they were a child or adult, he trained them to take responsibility for their own mental health by stepping back from their emotional responses and repatterning their brain by force of will alone. He called it *will-training*.

> **CRISIS**
>
> Never let a crisis be your excuse to hurt yourself.

He taught them that they were not helpless victims of a broken brain or chemical imbalance; it was by their own choosing that they were fearful, anxious, insecure, or any other emotional response that was inconvenient or unpleasant. Through his teaching, they came to see how their choices had destroyed their lives, and it could be through choices that healing would come.

His ideas, born of practical experience, were way ahead of his time (he died in 1954), and he was not highly regarded among his peers. His methods were unorthodox because he did not rely upon psychotherapy, electric shock treatment, or drugs. He chose to train his patients to exercise their wills to change the pattern of their thoughts and behavior. Psychiatrists at that time had no effective way of helping their neurotic patients, so they found a way to electrocute their brains, burning up the memory neurons so patients could not remember the things that troubled them. I know this was still quite popular in the early 1970s because we knew a woman who received this treatment and couldn't remember who we were. She couldn't remember much of anything. Shockingly, it is still practiced today, though on a smaller scale. It is a dreadful treatment.

Understand, I am not suggesting that there is never a need for a patient to be drugged into a mindless stupor. Just as some people must be incarcerated to control their behavior, some mentally disturbed people, who do not respond to will-training may need to have their minds incarcerated in drugs to prevent them from hurting themselves or others. Just know that it is not a "treatment;" it is a suspension of their human nature. All the fine doctors I have listed in this book do use drugs for their patients when they deem it necessary, but I have read enough of their literature to see that it is not their first choice for healing.

You can understand why Low's patents loved him for helping them regain control of their lives through simply making choices. It gave them a sense of dignity and control over their life as a permanent change took place.

He appeared to be practicing neuroplasticity before anyone knew the brain could change itself. He taught those paralyzed by a fear of going outside (agoraphobia) to open their door one inch wider each day, and once the door was open, to take one step further out onto their porch each day. He taught these fearful people to not think about themselves, but to focus on the wind, the warmth of the sun, the birds singing outside, the passing cars, and the feeling of being reborn. This technique now has a name—*mindfulness*—and is a popular method used by neuropsychiatrists to train people how to overcome mental illness.

Dr. Low was teaching his patients to introduce into their brains new feelings of pleasure to replace the old patterns of dread. He taught them to adopt a will to escape the chains that bound them. He used this same concept with those controlled by anger, bitterness, blame, lust, and eating compulsions. He worked from the premise of recreating "feeling memories."

Neurons that house the memory of feelings are powerful. The more of these feeling neurons that connect to our webs of memories, the more extensive our memories. What a shame if Lydia Rose were to introduce into her beautiful brain the damaging attitudes of envy and bitterness. **"A sound heart is the life of the flesh: but envy the rottenness of the bones" (Proverbs 14:30).** We once thought this passage and others like it were figures of speech. We now know that the Creator of the human brain and soul was giving us a scientific warning of the damage we do to our bodies by our stinking thinking.

For years, psychology tried to explain neurosis as a brain disorder. But how did the brain get disordered? You have heard it called chemical imbalance, but what are these chemicals that get imbalanced? They are the neurotransmitters we've talked about. The brain releases its chemicals in response to what we think. They get out of balance when our thinking is destructive. They get back in balance when we think as we were created to think. The Bible tells us what to think: **"Finally, brethren, whatsoever things are true, whatsoever things are honest, whatsoever things are just, whatsoever things are** pure, whatsoever things are lovely, whatsoever things are of good report; if there be any virtue, and if there be any praise, think on these things. Those things, which ye have both learned, and received, and heard, and seen in me, do: and the God of peace shall be with you" (Philippians 4:8–9).

Abraham Low taught his patients to think differently. They *thought* their way out of mental illness. **"For as he thinketh in his heart, so is he..."** **(Proverbs 23:7).**

AN EMOTIONAL CRISIS FOR LYDIA ROSE

As Lydia Rose left Mr. Director's office, she was dumbfounded and almost hysterical. She felt she had turned to wood, so stiff were her movements. Her hands trembled. She could feel her heart pounding in her head, and she was cold and hot at the same time. Her feeling neurons were on fire! She remembered she had just signed a year's lease on a very nice and expensive apartment, so her memory neurons jumped into the fray, and now her fact/numbers/logic neurons concerning money (a very different area of the brain) were all firing along with the feeling neurons. She would have to borrow money from her parents. The thought of her parents caused millions of synapse connections from her youth to fire, and so the new neurons began to wire together with the old. UGH...Lydia Rose just remembered that she had boldly posted on social media about how she was selected for the job from among so many others. She had revealed her dreams of grandeur of bringing herself to the attention of the renowned musician. Recalling the glamorous picture she had posted along with what she had written made

> *"* Of neuroplasticians with solid hard-science credentials, it is Michael Merzenich who has made the most ambitious claims for the field: that brain exercises may be as useful as drugs to treat diseases as severe as schizophrenia; that plasticity exists from the cradle to the grave; and that radical improvements in cognitive functioning—how we learn, think, perceive, and remember— are possible even in the elderly. *"*
>
> Dr. Norman Doidge, *The Brain That Changes Itself*

her legs so weak she had to stop and lean against the wall. She moaned as her brain fired up flashing thoughts of the hundreds of friends, events, and feelings that were now all wired together with this new network of feelings and thoughts. She was overwhelmed with defeat. Her mind began to replay every detail of the dreadful meeting. In this intense moment, Lydia Rose was reinforcing connections all over her brain. Looping is deadly.

The **amygdala** is considered the seat of emotion in the brain and is associated with impulses, aggression, and instinctive behavior. It is **not** where you want your wise decision and thought patterns to originate, but sometimes it happens.

As a point of clarification: Though the amygdala is responsible for the feelings, your emotions are not the source of how you "feel" about things. Your values—the things you deem most worthy in life—do not originate in the amygdala. They originate in the soul, which is not part of the brain. The brain is simply the physical mechanism by which the soul experiences the world and controls the body. The amygdala responds with emotions in accordance with how we value the things we experience.

Due to old connections, Lydia Rose's amygdala was in charge when the hormone **adrenaline** caused her heart to race, her blood pressure to go up, and the air passages in her lungs to contract, making it difficult to breathe. This explains the pounding in her head and cold/hot sensations. **Cortisol** is detrimental when it flows for an extended period. Over time, cortisol washes over the sensitive synapses like glue remover, dissolving the connections of feeling memories. Lydia Rose's brain connections will be damaged by cortisol, breaking apart tiny synapses, one connection at a time. Cortisol is not discriminatory, it harms whatever connections it flows through. The damage to her brain will depend on the length and intensity of her negative feelings.

Just as Abraham Low taught his patients, Lydia Rose can, by sheer willpower, stop her wild feelings, and in doing so she can stop the flow of these powerful brain chemicals. Lydia Rose is not a victim. She is responsible for her actions and for her reactions. Lydia Rose has a choice. She can change her attitude regardless of who she thinks is at fault and the whole experience can be a net positive, sharpening her awareness and better equipping her for life's hard knocks. **"For I say, through the grace given unto me, to every man that is among you, not to think of himself more highly than he ought to think; but to think soberly, according as God hath dealt to every man the measure of faith"** (Romans 12:3).

Biblical principles are in full accord with the science of brain health. But Low's will-training technique, though accurate to the physical and mental structure of the human body, cannot provide a force beyond the will. A relationship with Jesus Christ enables troubled souls to experience immediate victory and long-term healing of the brain.

It is worth saying again: we shape our brains with our thoughts. In his famous poem *Invictus* William Henley wrote, "I am the master of my fate, I am the captain of my soul." He was absolutely right as far as this side of eternity is concerned. We are indeed the captain of our soul. We have a choice to think one way or the other, to be guided by wisdom or by gut responses rooted in pride and self-centeredness. When God finished creation, providing us with body, mind, and spirit, we continued by forming our souls into what we shall be for all eternity. Lydia Rose was building her brain, the foundation of her future. Without the capacity to direct our thoughts and alter our conduct, God could not hold us accountable for our actions. We would be the product of forces over which we have no control, rendering it immoral for God to hold us in judgment.

> **"** His grief he will not forget, but it will not darken his heart, it will teach him wisdom. **"**
>
> J.R.R. Tolkien

Prior to the last 60 years, neuroscientists were unaware that negative emotions like bitterness cause a toxic drip of chemicals across our brain's connectors, eating them away and laying the groundwork for mental disease. Scans clearly show holes developing under the strain of negative emotions—shame, guilt, blame, hurt, bitterness, etc. Truly, **"...the wages of sin is death..."** (Romans 6:23). Bitterness, anger, and shame will bring a slow death. It is the nature of things. It is science—neuroscience.

Lydia Rose will have no memories in the areas that were eroded away. Gone are memories of playing with her daddy, maybe details of her language learning, and her acquired musical skills. With the drip of bitterness, connection after connection disintegrates. And the damage to Lydia Rose's tummy is felt right away. Microorganisms in her gut die off, leaving her immune system weakened.

Lydia Rose could choose to become a better human being, chalking this up as a learning experience. Or she could descend into stinking thinking. Research shows human nature seems to favor the latter, which is why God gave us clear instruction about how to think in Philippians 4:8.

It is situations like this that literally reshape our future mental and physical health. Lydia Rose could have been angry for a little while, but knowing she was at fault, she could have just relaxed. Relaxing takes a conscious effort. Some people are trained as children to exercise self-restraint, and some people have learned by experience that relaxation is a good idea. Some people have learned from God's Word to lay down their own rights and trust him. **"Wherefore, my beloved brethren, let every man be swift to hear, slow to speak, slow to wrath" (James 1:19). "...[L]est any root of bitterness springing up trouble you, and thereby many be defiled" (Hebrews 12:15).** Now we can see that God's instruction was given for our good. The more we learn of the human body and mind, the more we see that God's instructions found in the Bible were given to make us healthier, happier, and more successful. God was the first scientist, the first psychologist, and the inventor of neuroplasticity.

BAD LOOPING

Lydia Rose called her sister to talk about how ridiculous the whole thing was and how mad it had made her. It would have been nice if her sister had been an OLDER sister and willing to tell her that she should have obeyed the rules. Most of us are just sounding boards and not willing to speak truth when our friends need it the most. Over the next few weeks, poor, mad Lydia Rose had to find a job because the lease was binding, but finding a decent paying job proved very difficult, as there were few jobs that needed her talent. Lydia was not aware of the negative vibes—the nasty pheromones (more on these in chapter 18) she gave off to potential employers. They all detected something about her that said "trouble," although they couldn't say what exactly. Mysterious brain chemicals appeared to be leaving trails, or maybe it was the slightly bitter remarks she dropped here and there. Each rejection, each hardship, and each humiliation caused Lydia Rose more anger and stress. Her brain was getting smaller and her gut microbes were beginning to die. She was in a state of what psychiatrists refer to as *looping*. Looping never results in a healthier brain.

Rick Hanson, PhD, neuroscientist and author of *Buddha's Brain,* says,

Harmful behaviors such as complaining, if allowed to loop continually within the brain, will inevitably alter thought processes. Altered thoughts lead to altered beliefs, which in turn lead to a change in behavior. Our brain possesses something called the negativity bias. In simple terms, negativity bias is the brain's tendency to focus more on negative circumstances than positive. Negative stimuli produce more neural activity than do equally intensive positive ones. They are also perceived more easily and quickly.[92]

A BETTER SCENARIO

Suppose Lydia Rose called her mom instead of calling her little sister. Trust me, all moms want to coddle, but thankfully, most moms know that coddling is not always the best. Mom listens, offers suggestions about jobs, and tells her daughter that Dad has money in savings that needs a home (so she is covered financially), and then Mom asks Lydia Rose a few strategic questions: "You researched this school, didn't you? And they have a very high reputation of putting out some of the finest musicians? And Mr. Director has been there leading the charge for how long? And this is where your favorite international orchestra guy volunteers? Then why do you suppose Mr. Director asked you to teach in such an odd way, and why for only two weeks? What did you expect he would do when it was pointed out to you exactly how you were to teach the first two weeks and you then disobeyed? You should have trusted the guy I would have."

Lydia Rose needed to hear alternative pathways of thought. Mother was appealing to her prefrontal cortex (PFC), not her amygdala. She needed to

92 "Science Explains What Happens to Someone's Brain from Complaining Every Day." *Power of Positivity.* Retrieved from: www.powerofpositivity.com/complaining-changes-brain-anxious-depressed-research

be reminded that it was still the school she had highly regarded for many years, and the director was still the most successful man she knew in that field. Her mother's simple questions reminded Lydia Rose that she had been a little too high-handed and proud in her role as "hired" teacher. She was the weakest link in the chain but acted like she was a key member of leadership. Humble pie is not the tastiest treat, but it has an amazing healing effect on the brain. With a clearer brain, Lydia Rose was able to stop looping and spend time charting her course, and with a renewed vision, life didn't seem so bad after all.

Although she cried when her mama talked to her, Lydia knew Mama was correct and loved her above all. Her stomach started feeling better immediately. The cortisol stopped killing synapse connections and creativity returned. **"From whence come wars and fightings among you? come they not hence, even of your lusts that war in your members? But the wisdom that is from above is first pure, then peaceable, gentle, and easy to be intreated, full of mercy and good fruits, without partiality, and without hypocrisy. And the fruit of righteousness is sown in peace of them that make peace" (James 4:1; 3:17–18).**

HARD TRUTH

In our society, being kind is paramount, often to our detriment. Sometimes, those who love us best keep us in bondage by sympathizing with our emotional weakness and disappointments. They share our hurts to the point of becoming bitter and they, too, lose memory neurons. Those compassionate sympathizers are called enablers. Some of the kindest people I have ever known are enablers. As you can see from our two possible scenarios, Lydia Rose needed the hard truth and an understanding shoulder to cry on. Being an enabler is being the shoulder only. Lydia Rose and the rest of us need to see truth from someone with a PFC not blinded by a flush of caustic chemicals.

A mother can be an enabler by protecting her child from anyone who might cause emotional stress or by covering for her child's explosive behavior with excuses. If the sensitive (flight type) or angry (fight type) child grows up and marries someone who continues the enabling, it can lead to a lifetime of defeat, fear, uncertainties, laziness, or bitterness. Enablers think of themselves as more giving, forgiving, and loving, but every psychologist on earth agrees: it is never a positive thing to have a sweet, gracious, loving enabler on your team. Truth needs to take the lead, even when it hurts. For Lydia Rose's sake, Mama was willing to risk the relationship by not agreeing with her daughter's perspective. Truth is easy to uncover when the facts can be viewed apart from emotional hurt. Lydia Rose's mother led her down a path with questions that guided her to discover the truth and see circumstances from a larger perspective.

> **BLAME**
>
> If you blame someone else for your problems, then you are powerless to change anything.

If you have a loved one who falls into discouraged sadness, an ugly rage, or is in a state of bitterness, blaming others for messing up their life, don't coddle or talk away their pain. Worse, don't blame someone else for hurting them or not understanding them. You are setting them up for depression, violence, and/or a life of sickness and mental decline. Don't confuse blind loyalty with good counsel. Make sure your judgment is objective and based on truth. If you are as emotionally invested as they are, find a third party with a fully developed PFC who can be objective.

THE LITTLE BLACK BOX

The gut/brain connection also plays a major role in this downward spiral, as stress often causes extreme gut issues. Things can get complicated, for most of the immune system is found in the gut. Autoimmune diseases can take hold when a person's immune system is compromised by long-term stress or bitterness. The neurotransmitter serotonin is produced in the gut and is necessary for maintaining a positive outlook on life. Without a healthy gut, a person will be depressed. Spirals of hopelessness follow. As we've learned, nothing good comes out of bad feelings.

We now know that our brains are not little black boxes that are fixed from birth. They are wide-open windows, drinking in sunshine or storm. Mr. Director did not cause Lydia Rose's decline. He was only a minor player in her life.

LOOPING DESTROYS

It seems that a major default position for us humans is to blame someone else. It is a way to save our self-respect.

It takes conscious awareness to break the habit of blaming others.

Scientists have a name for it: **backward rationalization**. They document the fact that most people respond impulsively to negative experiences, and it is usually ugly. Being carried along by our impulses and acting or speaking inappropriately leads to frustration. So the brain comes to our aid by creating explanations for our bad responses and physically rewrites these imagined histories into our memories through a process called memory reconsolidation. This comes about because we want to believe that we are the good guy and the one we despise is the bad guy, so our brain simply rewrites the script. This process leaves most of our negative emotions unresolved and ready to be triggered at any time. These negative memories release constant, toxic neurotransmitters as our brain keeps trying to justify why we behaved inappropriately. This repeated reliving of the experience—*looping*—destroys neuronal memories. A well-known phrase says it simply: "Sometimes memory is downright creative."

Looping is destructive when it is self-justifying, but it is equally destructive when we have good reason to be hurt or resentful. The destruction caused by looping negative feelings is the same whether we are at fault or not. Looping one's hatred for terrorists who cause great harm still destroys brain cells.

Time is not a healer unless you choose healing. This is why the old style of counsel and therapy that relied on rumination and dragging up old hurts to talk about them often results in failure. Professional counseling that is built on who-done-it is looping. Counseling to see a clearer path and understanding how you can move forward is not looping. It is seeking to find a path out of turmoil or defeat.

Science has discovered what God knew all along. The Bible says we should be **"Forbearing one another, and forgiving one another, if any man have a quarrel against any: even as Christ forgave you, so also do ye"** (Colossians 3:13). And it says that if we would see long life and good days, we should not return the evil done to us: **"Not rendering evil for evil, or railing for railing: but contrariwise blessing; knowing that ye are thereunto called, that ye should inherit a blessing. For he that will love life, and see good days, let him refrain his tongue from evil, and his lips that they speak no guile"** (1 Peter 3:9-10). Everything the Bible commands us to do is for our good.

THE PREFRONTAL CORTEX, AGAIN...

Weaknesses in the prefrontal cortex (PFC) don't just magically disappear at the age of 25. We have all met adults who seem to be stuck in emotional immaturity, and they still hold on to offenses from their youth. If you could go back and review their developing years, you would discover that in their youth, they hated or resented someone, damaging their PFC. Instead of their youth being spent building their brain, it was spent in looping—breaking down their brain. That is WHY, for your child's sake, it is critical that you do not show bitterness or contempt for your ex—or anyone, for that matter.

Responding to the hard blows of life with shock, anger, hurt, bitterness, fear, or grief is understandable and normal. It is what makes us human instead of robots. Without some anxiety, some hesitation, some grief, we would be an empty container of neurons. It takes fear and caution to keep us from passing the car in front of us on a blind hill.

In 1921, the most extensive study on longevity was commenced. Over 1,500 children were chosen to be lifelong subjects. One of the major goals of the research was to see who would live the longest and why. After more than 90 years, researchers began the monumental task of organizing and analyzing the information and investigating the lives of those who lived to be centurions. What was their secret? I am sure the original researchers, who were long since in their graves, would have loved to have seen the results. The data they gathered revealed the startling conclusion that it was not the lack of tragedy and hardship, not genetics nor diet that caused longevity, it was a life of balance. That means you should worry enough to cause you to be on time, show up for work, and avoid the other woman because you don't want to lose your wife. Don't take foolish chances, and surely don't waste your life looping negative thoughts. Don't allow yourself to be swallowed up in anxiety, fear, bitterness, or anger. Basically, our ongoing reactions to the difficulties of life help shape us into the humans we will become.

One chief lifestyle that was noted among those who lived the longest and happiest was that they did not live carelessly. They considered the consequences of all their actions and weighed the long-term benefits of one option over another.

The data revealed that even in childhood, the character traits of conscientiousness, prudence, consistency, and dependability were manifested by those who would come to live the longest. The book *The Longevity Project*

> **DIMINISH**
>
> Our brains physically diminish in size as we stew, rage, and mope. Bigger is better. Choose happiness, forgiveness and gratefulness.

by Howard S. Friedman, PhD and Leslie R. Martin, PhD, says, "We have worried that perhaps nothing at all would foretell long life. This first finding demonstrated to us that a trait from childhood could be relevant to the health many years later."[93]

Training our children to learn from the hard things of life rather than being broken or hurt by them is essential to being a good parent. Every negative experience, from falling down and skinning a knee to painful events like losing a loved one, should be viewed as an opportunity to always focus on the good. Guiding children's thoughts so they do not loop is critical to their emotional stability.

A car wreck that brings long-term pain or sorrow can cause some people to question God, especially if the accident was caused by a selfish drunk or texter. This unthankful lack of trust directed against God brings looping that chews away neuronal connection after neuronal connection. A husband taking up with a young new girlfriend can bring a good wife to her knees in bitterness. If she allows her brain to loop, reliving words of anger, creating scenarios of revenge and other negative imaginations, it can damage her brain so that every relationship in her life will be tainted. For every one of us there will be occasions to feel slighted, abused, used, misunderstood, hurt, angered, crushed in sorrow, or sold out. If you so choose, all these occasions can be opportunities to let go, get up and smile, and then choose to forgive and start again.

FINDING BALANCE

True happiness and well-being come from a balanced release of neurotransmitters. We need to exercise judgment when judgment is appropriate. Otherwise, we frustrate our own soul. Likewise, we must show mercy and offer forgiveness when it is appropriate. Achieving enlightened balance produces lasting joy. This is amazing! The brain and body are exactly as you would expect, having been created by God, for the brain rewards righteousness and judges evil.

93 Friedman, Howard S., and Martin, Leslie R. (2012). *The Longevity Project*. New York: Penguin Group.

A disproportionate amount of any one chemical is not good for the brain and will erode the brain's normal function, damaging or destroying synapses, slowly killing the brain. Neuroplasticity shows how our moods, emotional and mental states, lifestyle, recreation, eating and sleeping habits, etc. affect the synapses and wire or unwire the brain.

Researchers now know that, in large part, we become what we feed our brain. Our thoughts (that's a scary thought), moods, reactions, as well as what we watch and read—all are grooving our brains. Equally important are our physical activities—singing, camping, swimming, laughing, playing, digging in the dirt, and more. These activities light up parts of the brain that are connected to our intellect, so when we get "back to nature," we are forming connections that make us smarter.

Who we know, love, or hate is also shaping and reshaping our brain. Who we spend time with determines how we feel or think on any given matter because we share a neural connection by means of mirror neurons. How we choose to respond to truth determines whether we are weak or strong, creative or dull, gifted or lacking, happy or angry, and a myriad of other things that make us who we are. The psalmist said, **"Blessed [blessed and happy] is the man that walketh not in the counsel of the ungodly, nor standeth in the way of sinners, nor sitteth in the seat of the scornful" (Psalm 1:1)**.

I CHARGE YOU

Do research with your children on the various neurotransmitters. Talk with them about things they do that could be harming their developing brain. Read Bible verses on the subjects of joy, thankfulness, and rejoicing. Have them make large cards that display the Bible verses, as well as a list of traits they want to practice in their lives. At bedtime, have the children share one thing for which they are thankful.

"And be not conformed to this world: but be ye transformed by the renewing of your mind, that ye may prove what is that good, and acceptable, and perfect, will of God" (Romans 12:2).

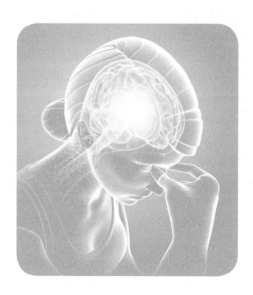

Concussions

You can't see the damge due to a concussion but the wounds are often debilitating both physically and emotionally.

Concussions are the most common and a mild form of brain injury. Sudden movement causes the brain to rapidly move back and forth, bouncing around inside the sharp skull. This damage can cause physical and chemical changes in the brain, which may appear as a negative change of personality.

Car wrecks, playing sports, and taking a fall can all cause concussions. They can even occur without the person realizing it. Headaches, memory loss, brain fog, delayed responses, dizziness, fatigue, and sensitivity to light or sound are just a handful of symptoms that a concussion victim may encounter. A child might have hit their head and cried a short time the day before; then the next day, they appear dazed, listless, tired, cranky, and are unsteady or possibly refuse to eat. They may be sleepy or just lack the normal spunk. The brain is hurting and struggling to perform. As in any part of the body, when there is an injury, a time of healing without emotional or physical challenge is needed.

Children playing sports can suffer repeated concussions over time and the cumulative effects can be costly. Dr. Gregory Hawryluk, a neurosurgeon and concussion specialist at University of Utah Health says, "We're starting to learn that perhaps these seemingly minor blows to the head, when they're accumulative, can lead to depression and behavior change."[1]

The best thing to do for concussions is to avoid activities that are likely to cause them. The next best thing is to wear head protection while participating in such activities. See a doctor if you suspect there has been an injury to the brain.

A LOOK INSIDE MY BRAIN

By Karen Sargent (the editor and proofreader of this book)

Last summer I was in a head-on car accident and got a concussion. Two years before that I was rear-ended and got a concussion. About ten years prior to that one, I was walking in the woods with my youngest child when a big walnut fell out of a tree and landed squarely on the top of my head. That's three concussions. There may have been another one around age eight or so when I was hit by a flying hammer, but back then we got bumps and bruises and didn't think anything of it. And then there was high school soccer where "heading" the ball was a practiced skill. We now know this causes mini-concussions.

So I've learned a bit about mild traumatic brain injuries (TBIs), and it's fascinating. If I could go back and do life over, I would study some kind of brain something. But since my problems now include learning difficulties and memory problems, I'm settling for what I can learn through my own experiences. Editing this book has been a real education.

While I've had a few concussions, the last one seemed to push me into a new realm of symptoms that wouldn't quit. Concussions are cumulative, meaning the damages build on one another over a lifetime. For post-menopausal women (which I am), the symptoms are more likely to last longer and turn into what's called post-concussion syndrome. I wasn't thinking much about this for the first few months after the accident; I just figured it was taking a little longer to get back to normal. Thank you, old age. But when six months went by and I noticed I was getting more emotional instead of less, was still having trouble focusing on work for more than an hour or so, and

1 https://healthcare.utah.edu/healthfeed/postings/2016/11/concussion.php

after two rounds of EMDR therapy my overall anxiety wasn't getting better, I decided to look for help.

It was at this point that I began reading through this book. One of an editor's jobs is fact checking, so I read every link and every reference, listened to every YouTube video, and even added some of my own research.

I spent the next three months reading extensively about brain mapping, synapses, pruning, neurotransmitters, and how we either help or hinder the process in developing brains. I read the story of Dr. Paul Bach-y-Rita's father, who suffered a massive stroke that damaged 97% of his brain stem, yet was able to re-learn enough to lead a normal life, even returning to his former profession of teaching. This story gave me hope that I could recover from my "mild" brain trauma.

By the time I finished working on the book, more than ten months had passed since the accident. My family doctor had mentioned neurofeedback, and I was ready to try what I thought would be my last-ditch effort.

But let me explain something. I have never been a "feel-y" person. I'm not emotional or in touch with my feelings and I don't dwell on them. I definitely don't talk about them. I'm very practical and the opposite of introspective. I can't (or won't) describe what I'm feeling. I hardly acknowledge it. I typically stuff it all down inside and just keep going.

So when post-concussion symptoms like emotional instability, anger, depression, anxiety, inability to focus, and trouble finding words and following conversations persisted, I thought there was something wrong with me. Not like I was a victim of this, but that there was something I was doing wrong to feel like this. I thought it must be my fault in some way, like I wasn't trying hard enough. I thought I must be a hypochondriac or imagining it or being a drama queen or that things were just a coincidence. I thought this for many months. Everything was my fault.

Two weeks ago I met with a psychologist who specializes in neurofeedback. He recommended I have a qEEG (quantitative electroencephalogram) so we could see exactly what electrical signals were going on in my brain. We would be able to see where there was not enough activity and where there was too much of each kind of brainwave. The woman who performed the test (Megan) did not know my story or what had happened to me. She didn't know any of my symptoms. She was just doing the test and would interpret the results with no bias.

KAREN'S BRAIN TEST RESULTS

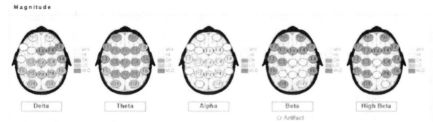

Eyes Opened Magnitude

Magnitude is the available power within a particular frequency at each site. It averages amplitude over time. The magnitude values are based on a statistical sample in addition to being cross validated with other major databases. The measures will indicate potential problems that may be present when either high or low (Niedermeyer and DaSilva, 2005).

Based on the information above and the full clinical report, some irregular brain wave activity is present within certain bands in different lobes of the brain.

Looking at the **Beta** patterns that are present, this individual may have symptoms such as emotional instability, negative rumination, excess worry (anticipatory), anxiety and/or hypervigilance.

The **Alpha** activity indicates possible challenges with chronic anxiety, sleep deficit, depression, low energy, and possible hypothyroid or inflammation issues (however, further testing would need to be administered in order to determine).

The **Theta** patterns suggest that there may be some difficulty with anxiety, OCD and/or rumination, learning difficulties, short term and sequential memory issues that generates poor attention.

Lastly, **Delta** patterns suggest challenges with short term and sequential memory, learning difficulties, language processing, and TBI.

When we met with Megan to go over the test results, she had diagrams of my brain activity. She showed me where areas of my brain were either not communicating enough or screaming at each other. The pictures showed where there was so much activity it's like a traffic jam. She said it appeared I had a TBI that affected my temporal lobes (she was correct). She described my symptoms to a T.

None of this was a surprise to me; after all, I'd been living with everything she described for many months. But there were a few things she said that surprised me. She mentioned that I probably had some sensory issues, like being hyper sensitive to light, sound, or smells. I definitely do, but I had convinced myself that I was just over-reacting. Scented garbage bags and lipstick are two things I can't stand the smell of.

While she was talking, all I could think was "It's not my fault." I'd spent months thinking I was the problem, I was the over-sensitive one, I was the one who just needed to get a grip.

I felt profound relief. The weight of all my self-accusation was suddenly lifted and I knew that none of this was my fault. A scientific test had proved that my symptoms were very real, and the relief was overwhelming. (Funny note: one of my symptoms is feeling overwhelmed. Ha!)

I've asked Ben many times in the last year if he thought I was just imagining the symptoms or dwelling on them too much or making things up. I was open to that possibility. He always assured me it was not me, not my fault, that my brain had been damaged and we were going to keep looking until we found something that could help.

Now that we know exactly how my brain is malfunctioning, neurofeedback can help fix it by rewiring what has been damaged. As long as we are alive, there is hope that the brain can heal.

"Thou wilt keep him in perfect peace, whose mind is stayed on thee: because he trusteth in thee" (Isaiah 26:3).

PARIETAL LOBE

Sensory input integration, spatial orientation, language process

FRONTAL LOBE

Cognition, decision making, problem solving, personality, emotional regulation

OCCIPITAL LOBE

Visual processing and recognition, reading

TEMPORAL LOBE

Auditory processing, long-term memory, visual memory, musical awareness

CEREBELLUM

Motion process, equilibrium, coordination, balance

BRAIN STEM

Regulates automatic body functions (breathing, heart rate, digestion, etc.)

For fascinating and telling images of how injuries and substance abuse damage the brain, visit Dr. Daniel Amen's website gallery at:

www.amenclinics.com/healthy-vs-unhealthy

Mindfulness

CHAPTER 16

*Neuroplasticity has taught us that thankfulness
is a key characteristic of a healthy soul.*

CHEMICALS AND HORMONES

Neurotransmitters are chemicals and hormones that control our feelings and moods. We control their release by how we respond and think. We unknowingly release harsh neurotransmitters when we allow our minds to be caught up in stinking thinking, brooding, stress, anger, fear, and any other negative thought or emotion. These chemicals wash over our synapses, reinforcing our moods, and can, over time, bring destruction to our whole body. We briefly discussed this in chapter nine. Remember my good friend who was losing weight due to stress? She was allowing her stinking thinking to destroy the natural flora in her gut. Remember my mama's wink when my dad yelled? She was taking control of her responses and in doing so, was causing happy neurotransmitters to be released, which helped reinforce her positive mood. She didn't allow herself, or us, to become stressed by my dad's lack of self-control.

It works like this: the sensation of pain, a thought, an odor, admiring a beautiful picture, seeing a loved one, a touch, throwing a ball, stress, or a physical task all cause an instant chemical release. Different chemicals are released depending upon our response to the stimuli, reinforcing our chosen mood or feelings. The speed at which these mechanisms function is unfathomable.

Neuroplasticity has allowed us to understand that there is more to humans than just a chemical response in our brains. Our mind can instantly dictate which neurotransmitters our brain releases. We are not victims of a broken body or mind. We can choose to wink, as my mother did. We can choose to forgive. We can choose to relax. We can decide to stop our stinking thinking and force our thought pattern into a productive stream. When our mind chooses a peaceful direction, the neurotransmitters that are released reflect that choice and reinforce the mood, making our peace and joy stronger. Of course, the opposite is also true. If we dwell on the negative, the neurotransmitters reinforce our mood. Once this knowledge became scientifically accepted, researchers rushed in to create an applied science to teach people how to use their minds to gain control over their mental weaknesses: anger, bitterness, depression, or any hurting emotional state. The new science is called *mindfulness*.

When you learn to control your responses, you control your neurotransmitters and you will be healthier, happier, and more successful. Employing mindfulness not only helps us achieve a stable emotional state, it has application in every area of life, allowing us to be more productive and creative. Here is a personal example of how using this knowledge can help you become an international winner.

INTERNATIONAL KNIFE THROWERS HALL OF FAME

Neurotransmitters are released in response to something that affects us emotionally. We are geared to respond to circumstances we perceive as either good or bad. The brain response is automatic, but we are not at the mercy of automatic responses. We have the power to control how we respond—thus, we control the function of our brain. Practicing mindfulness is how we control our neurotransmitters.

Mindfulness helped my husband, Mike, win the 2018 Knife Throwing World Championship sponsored by the International Knife Throwers Hall of

Fame. The skills that control the force of his throw, hand-eye coordination, judgment of the distance from target, elevation of the throw, and left/right alignment are developed and coordinated in the brain. You hear a lot about muscle memory, but the memory is in the brain, not the muscles.

My 73-year-old husband drove to Austin, Texas to compete in the 2018 knife and tomahawk world championships. There were over 65 men and women from around the world competing. For knife and tomahawk throwers, this event is equal to the Olympics. It was a furious, three-day competition with each contender having to throw many distances. It required strength as well as accuracy. After the first day, many of the throwers complained of their arms hurting. The last time Mike won a world championship was five years ago when he was 67 years old. At 73, he was well beyond the competitive years. Let's face it, like all old players, he was a has-been. He did not expect to win, though he still hoped to, and no one else expected it either. But there is this thing called mindfulness that he had recently learned as he listened to me retell all I was discovering about the brain.

After the first day, he had identified at least five men whom he considered to be better throwers than he. This caused him concern, releasing a neurotransmitter called **noradrenaline**, which works with **adrenaline** to produce the "fight or flight" response. He could have brooded on this problem and focused on self-doubt and the chemicals would have continued to flow. The overflow would have had a negative impact on his brain-muscle coordination. But for every negative "unhappy" chemical there is a positive "happy" one. His recent knowledge of neuroplasticity enabled him to focus and, as the throwers say, "get in the zone."

He dared hope for a third-place win. His previous wins caused the chemical **serotonin,** which imparts feelings of importance to be released. It is serotonin that often provokes young people to think they know it all and to be offended when challenged. Mike also had the neurotransmitter **dopamine,** which brings positive feelings with achievement flowing in his brain. The feel-good hormones were giving him confidence that this might be the year an old man beats all the young guys. This feeling of confidence aided him in focusing and gave him strength that comes from the brain patterning developed during previous wins.

For months before the throw, he had been making knives at his coal-fired forge, beating the hot metal into shape, seeking the perfect throwing knife. The physical labor had developed an old man into a strong, muscular athlete. He felt his knives were the best he'd ever had. He had been careful in what he had been eating and how much. He had faithfully taken his micronutrients. He knew he was as ready as he could be. Knowing all this gave him confidence.

All day he watched thrower after thrower perform. They were good—better than ever—and they seemed to be in the zone. His brain's hormones would ebb and flow, sometimes leaving him feeling excited to believe he stood a chance, and other times making him feel that he was not up to the task. Hormonal **endorphins** gave him a brief euphoria that masked physical pain, so even though his body was weary, he didn't feel anything but excited energy.

Mike tells how in practice before the tournament he had been applying the things he had learned about neuroplasticity. When it came time to throw, he was able to enter into a state of mindfulness, shutting out all thoughts of former victories or losses, ignoring his surroundings, not considering how he was doing or what others were doing in the lanes on either side of him. He was able to purge his mind of all negativity and form a connection with the knife and target that brought all the powers of his brain to bear on a single throw, one at a time, for the sixty throws that make up a contest. He was so focused that when he finished, he didn't have the slightest notion as to how he had performed. He couldn't even remember his throws—hits and misses. And yet he was in a total state of relaxation.

When they tallied up the results, it was too close to call without a recount. Finally, the name of the third place winner was announced; not him. The runner-up was called out...not him. Without him being aware, his momentary hope caused the release of a positive brain chemical, but in that same instant a negative chemical was released, bringing with it a sudden recall of the missed bullseye on the fourth round of throws. Finally, after a long pause, the name Michael Pearl was called as the winner of the 2018 Knife Throwing World Championship. The neurotransmitter **glutamate**—the most common excitatory neurotransmitter—exploded in his brain, followed closely by **serotonin,** which flows in when you feel important. **Dopamine** gives you a great feeling when you achieve what you desire, and it was ever present for this event. His elation was over-the-top and his grin couldn't be wiped from his face. A world champion at 73 years old with knives he had forged with his own hands! What a victory!

It has been several months since the big win, but the old guy is talking of how he is going to take the cup in Canada next year. Maybe he will. His neurotransmitters are still hard at work, based on the confidence and pleasure of thirteen previous world championship wins. All of this physical, mental, and emotional activity has built an amazing number of neuronal connections.

But knife throwing is good for more than the fun of the sport. It has also increased his mind power. His IQ is higher. He could have stayed home and watched blacksmiths on some YouTube channel and dreamed, thinking he was too old to start beating out metal in the blistering, August heat. But the act of forging the knives, practicing, and then competing created millions more neural connections because it involved body, soul, and brain. And the win...well, he almost had the brain of a teenager for a few weeks. He was so giddy, I thought his prefrontal cortex had been eaten. But not so—it had grown!

PROVEN SCIENCE

I could have left out the personal knife throwing story, but I am proud of my old man. He has been my favorite subject now for over fifty years. Just knowing he still "can" releases powerful neurotransmitters in my brain and likely causes me to function a little better as I write this book.

Researchers know that working as a team creates neural connections that identify with one another. Married couples who spend a lifetime together begin to think alike because their brains share so many "like" connections. We can be sitting on the couch and one of us can say a single word and both of us start laughing. There is a memory in our hippocampus that only we share, and it is too funny and too wonderful. There are millions of happenings that only our brains have created, and this bond is eternal. I wish I could give it as a gift to everyone.

MINDFULNESS

An increasing number of psychiatrists, not content with the limits of the traditional approach to therapy, are utilizing brain scans to note the changes that take place with our thinking patterns. In counseling, they have noted the growing number of people who simply do not have the brain pathways to feel empathy, thankfulness, mercy, love, forgiveness, and the like.

Why are some people devoid of what are considered normal human traits? Today's world, filled with noisy music, leaves the soul rattled instead of exalted. Raunchy TV corrupts the spirit. Filthy porn gives birth to a demon so demanding that eventually, a man will lust after his own flesh and blood. These things that steal away our basic human dignity are the common trend today. With the lack of family structure and community life—and most importantly, the lack of clean, clear Bible teaching—children are predestined to emotional failure. This is evident even to those who know not God, for it is manifest in lives filled with rage, bitterness, selfishness, unthankfulness, and unnatural nurture. **"...[T]he wages of sin is death..." (Romans 6:23).** That was once a passage we understood only by faith; today, it reflects the findings of neuro-researchers. People's brains are failing to develop the pathways for these normal human qualities, and humanity suffers.

Over time, the more astute psychiatrists came to recognize that no amount of counseling or drugs would "fix" people who lacked these basic qualities of life. The brain—the organ itself—would need remapping, hence the science of mindfulness was born. Researchers used the basic concept of neuroplasticity: "things that fire together, wire together." Doctors developed programs such as group meditation and therapy to help people see the value of gratitude, awe, joy, etc. When sharing in a group setting, mirror neurons are awakened to increase the depth of understanding.

Now there is an entire school of study on the subject of mindfulness. Dr. Daniel Siegel is a clinical professor of psychiatry at UCLA School of Medicine and the executive director of the Mindsight Institute. He is the authority on the subject of mindfulness.

The following is a list of courses he has designed:

- The Science of Happiness
- The Science of Joy
- The Science of Thankfulness
- The Science of Compassion
- The Science of Gratitude
- The Science of Kindness
- The Science of Empathy
- The Science of Love
- The Science of Awe
- The Science of Touch
- The Science of Heroism
- The Science of a Meaningful Life

> *" Thoughts lead on to purposes; purposes go forth in action; actions form habits; habits decide character; character fixes our destiny. "*
>
> Tryon Edwards

- The Science of Cooperation
- The Science of Spirituality
- The Science of Play
- The Science of Inspiration
- The Science of Forgiveness

This list of classes could be the outline for a series of Bible-based sermons. Amazing! Science has discovered that the human soul functions best when it is holy.

LEARNED OR NOT LEARNED

The thing that shocked the professional community was that these disorders (not showing empathy, mercy, love, forgiveness, etc.) are not the result of a brain condition inherent from birth. The lack of these qualities is the result of the culture in which people were raised—lack of training and lack of wholesome parental example. Remember mirror neurons—monkey see, monkey do. You can't bring forth sweet water from a bitter well. It is with good reason the Bible says, **"Train up a child in the way he should go: and when he is old, he will not depart from it" (Proverbs 22:6)**. As children, their brains failed to develop pathways of forgiveness, thankfulness, empathy, etc., which are essential to emotional and social normalcy. As small children, they were never trained to relate to others and to circumstances with patience and thankfulness. They grew up feeling entitled and assuming things should go their way. Their brains were hard-wired to be takers rather than makers, to be served rather than serve, to complain and demand rather than be thankful.

Stop and think about your child. Does he get irritated when he doesn't get exactly what he wants to eat, when he wants it? Does she get mad when she doesn't get a phone? Do your children enjoy helping you clean the house? Do they automatically respond in thankfulness when something good happens? Are you training your children in the science of mindfulness or the science of selfishness? Are you, as a parent, setting up your children to excel or to fail? Real success starts with thankfulness. This is science, and it is in full agreement with God. Why wouldn't it be? All truth is God's truth.

SIMPLE INSTRUCTIONS

Instructors teach mindfulness by helping students focus on the present. It is the mind filled with the moment. Mindfulness exercises begin by focusing on the mat you are sitting on, your breathing, the breeze stirring your hair or garments, sunlight and shadows, colors, sounds, smells—the experiences of your five senses. The experience then advances to meditating on one of the bulleted topics listed above, perhaps thankfulness. Many people have never experienced thankfulness, and their brains are undeveloped in that area.

As they sit there in a group setting, focusing on reasons to be thankful and actually feeling thankful, their brains develop new pathways, making thankfulness more likely in the future. The old hymn is scientifically sound when it says, "Count your many blessings, name them one by one."

> **OUTLOOK**
>
> The real winners in life are the people who look at every situation with an expectation that they can make it work or make it better.

You can understand why I say that I was stunned when I first started studying the secular science of mindfulness. It was as if it were taken straight from God's blueprint for our thought life as found in **Philippians 4:6–9: "Be careful for nothing** [don't worry or stress about anything]**; but in every thing by prayer and supplication with thanksgiving let your requests be made known unto God [don't pray with whining, but in thanksgiving that God is there standing with you]. And the peace of God, which passeth all understanding, shall keep your hearts and minds through Christ Jesus."**

This is a promise that if you practice keeping your mind full of thanksgiving, God himself will keep your brain.

"Finally, brethren, whatsoever things are true, whatsoever things are honest, whatsoever things are just, whatsoever things are pure, whatsoever things are lovely, whatsoever things are of good report; if there be any virtue, and if there be any praise, think on these things. Those things, which ye have both learned, and received, and heard, and seen in me, do: and the God of peace shall be with you."

Compare God's list to the list from mindfulness teachers. God says we will obtain peace by thinking on these things.

Psychiatrists and psychologists know that what is taught in mindfulness is foundational to the continuance of humanity. Those personal, human traits are what make nations and individuals survive and thrive. Marriage is built on mindfulness. **"[T]hink on these things."**

INTRINSIC VALUE

Mindfulness would not have become so popular if it did not offer something of intrinsic value. In our modern society, no one stops to smell the roses, and if they do, they are taking a selfie to document the occasion. The noise of life is constant from the moment we wake until the moment we restlessly fall asleep at night. This modern lifestyle is new to the human experience and is unhealthy to the brain, body, and soul. It is especially detrimental to the developing brains of our children. We have forgotten the pleasures of earlier times when we just sat and held our babies, sniffing their heads, thinking of nothing but their warm bodies and sweet odor. We are too busy looking at our phones to truly notice the emptiness in our souls. All this noise of life is costly. Doctors refer to this as the brain becoming "overstimulated." The modern lifestyle actually causes brain damage.

Humanity has come full circle. We have **"...sought out many inventions"** (**Ecclesiastes 7:29**), fought wars, created spaceships, and allowed higher education to "prove" there is no God, but all this doing is leaving a huge hole in our souls. Walking in peace and joy is not hard, complicated, or weird. It is a simple human ability—as consistent as a mathematical equation. If we are thankful, our spirit is full of joy. If our spirit is joyful, then our brain is not under attack.

CHILDBIRTH

Mindfulness has many applications. Childbirth is one that touched my life. In the 1950s, and even into the '60s, twilight births were standard. Doctors assumed it was better for the mother to be drugged into a twilight state when giving birth with no regard to the fact that the infant was also heavily drugged. There were so many horror stories of blue, unresponsive babies that it petrified the younger generation into going 100% natural. I was one of those freaked-out young mothers. In the 1960s, young hippie girls turned to a natural childbirth method that relied upon eliminating the stress and pain through focusing the mind. Several books were written from various perspectives. I stumbled across one and studied it as if it were pure gold.

THE CANDLE

"A candle that burns twice as bright, burns half as long" could aptly apply to our vagus nerve (the connector between the brain and the gut).

Forme it was. It taught that all you needed to do was learn to control your body with your mind and you would have a painless birth. The book said in order to gain complete control of your body, you would need to practice about 20 minutes a day during the last five months of your pregnancy. The expectant mother was advised to lie in a recliner and tighten up every muscle in her body and then start relaxing one toe at a time, moving up until you could relax any muscle in the body while everything else was tight. The hardest part was learning to relax your face muscles when some other area of your body was still tense. Once this skill was acquired, you would be able to visualize yourself in your favorite place of relaxation. My favorite imaginary place was lying on an air mattress in the ocean, rocking back and forth on the gentle waves, feeling the warm sunrays upon my face. As soon as I got to my visual place, I began the relaxation of each body part until finally, my face was relaxed. I practiced this visualization for months until I almost felt it hypnotized me. Did it work? It certainly did. I am a small woman and had big babies quickly and with complete ease. Two of my labors felt like they were less than 15 minutes. I am sure I was in labor much longer, but I was not conscious of any discomfort.

In 1 Timothy 2:15, we read a promise concerning childbirth: **"Notwithstanding she shall be saved in childbearing, if they continue in faith and charity and holiness with sobriety."** Saved in child bearing IF **they** (both the wife and husband) **continue** (a process throughout pregnancy) in three things: (1) **faith**—**"...that [God] is a rewarder of them that diligently seek him"** (Hebrews 11:6); (2) **charity**—benevolent giving of themselves to others; and (3) **holiness with sobriety**—righteousness of heart with a seriousness regarding God and childbirth. This promise is in accord with the laws of nature as God created the body-mind connection. The body is influenced by what we think. This principle will work in limited measure for anyone who can achieve the right state of mind. But God provides his children with a direct path through grace, to be sober, holy, and filled with faith and charity.

Thankfully, God responds to a little faith as if it were mountain-moving faith. At the time of my first pregnancy, I don't remember having a remarkable amount of faith or holiness, but God has a way of filling in the gaps with grace. My helping hand came in the form of a long, boring, poorly written book on childbirth. I read it as if it were the best thing ever penned. It taught me the art of mindfulness.

For those of you who are waiting to know where you can buy the book, you wait in vain. I can't remember the title or the author, and I am sure it is long since out of print. It was paperback, about two inches thick, and had few pictures. You would need to search by the year (1966–69). It might still be available from used book suppliers. From that background sprang the Lamaze method and the Bradley method of childbirth. I think the book was closer to the Bradley style. Before neuroplasticity revealed the effectiveness of mindfulness in pain control, through practical experience midwives were teaching pain control techniques that would in time be validated by science.

PAIN CONTROL CROSSOVER

For years after my first child was born, when other situations arose where I should have been in great pain, I seemed to have a high tolerance for pain. I thought it was just a product of my DNA. After my discovery of neuroplasticity, I came to realize that the training I did in preparation for my first birth had wired my brain to be able to ignore the pain. Pain requires neurons just like thought, memory, and movement. Pain is in the brain! Your mind can control your thoughts, your mind can control your movements, and your mind can control your pain!

If you suffer from pain due to monthly periods, don't take pain relievers that will damage your liver! Learn how to turn that pain circuit off using mindfulness. If you have headaches or muscle pain, learn how to use mindfulness to create pathways in your brain to subdue that pain. Of course, it is easy to say but it takes practice, which depends upon a strong desire. And of course, there will be times when your flesh jumps ship and you head to the medicine cabinet. I have. Don't be discouraged. Practice makes wide brain roads, and it takes time to get them well established! Try, try again.

PHANTOM PAIN

The proof that pain is in the brain is revealed in something called phantom pain. When someone has had an arm or leg amputated, they may still suffer pain in the limb that is not there. My daddy had his leg amputated, yet he was always fussing at me to scratch his toes. Several times a day, I would have to show him his stump so he would stop complaining. The feeling of the missing leg being there (and being itchy) was so powerful that he found it hard to believe his leg was gone. Amputation can also cause the brain to rewire in a haywire fashion, redirecting the pain to a lip, ear, or any area of the body. There are many fascinating studies you can read on the internet that show what researchers are doing with mirrors (or other mind-bending tools) to trick the victim's brain into stopping the pain. These studies make it clear how pain starts in the brain and how you can take charge and redirect it. Just understanding how the brain works in creating the sensations of pain will help you learn to control its effects on you.

Using mindfulness to take control of your pain, fear, anxiety, lack of sleep, anger, or any troubling issue is just smart. Read all about it! The internet is full of new research, just waiting for you to explore. Life gives back what you put into it. Put in a lot, and you get a lot out of it, sit around surfing social media, and you will get...well, not much.

I CHARGE YOU

Mindfulness is allowing the mind as well as the body to rest. The vagus nerve (pictured in the Brain-Gut Connection chapter) is a superhighway connecting all major body organs. Too much of any stimulus exhausts this major nerve. Too much sorrow, work, stress, and/or even trying to maintain a "get 'er done" lifestyle can lead to extreme health issues. People think entertainment is relaxing, but maintaining a vibrant vagus nerve (which serves the brain too) requires a time of total mindfulness.

"In every thing give thanks: for this is the will of God in Christ Jesus concerning you" (1 Thessalonians 5:18).

Homeschooling

CHAPTER 17

Neuroplasticity has taught us that homeschooling is most successful when done while singing, working, and sharing life.

KNOWLEDGE BEGETS KNOWLEDGE

A child's brain is the most alive when he has learned something—something he thinks is difficult and creative—and he knows others have taken note when he has mastered this feat.

When a beloved adult shows interest in what a child values, then the child feels what he has done or is doing is really important. These victories start on the most basic level; a baby learning to walk, a toddler putting up two fingers and saying two, and a four-year-old climbing on bars to prove how strong he is. But without someone special to share that moment, it is not so special for the child's soul or for his brain. This is an important point of neuroplasticity that can be seen on scans: good feelings tied with learning more than doubles the connectivity in the brain.

PUT YOUR EYEBALLS ON ME

A mother wrote a short note on Facebook that caught my attention. She said her four-year-old son was playing on the climbing bars while at the park when he shouted to his mom, "Put your eyeballs on me!"

Mother thought it was amusing. "I have my eyeballs on you."

"NO," he responded demandingly. "I can't see your eyeballs on me. Take your sunglasses off."

The need in a child's soul and his brain is for you—his parent—to look at him.

This evening I went to the park to swing. Swinging hard 50 times back and forth is good exercise for a senior citizen and it helps loosen up my neck, so I go most every day for a 5- to 10-minute swing. As I rushed to the swing set, I passed a dad sitting on the park bench. He was looking intently at his cell phone. There on the climbing bars was his four-year-old son, climbing, while constantly looking over his shoulder at his dad to see if his "eyeballs were on him." I could see disappointment in the little guy's face as his shoulders slouched and he sat still. My grandma instinct got the better of me: I hit the lazy dad violently over the head with my fanny-pack and told him to get his sorry self over there to play with his son.

Actually, I didn't really hit him, but I did think it real hard in case he had the gift of telepathy. Instead, I gently and sweetly said like the nice old lady that I am, "Your son would like his play a whole lot better if you climbed with him." The dad didn't take offense, nor did he take the obvious hint, mumbling, "Yeah, well . . .", and down his eyeballs went to the phone as if glued to the screen.

That guy is one dumb dad and someday he will be so sorry.

Face-time to a child is like sunshine to a flower or rain to parched soil. Jesus said, **"The light of the body is the eye: therefore when thine eye is single, thy whole body also is full of light . . ."** (Luke 11:34).

We tend to look at our treasure, and **"...where your treasure is, there will your heart be also"** (Matthew 6:21).

There is nothing like eyeballs on you to make you feel that someone is taking notice. It takes applause from those that matter to shift that tiny learning experience into other areas of the brain, thus building a network of knowledge.

What does this have to do with homeschooling? It is the chief ingredient to life, learning, and relationships. Success in any field of learning is opening the brain to many spheres of knowledge. Knowledge is built on knowledge, and knowledge obtained through shared emotional bonds opens many areas of the brain due to the huge neurotransmitter release. This is the principle of neuroplasticity in action: things that fire together, wire together. As we learned with Lydia Rose, this can work for good or evil.

A large part of education is remembering information. But there is more to it than retention of facts. There is reason and logic, imagination and creativity, but it is all contingent upon remembering. Millions of neurons may be involved in a single memory. One thought awakens many related thoughts, a giant network of experience and stored knowledge. If a small part of the brain is destroyed, the memories that are destroyed can usually be recovered from other places in the brain.

In a brief recap of our chapter about neurons, we learned how each neuron had thousands of tiny, cord-like tentacles sticking out of it. For every action or thought, those tentacles reach out toward other tentacles from nearby neurons. At the end of each tentacle is a synapse, which is like a hand that is always trying to grasp a hand from another synapse to form a communication link. To maintain long-term connections, synapses have to be glued together with a chemical. This chemical is called a neurotransmitter: "neuro" = brain and "transmitter" = information passer. There are over 100 neurotransmitters, but only about seven are major players we have discussed in this book.

MAJOR PLAYERS IN MEMORY

Neurotransmitters play a major role in our ability to learn and remember. The key to all learning is having the correct neurotransmitter flow when it is needed. Learning anything in a pleasant environment allows positive chemicals to wash over the newly established synapse connections. This glue-like neurotransmitter helps the memory stay connected.

The brain has many compartments and each compartment has a different function. The more areas of the brain involved in learning, the more accessible the memory. Remember the word picture example of learning the capitals of each state that we talked about in chapter 6? When a child is trying to learn a new word in a pleasant environment, that knowledge is stored in many happy places in the brain. If Mother is lightly scratching the child's head, serotonin (one of the positive neurotransmitters) is released. If there is music, a cool breeze, a pleasant odor of cooking, the sound of laughter in the background, the promise of good times to come later in the day, and the word being taught is linked to something the child enjoys, the memory finds lodging in many compartments of the brain.

The neurotransmitters do the same thing in your brain. If you are reading this book while lying on the couch totally relaxed, having just eaten a meal, your brain will be more open to receive the information than if you are trying to read while listening to your children fight in the background. The environment will affect the release of the neurotransmitters, which, of course, determines how much is caught. If you want to double the learning for your effort, then listening to the audio version of this book as you read along causes you to really tap into several areas of the brain. This means you will remember much more and have easier recall. We went over the specifics of this in chapter 4. This is how I study. The neurotransmitters seal the deal!

In homeschooling our children, environment is an important aspect to consider. If negative neurotransmitters are released in abundance, then some of those newly connected synapses will be washed with a corrosive chemical, cortisol, which will result in lost connections. This means there will be little or no memory or successful learning experience. Memory and learning are thwarted by negative emotions, tension, feelings of inadequacy, or fear of failure.

REVEALING SILLY QUIRKS

A middle-aged woman sat across the table from me, laughing at her silly quirk of hating to have someone stand over her shoulder while she worked on her computer. Even though she was laughing, I could detect that what she was saying wasn't funny to her. Some long-ago memories invoked a shiver, even as she told on herself. I asked, knowing the answer: "Were you home-schooled?" Another shiver. "Yes, and I was terrible. I just couldn't learn. I clammed up and my brain wouldn't work. It wasn't until I was an adult that I could really think straight. I have to say, I have vivid memories of my mom standing over me, tense and disappointed at my stupidity. I can still hear her saying in a suppressed, angry tone, 'Joanna, you are just not trying. Why don't you focus? You will sit here until you learn that word, and I don't care if it takes all day long!'"

GLUE OR CORROSION

It is not homeschooling that makes learning difficult, it is the teacher. I had a number of callous schoolteachers who invoked the same dread in me, but I didn't really like them, so the horror of disappointing them wasn't as detrimental to my psyche as it would have been if they had been someone whom I looked to for emotional support and love. This piece of information is significant. The inability to please the person you love can wreak havoc on the release of neurotransmitters—the very neurotransmitters that glue pieces of information together.

Basically, emotions decide our intellect. If schooling takes place in a tense environment, the next time the child sits down to do the exact same lesson, she will not remember what she was taught the previous day. In those sorry conditions, even Einstein would have struggled to learn to spell his name. In order to learn anything, synapses have to make contact and the contact needs to have the sealing chemicals to act as a bonding agent.

THE FAVORITE UNCLE

Many parents have said to me over the years, "I have obeyed the Bible doing what it says concerning training up my children in the way they should go but they still departed. God's Word is not true because I know I did my part." Blaming God is a scary game to play and it is really foolish. When you understand how the brain works, you can see where the problems arose.

The amazing ability of the brain can work in the child's favor or disfavor depending on who stimulates the release of neurotransmitters in their brain. Is there someone in your child's life that you dearly love, but hope with all your heart that your own son will not be like they are? Wish away, but wishes don't come true unless you carefully consider how your son's brain is being wired. It doesn't take physical touch to fire his brain. It takes someone who will take the time to look your child in the eye and show real interest in what your son is doing.

Let me introduce you to a kid named Larry. It doesn't matter what strikes Larry's imagination. It might be captured by fishing, playing cards, magic tricks, or face painting. Contrary to what is practiced today, it is not money spent, exciting adventures, or fun recreation that causes neurotransmitters to be released, it is the eyeball-time that a favorite uncle or friend spends intently listening to Larry talk that opens his very soul. When this happens, his brain will have millions of synapse connections that are being bathed with positive neurotransmitters released through the joy of success and being truly valued as a person. **This is the missing element in good parenting. It is the missing element in good homeschooling. It is the most molding, brain grooving force in a child's life.** We have always called it capturing a child's heart, but brain scans show us it is the brain that is captured. One section connects with another and then another until the whole brain is alight from the power of time invested, interest shared, and values established. If you are not investing in these things with your child, you can't compete with the favorite uncle, friend, or possibly even the negative influence that will take the time.

Neuroplasticity has a power of its own. The brain is alive with competition. Every synapse is vying for connections. The positive neurotransmitters are pouring over each fragile connection, gluing them into a lasting bond. If you are a mother, then God has called you to watch, pray, and be diligent and relentless in pouring your focus into your child's brain and, just as important, keep out the crud.

CRUD

Susy is eight years old and wants to learn martial arts. Susy's mama does her research and finds the best teacher available. The teacher has five stars from all the parents. Susy's teacher is not a pervert or even a bad man, so that is not the issue we are discussing. He is not crud per se, but he is the one who will unintentionally fill her brain with crud. Keep in mind, this example could be in art, music, or any other area of learning.

Young Susy really likes her teacher and for good reason. The teacher has learned that if he can win the child over to himself, then that child will work twice as hard in order to please him. The teacher knows that the child's success means his success. Susy loves seeing that she is really learning a skill. She loves the feeling of achievement. Mostly, what she loves is the fact that her teacher's eyeballs are always focused on her with an intense interest. He spends time discussing each of her moves and growing abilities. All these "feeling" areas of her brain release a flood of neurotransmitters which, as you have already learned, act like glue, reinforcing the synapse connections to wire her brain. Every time she improves, she hears him say, "Well done," which fires and wires her brain. In time, Susy's brain will become a web with connections in most every part. Because the teacher is part of all these areas of her brain, the mere mention of his name will cause her whole brain to light up. Why? You got it: things that fire together, wire together. Similar to electricity, if you turn on one switch that is wired to all the circuits, then all the lights come on. Over time, her teacher will laugh and talk about movies he has seen, and parts of the child's brain will record this attitude toward the things that are unclean, all the while changing her brain structure. His dislikes will become a part of little Susy's brain wiring, and her values will be shaped as surely as her brain is being wired. It is not her love for the teacher, but rather her intense love for her success and the attention that he gives her that causes Susy's brain to link to everything he values. All your prayers and Bible study to help her grow to be more like Jesus will not shape her brain as effectively as this one teacher. He has given her personal success and in doing so, opened an area of her brain that is wired to the many other areas that are touching her soul. Again, things that fire together, wire together and these wires are establishing brain patterns that are lasting.

Being a parent is not easy. It is a full-time, "I've got my eyeballs on you" job. Ask God for wisdom, seek counsel, and always be there when your child is being trained by an outside teacher so it can be your voice she hears calling out, "Great job!"

EXECUTIVE FUNCTION TRAINING

As we have learned in the stories of Lydia Rose and with Mike winning the knife throwing contest, we as adults can take control over our neurotransmitters. Learning how to control our neurotransmitters is an important part of a child's developing brain. As we discussed in chapter 6, this is what developing executive function is all about.

The classic marshmallow experiment revealed to us how some children have developed a measure of self-control, self-restraint, confidence, leadership, and other traits seen in successful, happy people. Through positive learning experiences, Mama is teaching more than facts; she is teaching how to overcome disappointment with determination, failure with success, laziness with hard work, and sadness with joy. Mama is the best person to instill confidence and success because her child means more to her than he does to anyone else. Learning to control your executive function does more for a person than allowing him to be self-disciplined; it gives him the control of his neurotransmitters which means he is the captain of his ship. He can control his moods (as well as his actions) and increase his brain power by releasing the chemicals that seal the synapse connections. Learning to control your neurotransmitters is the first step to never being addicted to anything because you have the brain power of self-control. This is an amazing facet that has been learned through the science of neuroplasticity.

GOOD NEUROTRANSMITTERS

It is not a lack of neurons at birth that makes a child less capable of learning or lacking in confidence, it is the environment in which learning occurs. All long-term learning must have positive neurotransmitters to glue the synapses together. And those neurotransmitters are released by our positive emotions, thoughts, and actions.

Homeschooling should be done in a spirit of joy, thanksgiving, fun, and participation. It should involve music, fellowship, group reading, group projects, and physical movement. Many areas of the brain should be stimulated at the same time so that the thing being learned will be stored in many areas of the brain. All night long that child's brain is reprogramming what he experienced the day before and cementing his synapse connections. Even in his sleep, he is rejoicing with his mom at the fun things that he learned, and his brain is growing. He is growing a BIG brain. This is real learning! This is what makes a brilliant brain and a stable human being. This is beautiful! If I were a young mom learning these things, I would stand up and yell, "YES! My children will have this and I will lead the way! My eyeballs will not be glued to my phone and my friends will not take my time; I will be glued to my children. I will help them gain self-control, self-reliance and self-esteem through many successful endeavors."

When you take a child by the hand and lead her to this success, you have her heart as well as her mind. You don't have to threaten her into performing at a certain level. You don't have to yell to get her to do her schooling or chores. She will love the person who makes her feel good about herself. She will cherish her time with you. She will have millions of brain connections that are all tied to you.

This is child training, this is real education, and this is life more abundant. If I had another life...I would do it all again.

In 1865, William Ross Wallace penned a poem praising motherhood that touched the heart of the entire world because everyone intuitively knew what he wrote is true. He wrote, "The hand that rocks the cradle is the hand that rules the world." I would add to his famous statement: "The mama who keeps her eyeballs on her children will raise up intelligent, confident, successful, and happy adults."

I CHARGE YOU

Purpose to keep your eyeballs on your children and not glued to a screen. Decide you will help them gain self-control, self-reliance and self-esteem through many successful endeavors. Likewise, decide you will never again get irritated at your child for having trouble learning. Make a list of things that can be done while your child is trying to learn. You could let them sit close to you. You could have soft music playing in the background. You could use their finger to trace a new word on their arm. You could smile and show them how proud you are that they are yours. This is the moment that you will choose to be a delight to your children, and it is the moment their brains will start drinking in everything.

"And thou shalt teach them diligently unto thy children, and shalt talk of them when thou sittest in thine house, and when thou walkest by the way, and when thou liest down, and when thou risest up" (Deuteronomy 6:7).

Addiction and the Brain

CHAPTER 18

Neuroplasticity has taught us that we are what we choose to be.

(Since my husband, Mike, has already done extensive study on the science of addiction and produced a video series on it, I asked him to write this chapter.)

By Michael Pearl

Neuroscience has blown the cover off the mystery of the addicted brain and has documented the process by which we become addicted and, thankfully, the process by which we can reverse course, change our brain, and overcome our most compelling compulsions.

Addiction is a brain problem. The hunger in the brain provokes the body to crave. Through various types of scans, scientists can actually see addictions at work in the brain and observe compulsive behavior. Researchers can read the map of your brain and know more about you than you know about yourself. Your neural pathways are a chronicle of your thoughts as surely as GPS tracking reveals where you have traveled, where you shopped, and what entertainment you sought. Past use is found to be a predictor of future behavior—barring an overriding choice of the will. The history of your thoughts and experiences is recorded in your brain map, and one day it will be opened as we stand before God. If science continues to advance, in a short time your most secret thoughts might be transparent.

The actual physiology of addiction is a natural, God-given function of the brain that is essential to our productivity and survival. When a person finds a bargain at a certain store, his brain marks the occasion with a flood of dopamine. This aids him in remembering the location and the experience, assuring he will return for more. When we successfully triumph in a difficulty, dopamine rewards us with a shot of happy chemicals, causing us to want to repeat the experience—thus, increasing our productivity. Those who achieve the greatest success and happiness in life are addicted to productivity, justice, mercy, love, grace, and faith. To some people, these virtues feel better than selfish indulgence, procrastination, or foolish wasting of time. It comes down to what the soul values. One man's pleasure is another man's shame.

The Apostle Paul made mention of the house of Stephanas saying, **"...they have addicted themselves to the ministry of the saints" (1 Corinthians 16:15)**. The house of Stephanas found it to be a very rewarding and pleasurable experience to lend assistance and encouragement. They were caring-and-sharing addicts, high on helping others.

I know an ex-druggie who finds great joy in giving the gospel to most everyone she meets. No one is ever offended because her pleasure in giving them the "good news" is so obvious, they are drawn into the moment. All addictions, good or bad, come about through the history of our choices. We want more of the thing that pleases us, and through repeated participation, the brain comes to depend upon it for a chemical release.

WHAT WE VALUE

There is a definite correlation between the amount of dopamine the brain releases and the degree of pleasure you experience. But, it is an oversimplification to define dopamine as just a pleasure-inducing chemical. Dopamine causes us to desire and seek out certain behaviors that we feel are satisfying. It provides encouragement to anticipate and do the things we value. It can cause us to rise to a high calling, invent something to help mankind, be the best parent in the world, seek a substance-based high, or repeat a destructive habit like texting, gambling, eating sweets, or using pornography. All addictions occur when a chemical or a repeated behavior gives us pleasure, and the brain marks the experience with an overabundance of dopamine. The dopamine conditions the brain to want more of the same—thus, addiction.

These chemicals do not determine what we desire and pursue, they merely assist and motivate us to do what is important to us. Dopamine doesn't tell us what to like, it just documents the things that give us pleasure and motivates us to seek more of the same. It is common for the addict to hate his or her addiction while craving more of it. The soul and spirit hate it while the brain and body crave it. **"For the flesh lusteth against the Spirit, and the Spirit against the flesh: and these are contrary the one to the other: so that ye cannot do the things that ye would" (Galatians 5:17).**

TWO KINDS OF ADDICTION

1. Substance Addiction

There are two kinds of addiction. The most obvious one is *substance addiction*. This occurs in response to chemical messengers introduced into the body, such as plant cannabinoids, barbiturates, THC, or CBD. These chemicals can be called "brain medicine" because that is the area of the body they affect. When you ingest them or inhale their vapor, you're allowing compounds produced by the plant to enter your body, travel through your bloodstream, and enter your brain. Once they arrive, these plant-derived compounds can influence brain activity by interacting with receptors on neurons. The artificial chemicals produce a rush of happy/motivational chemicals far in excess of what the body is capable of handling. Animal studies have demonstrated that CBD directly activates multiple serotonin receptors in the brain. Cannabinoids also indirectly increase the dopamine level in the brain by restraining that which inhibits dopamine neurons.

When we first take in a foreign chemical—nicotine, cocaine, alcohol, or heroin—the brain increases the output of feel-good, motivational chemicals. But the brain is designed to seek a balance between happy and sad chemicals, so when it realizes it is always going to be fed external chemicals, it slows down the production of its own. This is true of any substance that alters the mood and makes us "feel" better.

As with all medicines, these plant-derived chemicals can be helpful substances that can be used to bring healing or relief due to many types of medical issues. I know a little girl who was diagnosed with cancer when she was a baby. The harsh chemicals of chemo ravished her tiny body, leaving it in a state of high inflammation, which caused high levels of cortisol to be continually produced in her brain. This greatly complicated her health. CBD was used to change the chemical overload and thus, reduce the inflammation in her brain, allowing her body to heal. We are thankful for such interventions when they are needed, but when they are used recreationally, they can become an addiction.

Today over 50 percent of Americans are on some mind- or mood-altering substance and most of it is legal. In any given church, from horse-and-buggy Amish to staunch Baptist or devout Catholic, you will find a high percentage of the ladies and some of the men using some sort of brain-altering, feel-good stimulant.

2. Behavioral Addiction

The second kind of addiction is *behavioral*. Behavioral addiction, sometimes called "process addiction," refers to a person becoming addicted to certain activities through a process of repeated participation. These might include such things as shopping, playing video games, pornography, exercise, gambling, eating, and even texting. Whether the addiction is to a substance or an activity, studies have shown that both activate the part of the brain called the reward center, triggering the release of a cocktail of chemicals that give you a temporary buzz. A rush of pleasure from these chemicals can be just as compelling as a chemical substance dependency.

Happy motivational chemicals and sad stress chemicals are both essential for our well-being. When engaged in any activity that is dangerous—driving, climbing, diving, etc.—our brain responds to our concern with a release of cortisol, norepinephrine, or adrenaline. Likewise, when filling out our income tax papers, being interviewed for a new job, or walking in a dangerous neighborhood at night, the brain sharpens our responses with these so-called danger chemicals. A bipolar condition is a wide swing from too many happy chemicals to too many sad chemicals. A person in perpetual depression is overrun with sad chemicals and not producing enough serotonin, oxytocin, or dopamine.

The chemical imbalance happens like this: by our addictions, we artificially trick the brain into producing more dopamine. A brain high and a drug high are virtually the same. Dopamine has been called the morphine of the brain. The brain actually ceases to be able to maintain equilibrium without the excessive amount of stimulus input. Our actions, thoughts, and desires actually change the brain's chemical balance just like hard drugs do.

Unhealthy or wasteful process addictions are far more common than we recognize. It is easy to see them in others, but not so much in ourselves; especially when they do not rise to the level of requiring therapeutic intervention. Some addictions never do more than rob us of precious time, money, and energy that could be used productively elsewhere. Other addictions take a toll on our health—physical, mental, and emotional. All addictions have a negative impact on relationships to varying degrees.

When a person addicted to shopping is denied her crutch, she suffers a big "downer." So the shopper is highly motivated to continue her addictive behavior to maintain a level of "normalcy." The addicted shopper will praise herself for finding the best deals and buying smart. The overabundance of dopamine deceives her into believing a lie. Amazingly, as the pleasure subsides, the memory of the desired effect and the need to recreate it persist— grow stronger, even. The debt she incurs, piles of unused items, and the anxiety of being out of control cause self-loathing. Furthermore, the brain— which has adapted to the high level of dopamine—is now producing way too much cortisol as it seeks to bring balance. Depression hovers over her like a bad smell. This scenario is the same for any behavioral addiction, which can include the oddest things: running, golfing, fishing, gambling, social media, TV, etc. The development of all behavioral addictions is basically the same, except for one: pornography.

THE BRAIN ON PORN

Brain scans clearly reveal that porn makes a bigger footprint on neural pathways than any other behavioral addiction. It barrels down through the brain, laying claim to all the neurons it can capture, adhering as many neurons as it can to the porn neurons, leaving the lights out in parts of the brain. In time, the brain begins to shrink. Porn makes a path so wide and deep that other thoughts wandering across the porn path are diverted to explore the porn memory, thus, stealing brain cells. Porn is such an aggressive competitor that it snips away many normal working parts of the brain that allow our body to function, including the ability to have actual sex with a real partner. We receive many letters from women complaining of their husband's total inability to become aroused. This is only one area of the brain that gets stolen by the use of porn.

BRAIN DETERIORATION

Research in the United States has shown that 66% of men and 41% of women consume pornography on a monthly basis. That is two out of every three men. An estimated 50% of all internet traffic is related to sex.

A study reported in *JAMA Psychiatry* explains, "Men who report watching a lot of pornography tend to have less volume and activity in regions of the brain linked to rewards and motivation."

According to Simone Kühn of the Max Planck Institute for Human Development in Berlin, "We found that the volume of the so-called striatum, a brain region that has been associated with reward processing and motivated behavior was smaller the more pornography consumption the participants reported." Moreover, "the connection between the striatum and prefrontal cortex, which is the outer layer of the brain associated with behavior and decision making, worsened with increased porn watching." [94]

In other words, the part of the brain that is stimulated by pornography begins to lose connection with the part of the brain that makes moral judgments and decisions. The porn addict's brain loses touch with the reasoning, cautioning, and moral judgment part of the brain. In short, the porn addict will take risks that the non-porn-user would not. With the suppression of caution chemicals, the porn user's brain is a runaway subway car, with no thought of the danger. Another study showed "the volume of gray matter in a person's right caudate (in the forebrain) was negatively correlated with how much porn they view. In other words, high-volume porn viewers had less gray matter." [95]

If porn does this to an adult man's brain, what is it doing to our children's developing brains?

---

94 Seaman, Andrew M. (2014). "Porn may be messing with your head." *Reuters*. Retrieved from: www.reuters.com/article/us-porn-brain-changes-idINKBN0E82BK20140528

95 Hess, Peter. (2017). "This Is Your Brain on Porn." *Inverse*. Retrieved from: www.inverse.com/article/31799-brain-on-porn-erotica-neuroscience

THE CHILDREN OF SODOM

Throughout history, sailors have gone to faraway ports and discovered sensual sights far beyond those available in their villages and towns back home. But there has never been a time in human history when debauchery has been so affordable and able to be accessed anonymously by every person on the planet—including little children—as it is today. Ancient Rome became a place of depravity, like Sodom and Gomorrah 2,000 years earlier, but a night in Sodom or Rome would not have yielded one tenth of the eroticism offered to the homeschool boy while his parents sit in the other room reading their Bibles. Imagine a sci-fi world where the ten-year-old opens a door in the back of his wardrobe and steps into ancient Sodom or the debaucheries of Rome. Now multiply that by 100 and that is what is happening to hundreds of millions of children around the world. In the hands of a child, any digital tool that can access the Web is a direct doorway to damnation.

> **THE GREAT THIEF**
>
> Porn creates wide roadways in the brain which can grow to become so pervasive, it will interrupt all daily thought life. Its presence steals creativity, intellectual pursuit, and even natural sentiment toward your children. No man ever thinks he will become a victim to his use of porn.

We have seen many families raise eight or ten of the best kids on the planet. Their home is the perfect incubator for the growth of a godly, moral human being. But one of their children accidentally comes across porn or has it introduced to him by another kid, and he grows up to be a broken, lost soul. Years of prayer and careful training can be flushed down the toilet by that first viewing of pornography. Heroin holds an insignificant draw compared to pornography in the eyes of a 13-year-old boy.

THE ESSENCE OF EVIL

The porn of the internet is saturated with homosexuality, groupings of every combination, bestiality with every size animal (often killing the small ones with brutal sexual force, cruelty, and violence), and many porn sites specialize in the misuse of children and even babies. Blood, feces, and death linked to eroticism are all available with a single, accidental click. Men who view porn gravitate toward more and more aggressive sexual expression by virtue of the brain's need for higher levels of dopamine. The evidence of excessive porn use is clearly seen by the number of young children now being trafficked for sex. According to *USA Today*, <u>adults purchase children for sex at least 2.5 million times a year in the United States</u>. Arnie Allen of the National Center for Missing and Exploited Children reports that "The only way not to find this in any American city is simply not to look for it." And what man would do such a thing as rape a little child? Journalist Tim Swarens, who spent more than a year investigating the sex trade in America writes, "They could be your co-worker, doctor, pastor or spouse."[96] Otherwise ordinary men from all walks of life have destroyed their natural repulsion for the great evil of hurting a child in such a filthy manner.

God says in **Romans 1:26–28, "For this cause God gave them up unto vile affections: for even their women did change the natural use into that which is against nature; and likewise also the men, leaving the natural use of the woman, burned in their lust one toward another; men with men working that which is unseemly, and receiving in themselves that recompence of their error which was meet. And even as they did not like to retain God in their knowledge, God gave them over to a reprobate mind, to do those things which are not convenient." And in Mark 9:42: "And whosoever shall offend one of these little ones that believe in me, it is better for him that a millstone were hanged about his neck, and he were cast into the sea."**

"For God shall bring every work into judgment, with every secret thing, whether it be good, or whether it be evil" (Ecclesiastes 12:14).

A child who happened to open such an internet site would have his brain forever engraved with this repulsive evil. The stronger the shock, the more the brain retains the image. A young, growing brain that has a diet of this debauchery will not only develop incorrectly, it will shrink, and large areas will be left unused for brilliance, creativity, and normal body functions.

This is not a topic we can ignore, according to Amy O'Leary of *The New York Times*: "Jeanne Sager, a blogger, assumed it was safe to let her 6-year-old daughter, Jillian, watch 'My Little Pony' videos. But when she left the room for a moment, she heard something that didn't sound anything like a cartoon... Her daughter had stumbled upon a graphic video by clicking on a related

96 (2019). "The Essence of Evil: Sex with Children Has Become Big Business in America." *Health Impact News*. Retrieved from: healthimpactnews.com/2019/the-essence-of-evil-sex-with-children-has-become-big-business-in-america/

link listed to the right of the video player. It is one of the most common complaints of parents who discover that their children have been exposed to sexually explicit material online—that a few clicks on YouTube can land a child in unexpected territory, like a subgenre of pornography where popular cartoon characters, like Batman or Mario Bros., are dubbed over with alternate soundtracks and editing to show the characters engaging in explicit acts."[97]

If I were the devil, I would cause all parents to be careless or maybe just believe that their kid surely wouldn't look at porn. I would make sure all parents gave their children access to social media, video games, Netflix, Amazon, cable, cell phones, and the internet. And I would make parents encourage the kids to play as much as they wanted because I know that with that many baited hooks in the water, there would be no way they could escape.

Christian parents find it hard to believe that their lovely, well-trained, innocent children would seek out pornography, but they do. Research has revealed that 93% of boys and 62% of girls are exposed to internet pornography before the age of 18. Only one out of every 14 boys escapes exposure to porn. That is about the rate of families living outside the digital net. Pornography has almost reached 100% saturation. The average age a child first sees internet pornography is 11. What is your 9-year-old doing on the cell phone?

According to the booklet *Navigating Pornography Addiction: A Guide for Parents*,[98] 83% of boys have seen group sex on the internet and as many as 67% of children admit to clearing their internet browsing history to hide their online activity. A full 79% of accidental exposures to internet porn take place in the home.

Psychologies Magazine said in 2010 (almost ten years ago), "81% of 14-16-year-olds regularly access explicit photographs and footage on their home computers."[99] Surely, the percentage is higher now. Brains are being stolen and souls are being snatched while we assume our children are safe.

97 O'Leary, Amy. (May 9, 2012). "So How Do We Talk about This?" *The New York Times*. Retrieved from: www.nytimes.com/2012/05/10/garden/when-children-see-internet-pornography.html

98 Therapy Associates, PC. (2013). *Navigating Pornography Addiction: A Guide for Parents*. Retrieved from: static1.squarespace.com/static/5146816de4b04055d30999b8/t/569a9724d8af100e850 72fb2/1452971860313/Navigating+Pornography+Addiction-A+Guide+for+Parents.pdf

99 Payne, Ursula C. "The reality of online pornography and its effect on our Church and young people." Retrieved from: slideplayer.com/slide/10236919/

BRAIN DISORDERS

Sociologists and psychiatrists, scientists and neuroplasticity experts see and know how the brain is being drastically changed, and they are worried, as you should be. This is a self-inflicted disease for which there is a terrible price to pay. These science gurus are not concerned with the moral implications, it is the damage being done to the brains of chronic pornography users that alarms researchers. We are living through a great cultural paradigm shift in human nature, more dramatic than anything the world has ever experienced.

"Repeated consumption of porn causes the brain to literally rewire itself. It triggers the brain to pump out chemicals and form new nerve pathways, leading to profound and lasting changes in the brain."[100]

"Believe it or not, studies show that those who consume pornography more frequently have brains that are less connected, less active, and even smaller in some areas."[101]

If pornographic use is a deadly disease, we are experiencing a pandemic, with more than nine out of every ten children being infected. That is a spiritual holocaust. If Satan missed destroying their bodies in the womb (or shortly thereafter), today he gleefully kills their souls with pornography.

If I were a prophet, I would predict a great weeping of regret coming from millions of Christian homes. "If only..." I hear them cry. "If only!"

A child can recover from cancer. No one ever completely recovers from pornography. But through God's grace a few learn to be daily overcomers. That is what God offers and neuroplasticity explains.

KNOWLEDGE

As compelling as it may be, you are not enslaved to the brain you have created. Your child's brain can also be recovered. The first step of recovery is knowledge—you simply need to know what porn does to the brain. It should scare you! You will have to look far and wide among highly educated scientists to find one that is willing to indulge in porn. They have seen the horror

100 (2017). "How Porn Changes the Brain." *Fight the New Drug*. Retrieved from: fightthenewdrug. org/how-porn-changes-the-brain

101 (2018). "How Watching Porn Can Mess with Your Brain—Literally." *Fight the New Drug*. Retrieved from: fightthenewdrug.org/how-porn-can-mess-with-your-brain

of what it does to the brain, and even though they may not love God, they do love themselves enough to totally avoid porn. Knowledge is the first step to gaining control. People who have smoked cigarettes all their lives and have tried to stop a thousand times will suddenly find it easy to quit when they have cancer and know they will survive only if they never smoke another cigarette. Knowledge is a motivator.

REJECT

The second step to recovery is to stop feeding the beast, and over time the beast will get weaker and weaker. Neuroplasticity has revealed it takes about 45 to 50 days to eliminate a bad habit and replace it with a new, good one. Reject all actions and thoughts that take you down the porn pathway. Don't view and don't allow your thought pattern to feed the beast. Most people say, "I just can't help what I think." But you can. My wife, Debi, tells the story of our mutual friend:

"I had a friend (a lady) who was a porn addict since she was a young child. After becoming a Christian, she was often full of guilt because her brain kept going back to the porn filth. I only saw her every few months. One day, I was in her area of the state, so I drove by to visit. We were walking in a mall, talking, when she suddenly yelled very loudly, 'Oh Lord Jesus, cleanse me!' Well, I was somewhat startled, or maybe you could say I was shocked to the point that I totally lost track of what we were discussing, but she continued our conversation as if nothing had just happened. What? She had just yelled so loudly that everyone in the whole mall must have thought a bomb was going off. I guess she noticed the flabbergasted expression on my face because she grabbed my arm and laughed, 'Oh, I forgot, you didn't know. I started doing that about a month ago. Every time porn comes to my mind, I let 'er go. A friend told me that in about 50 days, I will have a clean brain. I only have 23 more days to go. He calls it, 'Blow your horn! 50 days 'til Jubilee.' I am willing to do anything it takes to rid my mind of that filth.' This was long before the science of neuroplasticity. People who want to be free find a way. I still know the lady after 45 years and she has remained free."

Science reveals that with 45 to 50 days of repetition, a new habit starts feeling normal and old patterns lose their compelling drive. Researchers call the recovery plan "Reject and Replace." Reject the cravings and replace them with new habits that are productive. For young men who have lost their ability to have a normal sexual response to their wives, this is good news. Reject and replace. Tell your wife your problem so she will understand, rather than pile on the emotional drama when you try and fail. There are many testimonials of recovery concerning this particular issue that can be found on the internet.

Remember, if you have been a porn addict, your brain is deeply grooved with broad neural paths, all leading to porn. You must **reject** that mental journey and overwrite the pathways with new thoughts, new ideas, and new actions. Addiction loves a vacuum. You must intentionally fill the vacuum with the thoughts and experiences you want to be grooved into your brain so there is no room for the addiction.

REPLACE

Researchers suggest "replacing" by stepping into a very challenging new field of learning. Music lessons five nights a week with hours of practice, judo, ballet, listening to the Bible being read by Alexander Scourby as you exercise, or do what the ex-addict that I wrote of earlier does: take up witnessing to every person you meet. Fill your life with so much new information and activity that every neuron in your brain is being challenged. Remember, "Blow your horn! Fifty days 'til Jubilee."

THE FINAL ANALYSIS

Addiction begins in the mind, so the cure must also begin with the mind. We can't expect there to be a physical cure for a mind/soul problem. In the final analysis, we do what we want to do, and no scientists or therapists can turn a screw in our brain or give us a drug that will cure an addiction that resulted from a thousand choices.

You cannot become addicted to something you do not value—with the exception of the unwanted administering of a narcotic. And even then, it has been shown that many people hospitalized and put on opioids for weeks are able to walk out of the hospital and never want to continue the drug. Their frame of reference did not allow them to find emotional pleasure in the sensations of opioids. The drug dulled their awful pain, but it did not fill an emotional vacuum. We can only become addicted to things that please us. Our addictions reflect our values—our heart.

Addiction is not an autonomous power unto itself. It does not control the soul or the body. If addiction were strictly physical, a person who has gone without drugs for two years would not seek reinforcement in NA meetings, where the focus is on the state of mind, not the body.

Addiction is a psychological symptom, a way to deal with a difficult emotional state.

Proof that addiction is a state of mind—a worldview, a reflection of one's self-image—is seen in the fact that people delivered from addiction for years can experience an event that stirs old, addictive cravings. Their bodies and brains have normalized. They are not addicted, but a life crisis rekindles the urge to go back to their old paths and immerse their brain in a chemical bath that changes their perception of reality. Unless you renew your mind—your self-image, your worldview—you will not progress beyond the wanting.

Your New Realities:

- You will live the rest of your life denying self.
- You will guard against temptation every moment.
- You will accept bad feelings as normal.
- You will form new neural connections with wholesome activities.

Good News:

You are not a victim of your brain chemicals or bodily addictions. You are the *cause* of your chemicals, and there is a force greater than your addictions.

"For what the law could not do, in that it was weak through the flesh, God sending his own Son in the likeness of sinful flesh, and for sin, condemned sin in the flesh: That the righteousness of the law might be fulfilled in us, who walk not after the flesh, but after the Spirit" (Romans 8:3–4).

THE BRAIN IS GOVERNED BY THE SOUL

Remember, our brain is said to be "plastic"—moldable, changeable, adaptable. It responds to our thoughts, so each brain becomes unique according to how we use it. The brain serves us by adapting to our choices, reinforcing our habits, and making them come to the forefront. We are what we think. We choose our thoughts and the brain conforms. The brain is a servant. Though the conditioned brain exerts a powerful influence, it is not the final determining factor in our thoughts and actions.

Researchers are well aware that there is something behind the brain that is more powerful than it is by itself, something they cannot observe or quantify. It is the soul. Every human experience is mediated by the brain, but the brain is second in the chain of command, subject to the soul. The mind (soul/spirit) is a separate entity from bodily processes and needs not be subject to the brain.

The brain is not moral or immoral; values are the domain of the unseen soul. The brain accepts our version of morality, treating our chosen behavior as normal, and assists our passions with a flush of happy chemicals that make us want more of the thing we choose as pleasure.

The history of the brain's use becomes the predictor of future choices. But at any time we can choose differently from the inclinations of the brain, though it is very difficult to defy the propensities we have built through a series of past choices. For example, there is no brain propensity greater than addiction to heroin, yet many people, for their own personal reasons, have chosen to ignore their neural addiction and act contrary to their driving impulses. We are never the victims of our brain patterning, but that patterning is predictive of 99% of our behavior—that is, until we decide in our soul to choose contrary to our most demanding impulses. We are the captain of our body, we are the master of our brain. But the brain, in a way, can be the enemy of change, for it demands a return to the well-established pathways of former behavior.

VICTORY OVER ALL ADDICTIONS

As mentioned above, the soul/spirit (researchers call it the *mind*) is distinct from the brain, and it is the first cause of all human thought and motivation. All humans of any religious or philosophical persuasion have the innate ability to do as they please—to reject the tug of addiction and choose the non-addictive lifestyle. That has been proven to be the experience of many over and over again. But most people are indeed weak in spirit and strong in fleshly compulsions. The flesh usually wins in a battle of wills—so much so that most people feel powerless to make desired changes. Jesus said, **"Watch and pray, that ye enter not into temptation: the spirit indeed is willing, but the flesh is weak"** (Matthew 26:41). The Apostle Paul, reflecting on his own experience, said, **"For I know that in me (that is, in my flesh,) dwelleth no good thing: for to will is present with me; but how to perform that which is good I find not. For the good that I would I do not: but the evil which I would not, that I do"** (Romans 7:18–19). After describing his struggles, he utters the cry of everyone who wants to overcome the flesh, and then he introduces the answer: **"O wretched man that I am! who shall deliver me from the body of this death? I thank God through Jesus Christ our Lord..."** (Romans 7:24–25).

Immediately following, Paul reveals the source of his overcoming strength: **"For the law of the Spirit of life in Christ Jesus hath made me free from the law of sin and death. For what the law could not do, <u>in that it was weak through the flesh</u>, God sending his own Son in the likeness of sinful flesh, and for sin, condemned sin in the flesh: That the righteousness of the law might be fulfilled in us, who <u>walk not after the flesh, but after the Spirit</u>"** (Romans 8:2–4).

Another time, addressing the Ephesians, Paul prayed, **"That he would grant you, according to the riches of his glory, to be strengthened with might by his Spirit in the inner man"** (Ephesians 3:16). And to the Philippians he said, **"I can do all things through Christ which strengtheneth me"** (Philippians 4:13).

Apart from Christ, a few special people, with plenty of support and a lot of willpower, can put down their addictions. But those who walk after the Spirit of God can put down all addictions, no matter how depraved and weak of character they may be (Romans 8).

Seeing powerful conversion and redemption stories has been the scenery of my life. I have been amazed at the radical changes that have taken place in the lives of those who are filled with the Holy Spirit of God. Observing the same thing in his generation, John said, **"Ye are of God, little children, and have overcome them: because greater is he that is in you, than he that is in the world"** (1 John 4:4).

If you are addicted to a substance or a behavior, you can lay it down when you choose to do so. The obstacle to making the hard choice is motivation. When you live for immediate gratification, you will not be able to act in ways that do not provide for that instant high. Two things are at issue: your chemical-dependent brain and the vacuum in your life without the addiction's instant high. Both must be addressed. If it were not for the vacuum of personal fulfilment, you could bully your way through 45 to 50 days of unhappy chemicals and be free, but the thing that brings the addictive behavior back is the gnawing vacuum. So replacing your addiction with wholesomeness is essential to your long-term victory. That is where being a real, born-again

Christian makes the difference. When you replace a chemical high with a Spirit high, you quickly create new neuronal paths of joy and fulfilment that leave no place for addictive behavior.

DID YOU KNOW?[102]

- 20% of all internet porn involves children.

- There is an average of 50,000 predators online at any given moment, on any given day.

- 69% of teens regularly receive online communication from strangers and don't tell their parents.

- 86% of girls say they can have online chats without their parents knowing.

- Roughly 116,000 child images online are requested daily.

SUGGESTIONS:

Those prepared are usually spared. Talk to your kids! Teach them about their brains and about the immense evil that is now trying to corrupt them. Three good resources can be found at nogreaterjoy.org:

1. *Sara Sue Learns to Yell & Tell: A Warning for Children Against Sexual Predators* (picture book)

2. *Samuel Learns to Yell & Tell: A Warning for Children Against Sexual Predators* (picture book)

3. *Science of Addiction and the Brain* (video)

102 This information came from www.vets4childrescue.org and www.guardchild.com/statistics

I CHARGE YOU

Decide right this minute to forgive those that have been weak, and resolve to be a helper; not an enabler, but a helper. Decide right this minute to forgive yourself when you have been weak. Stop seeking out those that cover for you and let them know you are ready to learn some basic executive function skills, like avoiding the marshmallows. Decide to be honest. Stop making excuses. Nothing is ever overcome until you are willing to be honest, first with yourself and then with others. Knowledge is power. Study gut health. Many addictions can be overcome with simple gut health. Now is the time to help your children learn self-control in all areas so that they never struggle with addictions.

"Now thanks be unto God, which always causeth us to triumph in Christ..." (2 Corinthians 2:14).

"For whatsoever is born of God overcometh the world: and this is the victory that overcometh the world, even our faith" (1 John 5:4).

What Makes Us Fall in Love

CHAPTER 19

*Neuroplasticity has taught us that we do not fall
in or out of love; it is a choice of the brain.*

PHEROMONES

You can't smell them, at least not in the normal sense that you detect an odor, but they are the most exciting non-smell you will ever detect. If humans are like other mammals, then it is the pheromones that subtly alter the behavior of those exposed to these odorless chemicals. Hormones work internally to affect only the individual secreting them. Pheromones are secreted outside the body and influence the behavior of others. They are the secret weapon that attracts a mate—so secret, we don't even know we are influenced by them.[103]

Over the last 50-plus years, pheromones have been studied and cataloged in a host of species across the animal kingdom. Pheromones have been proven to compel certain fish and moths to find mates. They are the trigger

---

103 Nordqvist, Christian. (2018). "What are pheromones and do humans have them?" *Medical News Today.* Retrieved from: www.medicalnewstoday.com/articles/232635.php

that drives a male dog to travel up to three miles across traffic, up and down hills, and through bodies of water to locate the female dog ready to breed. For animals, the primary method of negotiating hook-ups is regulated by pheromones. But do humans also secrete pheromones? Test after test proves something compels one particular human to be attracted to another.

DOING OUR OWN RESEARCH

For years, couples all over the world have taken the initiative to discover the truth of the matter by throwing sweaty T-shirt parties. As a girl enters the door, she is handed sweaty T-shirts to determine whether she wants to meet the owner. She sniffs until one smelly T-shirt gains her attention. If science were built on tests like this, the case for pheromones would have

been clearly established. All sorts of "non-scientific" tests have indicated a consistent pattern: Females choose the sweat from men who have completely different genetic patterns from them. Opposite pheromones attract.

A controlled T-shirt test in New Mexico took the research a step further by also studying the immune systems of the men by their sweat. The labs doc-

> **THE MASK**
>
> Almost all deodorants are perfumed, which means that most of us are masking our natural odor with a chemical concocted in a laboratory.

umented that the women who were at their most fertile time of the month preferred the sweat of not only opposite pheromones, but also the healthiest of the men in the control group. Hundreds of scientifically controlled research programs have been done with college students, documenting different aspects of what most influences a woman's choice when judging men's sweat. Many of the tests feature strange variables. In a study done by Steven Gangestad, PhD and Randy Thornhill, PhD, the volunteer men's hands, feet, ear length, etc. were measured to determine if symmetry between right side and left—in many animals, a sign of health, fertility, and longevity—was also important in human mating. Their findings were published in the *Proceedings of the Royal Society of London*: "Female volunteers (excluding any on contraceptives) preferred the smell of T-shirts worn by the most symmetrical men only if the women were at the stage of their monthly cycle in which they were more likely to become pregnant."[104]

Another study, done by Carole Ober, PhD, sampled the DNA of 411 Hutterite couples, all part of a religious sect descended from 64 people who emigrated from Europe in 1870. She proved that even in this closely related group, all the females chose the one man in this limited pool that had the greatest difference in the immune system. Ober stated that Hutterites somehow avoid marriage to partners with whom they share too many MHC (major histocompatibility complex) genes.

> *" How on earth are you ever going to explain in terms of chemistry and physics so important a biological phenomenon as first love? "*
>
> Albert Einstein

The smelly T-shirt research will continue as biologists conjure up more elaborate tests for measuring pheromones that the scientific world has yet to acknowledge. All the studies clearly confirm that the male exudes something that has a powerful influence on female responsiveness. Pheromones probably won't affect our lives because in this modern era, most everyone bathes or showers at least once a day, washing away that "thing" that nature has provided that sets us apart to the opposite sex. We then douse ourselves with masking chemicals. It has not always been this way. The historically famous warrior Napoleon supposedly sent a message home to his mistress, Josephine, stating: "I return in three days. Don't wash."

THE SCIENCE OF ATTRACTION

Love is all about the brain...and pheromones. We have all read of love at first sight, here's how it happens. In an instant upon meeting that special someone, this elusive wonder called pheromones sends an important signal to the brain, exciting the hypothalamus to produce dopamine. As if by magic, dopamine suddenly floods the brain bountifully, providing a rush of pleasure and feelings of reward. And then there is love—or at least, a measure of attraction.

There is more to our attraction than just pheromones. But if other concerns align, in that nanosecond with that amazing shot of dopamine, even the most reserved of us feel giddy. Our insides are warm with trembling

104 Berreby, David. (1998). "Studies Explore Love and the Sweaty T-Shirt." *The New York Times*. Retrieved from: www.nytimes.com/1998/06/09/science/studies-explore-love-and-the-sweaty-t-shirt.html

excitement, and, if we are young, maybe for the first time we experience a sense of euphoria. It is no wonder that thousands of poems are written and beautiful stories woven concerning the marvelous, thunder-struck moment called love. Science refers to these moments as "the phase of attraction." Of course, not everyone's moment is a "moment." Sometimes the "feeling" takes a while to develop...maybe the pheromones are confused by a fragrance the girl or guy is wearing, or maybe there is something deeper going on in a person's soul. Research shows that response to human pheromones can take a while to develop. Since there is much more to us than just animal responses, other factors will influence our attraction. Many times love comes softly.

The brain doesn't rest with a first response to pheromones; it keeps those accompanying neurotransmitters flowing. The steady flow of dopamine can cause you to lose interest in eating and have trouble sleeping. As we learned earlier, norepinephrine, which is known as the **fight or flight** hormone, kicks the body into high gear, making us feel alive and amazingly alert; no more brain fog, sluggish days, or off evenings. We are primed for love.

No wonder we all want to be in love! Brain scans reveal that the **caudate nucleus** fires like crazy when our dream guy or gal walks in the door. After almost 50 years of marriage and at 73 years of age, according to the finger pulse meter, my man's heart rate will jump 20 points within 5 seconds of me touching his arm. Now that is love magic! Neurotransmitters are a beautiful thing.

THE UPSIDE OF LOW SEROTONIN

Here's an odd thing about love: attraction seems to lead to a <u>reduction</u> in the hormone serotonin. Serotonin provides us with a feeling of being in total self-control. It is an important neurotransmitter that is believed to help regulate mood, social behavior, appetite and digestion, sleep, memory, and sexual desire and function. In the beginning of all love relationships, strange as it seems, serotonin levels drop very low. Scientists believe that this diminished level is what prompts the overpowering infatuation that characterizes the beginning stages of love. A normally reserved, self-disciplined person will still maintain their moral conviction and self-discipline, but even they, when they first fall in love, may act rather oddly and become quite obsessed. The self-regulator that controls our normally reserved social behavior is now not working so effectively. Without this drop in serotonin, many extremely self-contained people would never loosen up enough to find a mate!

The prefrontal cortex (PFC), our brain's reasoning center, lights up with extreme blood flow when in love. The amygdala, the highly emotional area of the brain that young people use for making decisions (since their PFC isn't fully developed) also gets very responsive. Basically our brain goes on red alert, telling it to move forward. Thankfully this low level of serotonin is temporary. As the relationship becomes secure, the levels of serotonin return to normal, although this can take up to two years of marriage. The higher our serotonin level, the more rationally we think. We can sleep, eat, and work again without being distracted. Love settles us at a more stable level.

THE DOWNSIDE OF LOW SEROTONIN

Many people live with low serotonin levels, which are linked to depression. Because serotonin is essential to regulate so many areas, a general lack of it can greatly impede a person's well-being. Serotonin is primarily produced in the gut, which helps explain why people with depression usually have gut issues. It is often noted that when stomach issues are resolved, the sad are sad no longer. Many leading psychiatrists are now giving micronutrients to their patients instead of anti-depressants.

Interestingly, people who are given to obsessive-compulsive disorder also have low levels of serotonin. Obsessive-compulsive behavior indicates extreme drives that may be expressed as addiction to drugs or porn, compulsive buying, gambling, reckless driving, sexual promiscuity, etc.

> **LOVE HEALS**
>
> Studies show that enhancing emotional bonds between people will help heal the limbic system.

This information leads us to another odd, yet likely, hypothesis. On the flipside of love, when there is a break-up after an attachment, especially if it is someone who is given to obsessive-compulsive behavior, it can cause a great amount of stress or depression and can even provoke a taste for revenge in the one cast adrift. Crimes of passion are all too common. This obsession can cause the person that has pulled the plug on the relationship to feel smothered by the one still clinging.

Love is divine, and love stinks...sometimes.

SCANS DON'T LIE

It is easy for us parents to think our teens don't feel as deeply as we do. Parents often think their young people don't have to deal with the emotional attachment drive of relationships, only the physical sexual drive. Not so. The video "The Love Competition: What Does Love Look Like in the Brain?" on YouTube,[105] shows several volunteers submitting to an fMRI scan to see whose brain is more activated when it comes to love thoughts. Researchers chose people from 11 to 75 years old and of varying relationship statuses. The researchers added the young, pre-pubescent boy as well as an old man well past his prime to see how their brains might differ from the others who were in the height of their sexually responsive years. Except for the child,

each contestant was told to concentrate on the person they really loved, or someone they once loved and wished they could have back, or someone they had their eye on and wished they could have. Since the little boy had not yet reached the awesome age of being stirred by the opposite sex, he chose to think about his newborn niece, whom he was allowed to hold for a few minutes earlier in the day.

> **BONDING**
>
> Oxytocin is sometimes called the "commitment neuromodulator" because it reinforces bonding. When males become fathers, a closely related neuromodulator called vasopressin is released. It drastically changes a man, making him a protector, caregiver, and a gentle dad.

All the participants were scanned for three minutes while they focused on their love, and they all came out excited from having stimulated their neurotransmitters through the intense love imaging. Each waited to see who among them had the most active love center in their brain. Amazingly, it was the old man whose brain was clearly most active with love.

He smiled when he saw that his brain showed the greatest activity and was eager to share his love story. He was just a young teen in 1961 when he first saw his sweetheart, but he knew immediately that she was the love of his life. There are many factors that may cause one to be attracted to a particular person. It may be a combination of a smile, the way her hair blows in the

105 (2016). "The Love Competition: What does love look like in the brain?" *Aeon Video.* Retrieved from: www.youtube.com/watch?v=p1npQEdTsF8

> *"* The chemosensory functions of the human nose are underappreciated. Traditional teaching is that the sense of smell detects volatile compounds, which may then allow the identification of substances that may be beneficial or harmful—such as good versus putrefied food. However, increasing evidence from research in other animals suggests that olfaction may serve another and more important purpose, that of mate selection in sexual reproduction; indeed, olfaction may be an essential impetus for evolution.[1] *"*
>
> 1 Bhutta, Mahmoud. (2007). "Sex and the nose: Human pheromonal responses." *Journal of the Royal Society of Medicine*. Retrieved from: www.ncbi.nlm.nih.gov/pmc/articles/ PMC1885393/

breeze, her social skills, or stored memories of past experiences. But we all know from what we have learned about pheromones that at that moment, the magic of her pheromones stimulated the release of the neurotransmitter dopamine in his brain. Love was born.

His ladylove was there with him in the lab, and no one would recognize her from the old picture he had brought with him to show everyone. He said he always felt his life was somehow blessed more than other people's because he was able to find just the right lady.

Love abides, love ignites, and love stays that way if the old brain keeps "thinking" loving thoughts. First come pheromones, then dopamine, and then, as long as the couple continues to think thoughts of love and good will, the brain will actually continue to produce the necessary neurotransmitters for the person to continue to feel they are in love. We will say more on this later.

The next great surprise was the second big winner. The 11-year-old boy's brain was almost as bright as the old guy's. Although there were no signs of hormones on the young boy's radar, his brain was lighting up like a Christmas tree. Love doesn't require sexual desire to produce neurotransmitters that make our brains show powerful feelings toward another. The brains of your young children are most likely producing lots of neurotransmitters, causing them to have extreme feelings at a much greater intensity than your own brain.

Reflect for a moment on a previous chapter, where we dealt with the subject of the unfinished PFC, the area of the brain that dictates judgment, wise decisions, and common sense. Perhaps you also recall the research we discussed earlier, which showed a group of teens and young adults incapable of discerning what emotion they saw on a face in a sketch. These young people do not have the physical ability to make accurate judgments, yet their pheromones are as intense as yours. Consider the powerful hormonal drive that stimulates their body and their mind, plus the intense feelings rising up in their brain...it is a wonder young people ever make wise decisions about marriage. This opens up a big Pandora's box in preparing sons and daughters to find a good mate for life.

THREE PARTS OF LOVE

Science breaks love down into three categories: lust, attraction, and attachment. Strong, healthy marriage relationships experience all three on a regular basis.

Lust

Most people think of lust as an evil passion. Not so. This term is used in the Bible to express righteous appetite (Deut. 12:15). God made our bodies to need sexual expression, especially men. It's as normal as the appetite for food. It is simple biology. Sexual hunger is an ever-present need, and God designed that it be fulfilled inside the bounds of marriage. It can be a holy lust that seeks fulfilment in the one to whom we are married, or it can be an unholy lust—a desire to fulfill the sexual appetite in an immoral manner—through perversions or outside of marriage.

The fMRI reveals a difference in the release of neurotransmitters in the brain of one who hooks up out of pure lust and one who has established a commitment to the other.

When there is no commitment toward the other person—no self-sacrificing love—the hormones testosterone and estrogen are the most readily available. Pheromones are not necessary in unholy lust. When a man driven purely by lust has an orgasm, his testosterone is diminished, so he has no further interest in the female. She is just a dumping place. Having dumped, his lust is satisfied and he moves on, always looking for the real love of his life, the one who touches the needs of his soul.

The female who was only the object of lust is different. Females are more sensitive to the effects of oxytocin, a bonding hormone that is released upon intercourse. This release of oxytocin will cause her to desire a deeper commitment in the relationship, but without his continuing sexual interest, she will have no hold on him, and he will likely never develop tender feelings toward her.

Attraction

The first state of attraction is seeing someone you hope to get to know for possible attachment. Both male and female will look for opportunities to spend time talking and visiting with that person, hoping the relationship will continue. This hope releases dopamine and norepinephrine and can decrease the normal amount of serotonin. If sex happens early in the attraction stage, the male will likely lose interest before he has a chance to develop enough neurotransmitters to want to take the relationship further.

Attachment

Neurotransmitters oxytocin and vasopressin are released in the brains of both the male and the female when they "think" they have found their long-term mate. Just the act of thinking the other person is going to be your lifetime mate provokes the brain to release the neurotransmitters that make the couple want to stay together. The brain assists the commitment. When the male makes this commitment his testosterone levels drop, which helps keep him from being distracted by other females. Also, the attachments he wants to form will need high levels of oxytocin. High testosterone can block oxytocin, so the lower levels of testosterone will allow oxytocin to rise. Now his brain will release neurotransmitters that cause him to develop a protective instinct toward his mate, and she develops a need to please her man. After the couple has been married for a year or two, giving time for the lust and attraction hormones to be totally satisfied, then oxytocin and vasopressin take a leading role, which provokes feelings of bonding or being one with your spouse. It is the "spouse thoughts" that release the oxytocin and vasopressin hormones, and it is their continual thoughts of being one that cause these hormones to stay high. The brain hormonal output is actually regulated by thoughts. Now the attachment phase is complete.

Isn't this all amazing? God made us so complex. Our brain and body assist us with our goals and aspirations. We decide and the brain complies. **"We are fearfully and wonderfully made...And that my soul knoweth right well" (Psalm 139:14).**

MIND-WANDERING CHANGES THE HORMONES

Divorce comes about when a man or a woman begins to mentally play with the idea of being with a person other than their spouse. Let's stop right here before we go on and describe how the brain works when it processes infidelity. The Christian, led by a higher law and directed by the Holy Spirit, will check the first inclinations to mentally play with the idea of being with another person, for our Lord said, **"But I say unto you, That whosoever looketh on a woman to lust after her hath committed adultery with her already in his heart" (Matthew 5:28).** But for those who travel that road, here is how the brain works.

Sometimes with men, it is simply a matter of a hot female stirring his lust—lust being a body that just needs to use a body. Men's senses are most provoked by what they see. Women often don't feel like they are responsible for a man's sexual struggle, but God will judge according to the fruit of our doing, not according to what we think or feel. More often than not, when a man is captured by lust for another woman, he has no interest in attachment. God says, "FLEE youthful lusts."

LOVE

Our attachments bring us the greatest joys and the most painful sorrows.

The brain follows suit, adapting to our thinking. The constant sexual tug from viewing another female can change the neurotransmitters in the brain, even when a man truly loves his wife. Infidelity statistics from 2018 say that 36% of married men admit they are guilty of adultery. Remember what was written about lust? The sad thing is many wives are so emotionally damaged by their husband's infidelity that the marriage is destroyed. Regret is an ugly word that is not easily deleted from the pages of our lives.

It is not uncommon for wives to wander in their thought life, which also results in neurotransmitter disruption. Infidelity statistics from 2018 say 21% of women admitted to affairs. As a rule, women don't fess-up as readily as men, so this percentage is doubtlessly higher. Women don't struggle with being provoked visually as much as men do. A woman's weakness is her need to be desired. She thinks, and the brain responds in kind. Simply thinking about infidelity causes the brain to stop releasing the same amount of oxytocin and vasopressin—the attachment hormones—and without them a person will stop feeling bonded to their spouse.

God says in **Proverbs 23:7, "For as he thinketh in his heart, so is he..."** Since this thinking process actually disrupts the flow of oxytocin and vasopressin, it causes the "mind wanderer" to feel as if he or she has fallen out of love. In a way, they have. The "mind wanderer" will often blame their spouse because of the brain's natural tendency to avoid being the guilty party. Love attachment starts and stops in the brain. Infidelity and divorce start with thoughts. The brain doesn't cause our behavior, it just adapts to our thoughts and makes it easier for us to do our heart's desire. That is why Jesus said that when a man looks and lusts, that he, **"...hath committed adultery with her already in his heart" (Matthew 5:28)** for it takes place in the brain before it takes place in the body.

DENNY AND RENEE

Denny and Renee met at a church camp. There was an immediate spark. Renee was a very attractive, sweet, virgin girl and had no idea why none of the homeschool guys had ever shown any interest in her. She caught them looking from time to time, and they often spoke to her, but no one ever pursued her. What she didn't know was that she dressed way too sexy for a regular guy to think straight when near her. Unlike most of the yokels there at camp, Denny was suave, in total command, and very assertive in pursuing Renee. She didn't know that though Denny talked the talk, he didn't walk the walk. The way a girl dresses and acts attracts a certain kind of man. Of all the guys at camp, she attracted Denny. I often tell young girls if you want a true prince, you need to be a princess in manner and in dress.

Denny had classic obsessive-compulsive behavior, but Renee had no clue. From the start, Denny was confident and aggressive, sweeping Renee along, causing her to be thrilled with love. Her natural drive made her want to please him, and he made it clear that the way he would be pleased was sex. It was about this time she learned that two years earlier, he had met another girl at church and that girl now had his baby. This gave her pause, but didn't stop "love." Anyway, who could resist Denny? He was so strong and forceful. She was shocked at how mad he got when things didn't go his way. In her entire life, she never remembered her dad getting mad like that. This was a little scary, but even that didn't stop the love! She was on a dopamine rush without the serotonin to balance it out.

Her parents weren't happy with the situation. Somehow they picked up on serious issues that Renee seemed to miss. Renee loved her parents, but she knew Denny was the one. He had big mood swings and extreme ups and downs that hinged on whether or not things were going his way. He made it clear he liked to show her off to his friends, and the more of her showing, the better. This seemed the opposite of a man who wants his special girl just for himself, but for Renee, that wouldn't stop love!

There were lots of signs that this might not be the direction Renee needed to go, but she was so thrilled with love, the guy's problems didn't matter. Nothing could stop love! Love cures all—doesn't it? Girls can be so silly sometimes. Renee was really in love with love itself—not with the man. She was body surfing in hormones.

Denny and Renee did marry, and almost immediately, Renee began to live in terror. She believed once married, always married and don't dishonor your man by telling anyone bad things about him, even if he is violent to the point that you fear he might kill you. By Divine Providence, a truck full of men were passing by and saw Denny in an act of violence toward his wife. The law was called.

Denny is back in the game hunting now, most likely visiting new churches for the next vulnerable, hot virgin. Renee has since learned that there were at least three girls he found at churches and discarded after use. She has been advised by law officials and professional counselors that, until he finds a new girl, his first concern may be revenge on the last one who dared to humiliate him. Statistics say that one in four females suffer violence at the hands of the man with whom they have been intimate.

The moral of this terrible story is twofold:

1. Trust counsel, take heed to warning bells, and don't get caught up in feelings because sometimes those neurotransmitters are lying to you.

2. Guys who are scared, shy, and act like dumb yokels are likely the good guys. **"Be sober, be vigilant; because your adversary the devil, as a roaring lion, walketh about, seeking whom he may devour"** (1 Peter 5:8).

BELINDA AND RALPH

In all honesty, Ralph never considered Belinda as a possible wife. She was attractive, kind, and charming, but there just was not that shot of pheromones sparking the attraction. Now, Ginger was a whole different thing! When it came to Ginger, Ralph had a serious flow of pheromones, but he had enough sense in his half-developed PFC to know she was not good wife material. She was so fine to look at, and she was full of laughter and conversation, sweeping him along with fun and entertainment. With a steady dose of looking at Ginger, Ralph was beginning to develop a strong bodily need. His testosterone was running high, as was his dopamine. And her constant company at church functions where she hung on to his arm made him feel she was his woman! This was beginning to release the needful neurotransmitter oxytocin to help him overcome his reluctance in choosing her for his life partner.

Ralph's parents were becoming concerned. Ginger was always at church youth functions, but had never shown any real interest in the things of God. Plus, she was super flirty, dressed in a way to attract men, and, to top it off, she appeared lazy. She was also known to spend money unwisely. Ralph's mom and dad had a conversation with him, pointing out these issues and reminding him to flee youthful lusts. But Ralph had almost passed the point of no return. His brain was adapting to his lusts. Ginger's cute giggle, short skirt, and squirm against Ralph's leg was quickly paving the way for future little Ralphies.

Ralph's wise parents decided to put a challenge before their son: "Have you ever considered Belinda as a wife? If you step back and really notice, you will see that she is a very pretty girl, and she actually has a great figure, she just doesn't display it. Have you noticed how she is always helping out at church, babysitting or cleaning the rec room? She will be a great mother, and a man would not be concerned about her being a flirt." They asked their son to begin praying and asking God for wisdom concerning Belinda. They also asked if he would be open to them inviting her to travel with them on a three-week mission project so Ralph could get to know her better. Ralph wasn't against Belinda, but neither was he really interested. Yet he loved and respected his parents, so he was willing to be nice and get to know Belinda— thinking nothing would come of it.

Going on a mission trip often opens up a young person's eyes to the plight of other, less fortunate people. It can bring on a sobriety that would otherwise take years to acquire. Because Ralph's parents had planted the idea of Belinda in his head, he couldn't help but visualize her as a possible wife. She was sweet, although she was so shy it was hard to get her to talk. But after a few days of working together, she did open up a little. He enjoyed watching her work, really getting into the project and pulling her share and then some. Working with another young person when they are helping those in need has a way of allowing you to see the quality in them. Slowly, respect and admiration for the fine person that she was began to release the neurotransmitters that resulted in attraction that his pheromones had failed to provoke. This new appreciation for Belinda made him see Ginger for who she really was, and he realized that he wasn't so impressed with her silliness or sexiness anymore.

> ### TOLERATING
>
> In many ways, we teach people how to treat us by what we tolerate and what we refuse to tolerate.

When he came back from his trip, several of the guys teased him, saying he was lucky to get back when he did because Ginger was casting her charms on Jerry, and Jerry was moving in fast. This information caused Ralph to do a quick mental evaluation of his feelings. He realized he wasn't even jealous or mad at Jerry like he might have been just three weeks earlier. It was almost a relief to think that if he had married Ginger, this might be his life—always having to hover over her to make sure she wasn't flirting with some other guy.

His wise parents had planted an idea in his head and had provided an opportunity for him to get to know this shy gal. Thankfully, through this he had gained some insight and wisdom about what kind of girl he really wanted to spend the rest of his life with. Ralph and Belinda married and lived happily ever after.

The moral of this story is twofold: Pheromones can't always be trusted to help make good decisions, and wise parents might need to help love along.

RACHEL AND MOSES

Moses had been earnestly wife hunting for several years but just couldn't quite find what he was looking for. Moses wasn't young or easily impressed. Plus, seeing the misfortune of several of his friends stuck in hard-to-deal-with marriages had built in him an extreme fear of making the dreadful

> ## LOVING IS...
>
> Loving is not looking for a friend so you will not be lonely. Loving is not looking for someone to pour into you. Loving is not waiting on others to love you. Loving is finding someone who has needs and filling them. God designed us to be givers. He designed us to go out and find others to pour into. Life is loving and giving yourself to others, and in return, love is reciprocated.

mistake of marrying someone who was not suited to him.

He had been to several homeschool shindigs and met many fine girls but had passed on all of them. He spent a lot of time thinking and asking himself questions. How would he know which girl would be a good match for him? How could he really know what was God's will for his life? What if he messed up some girl's life because she couldn't stand his weird peculiarities? Everyone in the family fussed at him for being so messy and told him that no wife would tolerate it. And there was the issue of having weird ideas about food: everyone he knew teased him about what he would and would not eat and said it would drive a girl crazy having to cook for him. What if he married someone who was really irritated about such things?

Moses had been born and raised strict Amish—a hard worker. He was saved when he was twenty and that was when he began reading and loving the Bible. He was a good catch, he just didn't know it.

He was at another shindig wife hunting again when the pheromones hit him like a ton of bricks. It happened as he was leaving the volleyball court, heading to help in one of the outdoor ministries. A really gorgeous girl stopped him at the gate and said, "Hey, I read your Facebook page where you posted a sermon. It was great and really blessed me." Here he was, standing face to face with a beautiful girl who was blessed by the message he had posted. It would take a full-blown explosion of pheromones for Moses to get past his fears of messing up in the marriage department, and here they were, going off like fireworks. Moses promptly forgot he was due to help in the other field and that he had the equipment they needed. Without him, 100 people stood and waited in the hot sun. Maybe he did remember but just didn't care. The young couple talked.

However, months passed and Moses dragged his feet. How could he know if she was right for him or him for her? Too much introspection almost made him change his mind. He sought out counsel, and wise counsel assured him that she was the best thing that had ever come his way. He complained, "We are so quiet, shy, and scared. We can't even get to know one another! It is just not going to work!" Fortunately for Moses, his neurotransmitter dopamine drove him to try again and again to get to know the beautiful girl who seemed too good to be true.

Finally, after several uncomfortable occasions of trying to enjoy one another's company, they began to relax and talk. The neurotransmitter oxytocin began to be released into his brain, and he knew he couldn't live without this beautiful lady. The rest is history. Never has there been a sweeter, wilder, and more wonderful love story except, of course, mine and my man's.

The moral of this story is: When everyone can see the other person would be a good match, even if you are both too shy to talk, try anyway because there is a glorious wonder awaiting you.

I CHARGE YOU

You can control your neurotransmitters. If you don't have a natural response toward your husband, then practice "hot thinking" instead of stinking thinking! Having a good attitude about him is a good start. Good sex starts in the brain as it releases positive neurotransmitters. Get your brain in gear by doing some planning of the dress, the setting, the food, the fragrance, and the timing. Your brain, to a great degree, will be in control of his brain because his brain will know something has changed for the better.

Marriage is two people becoming one flesh...hello? Did you just read what marriage is? Two people becoming one flesh. A good marriage, to a great degree, is good sex. We can control our neurotransmitters by what we are thinking, and it is these chemicals that make being married extra special. As I said, good sex starts in the brain and ends with a satisfied sigh.

GOD SAYS

The Apostle Paul discussed marital passion in 1 Corinthians 7:2–5 saying that, [in order] **"...to avoid fornication, let every man have his own wife, and let every woman have her own husband."** He assumes the power of lust to be a given. And he took it further by saying that the act of sexual surrender in marriage is a benevolent act toward one's spouse: **"Let the husband render unto the wife due benevolence: and likewise also the wife unto the husband."** And for those who feel that it is their right to withhold sex from their partner, Paul warns, **"The wife hath not power of her own body, but the husband: and likewise also the husband hath not power of his own body, but the wife."** To withhold natural sexual gratification is a crime called defrauding: **"Defraud ye not one the other, except it be with consent for a time, that ye may give yourselves to fasting and prayer; and come together again, that Satan tempt you not for your incontinency."** Paul implies that a husband or wife who is the victim of sexual defrauding is in danger of temptation from Satan. The first line of defense against fornication (adultery, pornography, self-pleasing, etc.) is a cheerful, eager marriage partner. The assumption of the entire passage is that lust is natural and to be expected and that a ready and willing partner is the God-ordained prevention for temptation. (My husband and I have written several books along these lines. They are listed in the back of this book.)

The first of the three categories of love is lust—a natural, God-ordained passion that can be exercised righteously within marriage or can be sinful if indulged outside God's lawful bounds.

"Charity suffereth long, and is kind; charity envieth not; charity vaunteth not itself, is not puffed up, Doth not behave itself unseemly, seeketh not her own, is not easily provoked, thinketh no evil; Rejoiceth not in iniquity, but rejoiceth in the truth; Beareth all things, believeth all things, hopeth all things, endureth all things" (1 Corinthians 13:4–7).

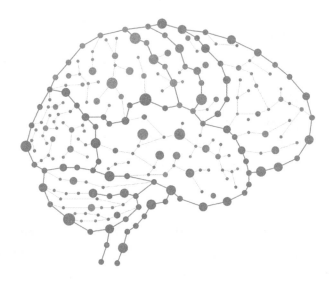

Now You Know

Neuroplasticity has taught us that we are indeed the captain of our ship. Whichever way we direct our brain is the way we will go.

THE BABY GIRL

Some people through no fault of their own have broken bodies, and some people are broken psychologically. Many years ago, we were asked to counsel a good family. Their baby girl had started obviously masturbating every time she was put down to rest. The parents were baffled. I am aware that for the last number of years (since the advent of vibrating toys and, of course, since porn has become so rampant) it has become a common occurrence. But back then there was no literature to be found on the subject. We had no clue. A week later the mother called, crying. She remembered that months earlier, a young man who was a close family friend had offered to entertain their demanding baby girl so the rest of the family could go on an outing. He offered his babysitting services several more times. In those years before internet pornography, it was hard to imagine a man would sexually stimulate a tiny baby girl. What kind of human being would do that? There was no use to speculate or accuse.

Many years passed and that baby became a teenager and then a woman. She grew to be a tender, kind human being, but, though she came from a very conservative background, her manner and style of dress and stance were overtly sexual—awkwardly so. Oddly, for many years she made a point of avoiding going out in public, especially without her husband.

God says, **"It were better for him that a millstone were hanged about his neck, and he cast into the sea, than that he should offend one of these little ones" (Luke 17:2).** Can you imagine the wrath of God stored up against men who are responsible for using children?

NOBODY PLAYS IN MY SPECIAL PLACE

Years ago, a young couple asked if they could live on our property until they got on their feet. The guy had serious health issues and seemed mentally about to break. Looking back, I can clearly see that his gut was in trouble. The gal was full of energy and was extremely intense. I didn't know how to identify mental health issues at the time, but somehow I knew this sweet gal was nuts. One day we were in the garden picking vegetables and I asked her, "Why did your parents let you marry at 16 years of age to a guy they had just met?" Her parents were homeschooling, conservative people, so it seemed odd.

She just shrugged her shoulders and said matter-of-factly, "My dad wanted me gone because he was afraid I would burn the house down and kill all the kids."

Now, that was not the answer I expected, and I tried not to sound stunned when I asked, "Why would he think that?"

Her answer was quite forthright: "I don't know how, but he found out that I burned the barn down when we moved from the last place, and then he remembered the other place we lived had burned when we moved. I always had everything ready so I could light it when I knew everyone was in the car and there was no chance anyone would be hurt. I told him I would never hurt my brothers and sisters. He just didn't understand that I didn't like to think about other kids playing in my barn. It was my special place, so when we moved, I just burned it down. It was old, so I didn't see the problem."

Yes, some people are broken and need healing. We moved them off the property as soon as possible and really expected the trailer to be a pile of ashes. Obviously, it was not a special place because it was still standing after they were long gone.

Clearly, some people are abused and misused and suffer overwhelming grief or turmoil and maybe have had some serious bumps on their heads, leaving them with odd mindsets, weird ideas, brokenness, and anxiousness of spirit. Although they are broken, and thus, have a higher mountain to climb, they can still climb. God is there for them in a special way. **"To appoint unto them that mourn in Zion, to give unto them beauty for ashes, the oil of joy for mourning, the garment of praise for the spirit of heaviness; that they might be called trees of righteousness, the planting of the LORD, that he might be glorified" (Isaiah 61:3).**

The baby girl grew up and became an excellent wife, mother and grandmother because she had learned how to make wiser life choices. The barn-burner and her husband started an orphanage about 25 years ago and to the best of my knowledge they are still faithfully serving the young urchins that once ran amok on streets of Bangkok. Neither the molested baby, now grown, nor the barn-burner's brains are stuck in brokenness any more than Pedro Bach-y-Rita's brain was stuck in paralysis after his stroke.

MY LIST OF FAVORITES

People are not born angry or depressed. It is hard to take responsibility for our actions and reactions, moods and feelings. It is easier to blame others. It has become popular to have a therapist with whom you can be yourself, without judgment, voicing all your insecurities and hurts, searching your past to find who is responsible for your psychological condition. Therapists can be extremely helpful if they lead the patient to be honest and take responsibility. I like Dr. Amen's approach in doing SPECT scans, instead of just wondering what is happening in the brain. I love how Dr. Low taught his patients to open the door a little wider each day and take one step at a time, thus overcoming fear. Of course, the first stage to mental or physical healing would be to utilize the information found in Dr. Emeran Mayer's books concerning healing the gut to heal the brain. And while I am giving my list of all-time favorites, in my humble opinion, the fascinating research conducted by Julia Rucklidge should go down in the medical text books as a game-changer. She demonstrated that taking high quality micronutrients is more effective for long-term mental health than using any of the medication available today. This research should be duplicated on a large scale as it appears to be so pivotal in mental health.

Neuroplasticity researchers have come to our aid and become God's assistants, revealing that we are responsible for what we choose to think. God (and now science) is calling us out of that stinking thinking mindset. Isn't it fascinating that the life and spirit to which God calls us just happens to be the perfect environment for a healthy body and mind? **"For God hath not given us the spirit of fear; but of power, and of love, and of a sound mind" (2 Timothy 1:7).**

THE BOYS FROM BOSTON

Eighty years ago, a far-sighted Harvard professor, Dr. Clark Heath, started a study called the Harvard Study of Adult Development. He enlisted 268 Harvard sophomores in 1938 during the Great Depression to see what could be learned from a longitudinal study as to what makes a good life. Unlike the vast majority of lifespan studies, this one has continued even to this day. Now the children and grandchildren of these men are being studied.

Each man was contacted every other year by researchers gathering information on their health, private life, hopes, dreams, disappointments, fears, failures, loves, and many other questions. The researchers visited them in their homes so they could do their own profile of the husband/wife relationship and their relationships with their children. They also gave detailed accounts of the style of living for each man. Blood tests, doctor's reports, divorces, death of spouse or children, disease, fighting in wars and the effect it had on the men, triumphs, and failures were all carefully recorded. Years passed, decades came and went. The study had four directors over the years and a multitude of researchers who gathered seemingly random information, slowly building a profile of the life of 268 men. But even with the most primitive of medical research, truth was still becoming more and more obvious. Trends began to take shape that were not expected.

Researchers began to wonder if the results could have been skewed since all the volunteers were Harvard men—educated, wealthy, and born with more than their share of potential. Researchers surmised that a totally different strata of society would likely yield a different set of statistics. They would start another study from a group that was not so privileged.

In the 1970s, 456 inner-city, low-income boys ages 12 to 16 were enlisted as part of the Glueck study. The same set of protocols used with the Harvard men were used with the less-privileged group. Their questionnaires, doctors' reports, blood tests, X-rays, home visits, etc. were compared with those of the Harvard men. As medical science advanced, MRI and fMRI brain scans replaced anthropometric measurements of skulls and brows.

Over the years, some of the men were killed in war or accidents, and some dropped out of the study, but most of the men continued sharing their lives. Through these two parallel studies, we have learned the single factor that is most predictive of a happy, long life.

Research revealed that the men who were content and thankful in their relationships had experienced the same mishaps, sorrows, and failures as the men who considered their life to be miserable. It was not the different degree or intensity of family bickering in the happy men when compared to the miserable ones that set them apart. They discovered that it was not the pains of life that destroyed joy, but rather, the reaction to those pains. It was a lack of contentment in relationships, regardless of the circumstances.

The words that jumped out to me as I read the reports from the long-living men were content, satisfied, forgiving, long-lasting family ties, good friends, and enjoyment in simple things. The word that stood out in the files of those men whose lives were cut short was loneliness.

The Apostle Paul, reflecting on his hardships, said, **"But godliness with contentment is great gain"** (1 Timothy 6:6).

The men who were most content were NOT chasing happiness, fulfillment, money, or fame. They were thankful for their family, friends, and life. They obviously had learned to forgive and forget when upsets in relationships came their way, rather than cut off the offenders.

Dr. Robert Waldinger is the fourth leading director of the study, a psychiatrist at Massachusetts General Hospital and professor of psychiatry at Harvard Medical School. He said of the data gathered from the last 80 years, "The surprising finding is that our relationships and how happy we are in our relationships has a powerful influence on our health. Taking care of your body is important, but tending to your relationships is a form of self-care too. That, I think, is the revelation."

The men in both groups who reported being closer to their family, friends, or community tended to be happier and healthier than their less-social counterparts. They also tended to live longer. Those who reported being lonelier, were less content, and their health declined sooner.

Researchers have pored over mountains of data on the men in the study, including vast medical records and interviews, searching for that elusive magic that makes a long, sweet life. Dr. Waldinger said in a TED Talk titled *What Makes a Good Life? Lessons from the Longest Study on Happiness,*[106] "When we gathered together everything we knew about them at age 50, it wasn't their middle-age cholesterol levels that predicted how they were going to grow old. It was how satisfied they were in their relationships. The people who were the most satisfied in their relationships at age 50 were the healthiest at age 80." The study showed that the role of genetics and long-lived parents and grandparents proved less important to longevity than being content with their relationships in mid-life.

Incredibly, researchers were able to look back into the studies of all the men when they were 50 and successfully calculate who had lived happy, healthy, clear-minded lives into their 90s.

THE PLAN

If we want a better brain, we need a plan.

We are creatures of habit, so establishing a new routine is foundational. We will probably fail to do all that we should, for we are fighting against years of brain patterning. But fire enough synapses and you will wire new pathways in your brain. Purposeful people—though not perfect—are happier and live longer. Remember my friend who had been a porn addict and yelled in the mall? Sometimes it takes extreme measures to break a bad habit. How far are you willing to go for the good life?

Your ship goes in the direction you chart, and it takes time and effort to change the direction. If you chart a different course, then change is needed, and that change needs to come from within YOU, not from the outside. Don't wait for the environment to change. It is easy to think that if we just had a different life situation we would be happy, but as the apostle Paul said, **"I have learned, in whatsoever state I am, therewith to be content" (Philippians 4:11)**. Don't think that changing partners or locations will improve your life. When you do that, you just bring your old mindset into the new circumstances and add new conflicts to the mix.

Choosing to improve brain and body is a personal decision. Both weak and strong can do it. Those that have had sorrow can have beauty for ashes. The fact that you have read this book to the end speaks to the fact that

106 Crocco, Kyle. (2018). "What makes a good life? Robert Waldinger has three lessons for you." *BigSpeak.* Retrieved from: www.bigspeak.com/makes-good-life-robert-waldinger-three-lessons

you have the gumption and perseverance to take the steps to build a better brain. You are seeking knowledge. You are already among the overcomers.

"For whatsoever is born of God overcometh the world: and this is the victory that overcometh the world, even our faith" (1 John 5:4).

I CHARGE YOU

There are things that you have learned that can help you thrive. You can lay this book down and next week, you will scarcely remember what you learned, or you can re-read portions that you know will help you. Make a to-do list, talk with others about what you have learned (which will reinforce your brain), and maybe even teach through the book with other mamas. Use social media to share what you have learned. The choice is yours. I charge you to charge ahead to do what you have never done before. Be all that you can be, and when you learn and grow, your children will be right there beside you, thriving.

"And ye shall know the truth, and the truth shall make you free" (John 8:32).

Eternal Things

"For what shall it profit a man, if he shall gain the whole world, and lose his own soul?" (Mark 8:36)

An understanding of the science of neuroplasticity is a wonderful tool that enables us, in some ways, to understand the physiology of our mental and physical self. If we earnestly apply what we learn, it will enhance the body and mind of us and our children. Knowledge is power to effect change. My hope is that your imagination has been stirred to the point that you will continue to learn. But this is not the end game.

With the best of all possible brains, we remain incomplete for we are a three-part being: body, mind, and spirit. The brain is the mechanism that allows the soul and spirit to function in this body of senses. Sometimes it is the spirit that needs healing, not the brain. Character does not reside in the brain, it is the attribute of the human spirit. **"God is a Spirit: and they that worship him must worship him in spirit and in truth" (John 4:24). "Now we have received, not the spirit of the world, but the spirit which is of God; that we might know the things that are freely given to us of God" (1 Corinthians 2:12). "(For the fruit of the Spirit is in all goodness and righteousness and truth;)" (Ephesians 5:9). "For God hath not given us the spirit of** fear; but of power, and of love, and of a sound mind." (2 Timothy 1:7).

We are born without the Divine Spirit. God gives his Holy Spirit to those who believe upon the Lord Jesus Christ. Then we are whole. Not perfect, but complete, able to overcome life's challenges, and triumph in this body of weak flesh. If you have not yet received the Spirit that is so freely given, there are free resources that will enable you to take that step to wholeness and spiritual healing.

"If any of you lack wisdom, let him ask of God, that giveth to all men liberally, and upbraideth not; and it shall be given him" (James 1:5).

Somewhere along the trail of life
if we are to find health and happiness,
we must come to believe that the person we
are and will become is the one we are creating
by our own personal choices.

Acknowledgements

Clint Cearley read my first rough draft. He dumped part of my writing as negative dross and told me which areas to expand. He studied and researched along with me so he could be knowledgeable enough on the subject to proof for accuracy. As he studied, he found additional research, quotes, and data that proved helpful. Then, as a renowned artist, he laid the book out in such a way as to enhance one's reading pleasure. Lastly, he used his art ability to further communicate the message. He also edited and proofed. Clearly, Cearley is a very important part of our team.

Karen Sargent has been my editor and proofer for years. Her work is invaluable. While I was writing this book, she had two car accidents, two years apart with each resulting in a brain concussion. Without the information she had already edited she would not have realized how profoundly the concussions affected her and she would not have had the information that healing was possible through therapy. Her misfortune greatly increased my desire to communicate this message to those who might otherwise never see the value.

Chris Barrett is new to our team and has proven to be a real asset. He is an extreme perfectionist in editing and proofing. We can all thank him for making the book more readable. Thank you, Chris.

And to the Mama Bloggers, *Facebook Queens,* and *other Social Media Supremes,* thank you for passing along the word of this book. Your videos and stories telling how much you learned from the book spread the word like a firestorm. You little mamas can now change the world in the space of a few hours. If you feel that what you have read will lift a fellow sister and help her stand stronger, healthier, and happier, continue spreading the word to help the book go viral! You are the movers and shakers. I am glad to have you all on my team!

Resources

Recommended books, videos, and experts on the subjects of neuroplasticity, behavior, mental health, and gut health

BOOKS

The Brain That Changes Itself: Stories of Personal Triumph from the Frontiers of Brain Science – Dr. Norman Doidge

Of all the books I read on the subject of the brain and the many lectures that I sat through, this book captures the wonder of neuroplasticity's discovery and development. Dr. Doidge introduces in a personal way the best of the scientists that made neuroplasticity well-known. He writes with creativity and skill. This is the one book you will want to read if you want to know more about neuroplasticity. It deals with some heavy sexual issues and shows how destructive porn is to the brain, so it is for mature audiences.

The Brain's Way of Healing: Stories of Remarkable Recoveries and Discoveries – Dr. Norman Doidge

This book is a treasure-trove of the author's own deep insights and a clear, bright light of optimism shines through every page. He describes natural, noninvasive avenues into the brain provided by the forms of energy around us—light, sound, vibration, movement—that can pass through our senses and cause our bodies to awaken the plastic brain's own transformative capacities without surgery or medication.

Soft-Wired: How the New Science of Brain Plasticity Can Change Your Life – Michael Merzenich, PhD

Merzenich has been referred to as the "father of neuroplasticity." He covers many of the different experiments that were done to prove that the brain was indeed plastic and could change itself. He has several interesting lectures on YouTube. Anyone who is seeking to know more on this subject should become familiar with Michael Merzenich's work.

Change Your Brain, Change Your Life: The Breakthrough Program for Con-
quering Anxiety, Depression, Obsessiveness, Anger, and Impulsiveness
– Dr. Daniel G. Amen

This is a highly entertaining and informative book.

Feel Better Fast and Make It Last: Unlock Your Brain's Healing
Potential to Overcome Negativity, Anxiety, Anger, Stress, and Trauma
– Dr. Daniel G. Amen

Unfortunately, many people turn to self-medicating behaviors such as
overeating, drugs, alcohol, risky sexual behavior, anger, or wasting time on
mindless TV, video games, internet surfing, or shopping. And even though
these behaviors may give temporary relief from negative feelings, they usually only prolong and exacerbate the problems or cause other, more serious
ones. I recommend Dr. Amen's book to anyone who wants to learn about
bringing healing to the body and the mind. He shares the recommendations
he gives to his own patients.

Mental Health Through Will-Training – Dr. Abraham Low

While this is an older book, it is a great resource for the explanation and application of cognitive behaviors and self-help techniques. This book is recommended for those who want to get control of their life and for those that
help them.

The Mind-Gut Connection: How the Hidden Conversation Within
Our Bodies Impacts Our Mood, Our Choices, and Our Overall Health
– Dr. Emeran Mayer

Dr. Emeran Mayer is one of the most renowned leaders, speakers, and writers on the subject of the gut-brain connection. His book is critical reading
for anyone experiencing any emotional turmoil, physical illness, or allergies.
Most of the immune system is in the gut, and many hormones are made in
the gut. All nutrients that provide fuel for the body to function are processed
in the gut. Dr. Mayer's book will help you understand how and what you must
do to get and stay healthy. This book is recommended reading for everyone.

The Longevity Project: Surprising Discoveries for Health and Long Life from the Landmark Eight-Decade Study
– Howard S. Friedman, PhD, and Leslie R. Martin, PhD

This is the story and the results of a study in which researchers wanted to find out who lived the longest, happiest life and why. I recommend this as a school project for homeschoolers (and their mamas).

The Art of Roughhousing: Good Old-Fashioned Horseplay and Why Every Kid Needs It – Dr. Anthony T. DeBenedet and Lawrence J. Cohen, PhD

Roughhousing is a form of nurturing and building close connections. Daddies seem to come by this form of nurturing naturally, but many mamas are raising children alone and need to know why it is an important aspect of childhood and how to go about including it. I recommend this to parents who mistakenly think that roughhousing is being naughty.

Healing and Preventing Autism: A Complete Guide
– Jenny McCarthy and Dr. Jerry Kartzinel

Jenny is the mom of an autistic child. The story of how she researched and fought to get her son back from the murky world of autism is well known. Dr. Kartzinel was willing to pour his life into finding a reason for the disorder and a way to bring healing to autistic children. Together they offer practical solutions. I recommend this book to anyone with a child that has any signs of autism.

SPEAKERS

Dr. Paul Bach-y-Rita on YouTube

Of all the great scientists and doctors studying the field of neuroplasticity, Paul Bach-y-Rita had the greatest zeal to know the truth and to pass the information on to others. I recommend you seek out anything you can find that features Paul Bach-y-Rita and watch it with your children.

Kati Morton, LMFT on YouTube

She is a licensed therapist with short, positive, educational videos on mental and behavioral conditions. I recommend watching several videos from any music therapist as well.

Dr. V.S. Ramachandran on YouTube

Dr. Ramachandran is a neuroscientist known primarily for his work in the fields of behavioral neurology and visual psychophysics. There are several videos available in which he lectures on brain damage. In one of the videos, he explains the connection between cerebral tissue and the mind using three startling illusions as examples. His lectures showing the use of mirrors to bring relief from pain are also quite interesting. This is the scientist who came up with the theory that mirror neurons have something to do with autism. I love his example of a talking pig—it is worth searching for. I recommend this doctor's lectures, but beware of his Eastern spiritualism.

WEBSITES

BrainHQ.com

Created by neuroplasticity expert Michael Merzenich, PhD, this website offers a full range of brain exercises to help improve everything from your brain speed and memory to social skills and hearing in a crowded room. For $8 a month, it's a great (and fun) investment for your brain. I can certainly see this training program has changed the face of our prison system, police force, and fire departments where it has been implemented. I would suggest that parents NOT use the school curriculum for children over the third grade because it is obviously geared to changing the brain toward a humanistic perspective, which clearly does not include God.

FightTheNewDrug.com

A non-judgmental, non-religious, science-based movement and resource on the harmful effects of porn on the brain, relationships, and society. "Porn Kills Love" is their motto. I recommend this to any couple where the husband has lost his ability to perform sexually. The letters that come in to our ministry reflect the issues that families are facing. Obviously, this is a huge concern that has become a real problem. Men and women are finding help through this site.

About the Author

Debi Pearl grew up near Memphis, Tennessee, during the 1950s and '60s at the height of the hippie revolution and the Jesus Movement. The forced draft due to the Vietnam War brought a sense of eternity to the youth, provoking them to seriously consider their souls. It was a time of great movement of the Spirit of God. As a teenager dressed in a tie-dye tee shirt and long, drooping peasant skirt, she stood on the highways and byways sharing the gospel, seeing miracle after miracle of God's amazing grace. Some of what you will read in her work reflects this glorious time.

She married her life mate, Michael Pearl, in 1971. From that day forth, they have functioned as a team in ministry, art, and writing. For the first fifteen years of their life together, they worked as professional artists while ministering to the military. In 1990, the Pearls moved to rural Tennessee right in the middle of an Amish community. The next several years were spent gardening, canning, studying health and herbs, homeschooling, and being a local midwife. God eventually led Michael and Debi into the ministry of writing about homeschooling, child training, and family relationships. Their first major book, *To Train Up a Child*, was published in 1994. It is now sold all over the world in over 15 languages.

Since that time, Debi has authored or co-authored many books with Michael. Debi's bestselling book, *Created to Be His Help Meet*, has been extremely successful worldwide. It is the first book in the *Created* series. To date, over one million copies of her books have been sold in over 20 different languages.

The Pearls established No Greater Joy Ministries, Inc. (NGJ) after the publication of *To Train Up A Child* to better facilitate sales of their books. The largest project that NGJ has ever been involved in was the publishing and subsequent translation of the 336-page, full-color book *Good and Evil: The Ultimate Comic Book Action Bible*. To date, *Good and Evil* is in print in 52 languages with the goal to reach 100 total languages, some of which are currently in the translation and publication process. *Good and Evil* is sold to every country in North and South America, and most countries in Europe, Africa, and Asia. It is also used by missionaries all over the world. Through a program the Pearls established called Light Bearers, the book is distributed free of charge to thousands of prisoners every month here in the USA. Chaplains write NGJ continually saying that of all the books and literature available in the prison, the *Good and Evil* book is by far the most favored.

The Pearls are busy doing life with their 5 children and 25 grandchildren (and counting).

Product Catalog

Further reading and study materials by Michael and Debi Pearl

Created to Be His Help Meet

As you have probably discovered, you don't just marry "the right man" and live happily ever after. A good marriage, just like anything worthwhile, takes doing the right things every day...every hour...every moment. This book reveals God's plan for obtaining a heavenly marriage.

Preparing to Be a Help Meet

Being a good help meet starts long before marriage. It is a mindset, a learned habit, a way of life established as a young unmarried girl. Bonus! Complete Teacher's Guide included for women's study groups.

Created to Need a Help Meet

All men know that they need their wives sexually. What most men don't know is that they need their wives emotionally, spiritually, and mentally in order to be well-rounded, thoughtful, balanced and motivated men. An Amazon reviewer called it a "...gritty, witty, no-holds-barred excursion into relationships and marital bliss."

In Search of a Help Meet

Choosing your life's partner is one of the most important and life-directing decisions you'll ever make. This book may save you from making the biggest mistake of your life. Written for young men.

Create a Better Brain through Neuroplasticity – Audiobook

Whether you want to increase your memory and recall by utilizing a different part of your brain or share with someone who loves to listen to audiobooks on their commute, *Create a Better Brain through Neuroplasticity* is available as an audiobook MP3 CD, iTunes audiobook, or digital download!

Samuel Learns to Yell & Tell
and *Sara Sue Learns to Yell & Tell*

A child predator loses his power when he loses his cover. These books will equip parents and children to arm themselves against predators. They are written in a musical rhyme and rhythm that children love. They will also be more inclined to remember what they read by this type of writing.

FREE BIBLE TEACHING AND RESOURCES

Goodandevilbook.com

God chose to introduce Himself to mankind not through principles, concepts, or doctrine, but through stories of prophecy, war, mercy, judgment, miracles, death, life, and forgiveness. This amazing book takes you through the Bible chronologically, retelling key events in an easy-to-grasp, illustrated comic book format.

Ngj.org/romans-yt

Are you ready to study and understand the Bible like never before? Be enlightened, encouraged, and transformed as Bible teacher and author Michael Pearl of No Greater Joy Ministries brings the Scriptures to life, verse by verse!

Ngj.org/am-i-saved

This is a three-message set: *Born Again, Am I Saved?* and *Except Ye Repent!* It discusses the nature of repentance and faith as it pertains to salvation. If you have ever had questions about your salvation, these messages have been designed to explain salvation clearly.